*From Generation
to Generation*

DISCARDED

From Generation to Generation

Understanding Sexual Attraction to Children

✦ ✦ ✦

Anne Stirling Hastings, Ph. D.

The Printed Voice

© 1994 Anne Stirling Hastings

All rights reserved.

Published by:
The Printed Voice
98 Main St., No. 538
Tiburon, CA 94920

Cover Design:
Kathy Warinner

Text Design:
Tori Hernandez

Library of Congress Cataloging-in-Publication Data

Hastings, Anne Stirling, 1943-
   From generation to generation : understanding sexual attraction to
children / Anne Stirling Hastings.
      p.   cm.
   Includes bibliographical references (p.   ).
   ISBN 0-9637891-4-7: $9.95
   1. Pedophilia. 2. Child molesters--Psychology. 3. Child sexual
abuse. 4. Adult child sexual abuse victims.   I. Title.
RC560.C46H37 1994
616.85'836--dc20
                                                      94-16582
                                                         CIP

ISBN: 0-9637891-4-7

Printed in the United States of America
10 9 8 7 6 5 4 3 2 1

For my father,

and all people who are sexually attracted to children.

The identity of those whose stories are told here have been protected by changing identifying data. In addition, each has been given an opportunity to read their stories and make changes that will allow the story to be valid even while altered for protection.

TABLE OF CONTENTS

Foreword by Anne Wilson Schaef, Ph.D.

Introduction 1
Chapter 1
We Are Half Way Through a Cultural Shift *15*
Chapter 2
Women Who Have Sexual Feelings for Children *29*
Chapter 3
Ignoring the Sexuality of Children is Harmful Too *63*
Chapter 4
The Father Who Used His Daughter as His Lover *79*
Chapter 5
The Other Parent Who Didn't Know *99*
Chapter 6
*A Man's "Covert" Sexual Relationship
   with His Daughter* *125*
Chapter 7
When a Mother Is "Only" Attracted to a Child *133*
Chapter 8
Falling "In Love" with a Young Person *145*
Chapter 9
Why Adults Are Sexual with Babies *163*
Chapter 10
Sibling Incest *173*
Chapter 11
Children Who Are Sexual with Children *189*

Chapter 12
  The Non-Recovering Pedophile *201*
Chapter 13
  Treatment for Male "Sex Offenders" *207*
Chapter 14
  Women "Offenders" *225*
Chapter 15
  "Behavior Modification" Treatment of Sex Offenders *241*
Chapter 16
  Drunk and Homeless:
    The Man Who Had Sex with His Stepson *257*
Chapter 17
  How Our Culture Perpetuates Sexual Violation *269*
Suggested Reading **285**
Support Groups **287**

FOREWORD

I feel honored to write the foreword for this important book. Truth-speaking is a necessary function in any culture and speaking the truth in a culture where dishonesty is the norm is a particularly courageous act. Yet, it is only because of the few people who are willing to bring healing through truth that any culture is able to move out of the morass it has created for itself.

Anne Stirling Hastings points us to another problem that is rampant in today's culture which, I believe, must be named and addressed. That is that we have developed into a culture of victims and perpetrators. Even *Time* magazine had a lead story about this phenomenon in the last few years. We have evolved our understanding of ourselves and one another from modern psychology and, therefore, mechanistic science. Mechanistic science only focuses upon the external or that which can be observed and measured. Over the last few centuries, this external focus has resulted in a society of people who look outside themselves for the reasons that they are the way they are and consequently, they also look for healing to come from somewhere external to themselves. Of course, these are characteristics of an addict and they are also characteristics of the victim-perpetrator. A society of victims is always looking for someone on whom they can perpetrate. In fact, having been a victim gives license to become a perpetrator and, hence, perpetrate on anyone who, we believe, has victimized us. We have failed to recognize that all perpetrators have been victimized and all people who see themselves as victims will, as they see it, justifiably become perpetrators. I call this the victim-perpetrator dualism. There is no way for any healing to happen when we are stuck on this dualism. Also, nowhere in the culture are we more stuck on this dualism than with anything having to do with sex.

Anne Stirling Hastings has effectively helped us remove ourselves from this dualism with respect to persons who are sexually attracted to children. First, she helps us see that these people are not monsters, as we would like to believe. They are people like us. They are people who grew up in a sexually-addicted society, who received confusing messages about sex from early childhood, and who probably have experienced sexual abuse as children. They are...ourselves, our family, our neighbors, and our friends. She helps us know this truth by her willingness to risk exposing herself and sharing her own explorations and truths. This is a great gift.

In addition, Dr. Hastings gives us hope. Not only are the people struggling with these issues open to help, *they can be helped*. Her own work personally and professionally leads the way.

Traditional psychology has not had much success with treating "sexual deviants." In fact, they have been described as untreatable. Yet, we have here in this book another story, which suggests that it is not the people but what we have been doing with them. Dr. Hastings has found something that is working and she shares it with us.

This is not to say that I agree with everything in this book. I do not. The author and I disagree on the usefulness of psychotherapy in the healing process. I do not believe that true healing is possible in that model. I have developed a model of healing that is not based upon mechanistic science nor psychotherapy, which I call *Living in Process*, which has also proved quite successful. Frankly, there is so much to be done in this and other areas, I welcome diversity.

I applaud this book. On reading it, I was struck by the truth and compassion contained within these pages. There is information, yes. Much information, good information...information that professionals and non-professionals need to read, for no one in this society is unaffected by the issues described. And, there is more than information. There is caring and, most of all, hope. A saying of Jesus has carried me through much of my life. "You shall know the truth, and the truth shall make you free." It seems relevant to this book. There is truth here, and only as we face the truth can we hope for healing and freedom. No longer can we ignore the damage that exists at every level of a sexually-addicted society. No longer can we ignore that all of us are affected and damaged by a society that uses sex as a drug and perpetuates generations of damage resulting in a society that no longer has any operational understanding of true intimacy with ourselves or anyone else.

Of course, to stop with knowing the disease inherent in the society is to avoid the problem. We must recognize the role of society and we must focus on healing and changing ourselves. We must, each of us, start inside and accept that the shock waves of change move out from the point that is ourselves to the world we can create if we start at the starting point. Anne Stirling Hastings has demonstrated this process admirably. She has made a dangerous leap, and broken through society's denial by doing her own work—openly sharing her own journey—embracing the path of recovery and sharing her own recovery and healing.

This book is, I believe, a giant step forward in understanding a phenomenon much bigger and more pervasive in our society than we want to believe it is. This book opens a door. Many will follow, and it will be important to remember that this was the first.

ANNE WILSON SCHAEF, PH.D.

Author of *Women's Reality, When Society Becomes an Addict,* and *Beyond Therapy/Beyond Science*

ACKNOWLEDGMENTS

Laurie Harper actively searched for a publisher for 18 months, facing ongoing reactions to the content of a book that was repugnant to editors. She supported this project with her time and creativity as well as her personal commitment to knowing this information should be in print.

Leslie Keenan, editor and publisher, saw the early chapters, and found this project to be consistent with her own desire to provide information that is essential to global healing. I appreciate our continuously developing, non-hierarchic, cooperative relationship. We are figuring out how to produce books and tapes from a place of equality, living our recovery process as we discover how to create businesses and products from the philosophy we both aspire to. Our relationship works so well that we often don't notice it.

Jill Seipel supported this work with her natural compassion for people who have sexual attraction to children, and her supportive and helpful attitude. Her matter-of-fact approach to this controversial subject provided me with a mirror for my own such unpopular attitude. Jill also spent many hours in interviews, and critiquing the manuscript, providing reassurance that I wasn't making things up in order to affirm what I believe.

Louisa Turner and Cindy Ruschin's encouragement and support has been affirming and valuable.

Matthew Grace spent hours at the library searching out information. I appreciated Matthew's constant reflection of the need for this writing, and his ability to climb into my head and search the library in a way that felt as if I were doing it.

Jamie Compton's willingness to be honest about his negative as well as positive reactions has been ultimately supportive.

He embraces his own sexual healing, and joins me in knowing how vital sexual recovery is to our world.

Rex Holt, my mate, continues to support me in all aspects of my work. He listened to chapters when first written, fed back to me what I was saying, and took for granted that I would do what I needed to do.

Anne Wilson Schaef's conceptualizations about addictive culture and the possibility for recovery at a cultural level provided the context for my understanding. Her mirror for my "knowing" is reflected on every page. I am deeply appreciative of her foreword. Her voice belongs in this work. Anne pointed out to me that I was not in my integrity when, early on, I changed the name and theme of the book in an attempt to make it palatable to publishers and readers. She reflected back to me the need to be true to what I was saying.

In order to maintain their confidentiality, I can't name the women and men I interviewed. This prevents me from describing each one in glowing terms, thanking them for coming to me with their stories and for being willing to tell, especially to a person who was going to put their story in print. Given the possibilities for conflict and bad feelings, there have been few. Instead, many of my months were filled with passionate stories of people who know how to heal themselves from sexual feelings for children. From these people came deep hope for cultural change and affirmation of my original thesis—given the right circumstances, individuals can give up sexual interest in children.

Introduction

We live in the midst of a vast cultural shift that began little more than a decade ago. We are becoming aware of the prevalence of incest and other adult/child sexual interaction that has been going on for centuries. We once thought it was rare, something done by only a small number of seriously disturbed people—mostly males with female children. We now know that at least one in five people have had sexual contact with adults when they were children. As the definition of sexual contact broadens, and the biases of experimenters are confronted, we will find this number to be much higher than we now realize.

The idea of adults having sexual contact with children is so abhorrent to those who grew up in our culture that cultural denial of its extent and severity is strong. As a result, it has been difficult for anyone to admit an adult was sexual with them in childhood, or even to remember it. But as more books are written, more experiences are shared, and more therapists trained, the stories are coming out. It is clear now that such things commonly go on. People who want to remove the effects of these childhood experiences from their adult lives can seek help to do so. As more and more people speak out and learn their own truths, our culture will continue to shift. We are becoming conscious of the truth of incest, and through this consciousness, we will change.

WHO IS SEXUAL WITH CHILDREN?

There is one very large missing piece, however. *Who are the people who are sexual with children?* Therapists' offices are filling with people who come to learn about how adults were sexual with them, but very few come to find out how to no longer be sexual with children. The price is too high.

First, adults who are sexual with children (ASC's) will immediately be reported to Child Protective Services and subjected to an investigation. Second, their shame is so intense that it seems impossible to tell the story in order to find help. Third, their lives and the lives of their families will be seriously disrupted, and few are willing to face this outcome. ***The result is that we are only learning about one half of the picture, and the other half is still very difficult to see.***

Those who treat sex offenders ("sex offenders" is a term for those who have been prosecuted and have gone through the legal system) see a biased sample—ASC's who have been reported. Most of these people are at the more serious end of the continuum, performing acts that are more likely to be reported. Women are rarely turned in to Child Protective Services (CPS), because our cultural bias tells us that women are not capable of such acts.

Among the men are many who cannot see that they have harmed anyone, or who are so filled with shame they are unable to engage in meaningful treatment. Psychological defenses of denial, minimization, and rationalization are used creatively so that the person himself often doesn't know the truth. The result is the emergence of a common view that those who are sexual with children are a difficult group to treat. The real truth is, most people who are reported are not able to use therapy well because of their intense shame, our culture's shaming, and the lack of treatment programs that adequately address their needs.

THE PREVALENCE OF SEXUAL ABUSE

Research on sexual abuse is still in infancy, and there is almost no information focusing on the ASC's. Of journal articles on the subject of sexual abuse I could find, over a third were written in the past three years. The other two-thirds covered a span of many decades, pointing out how the subject was neglected in the past as scientists were unaware of the magnitude of the problem. About 95% of these article titles refer to the children who are sexually abused. The remaining one in twenty addresses the adult who is sexual with children, most often the adult who goes to prison and is difficult to treat. The average ASC is not examined. Of these one in twenty, *only two studies inquire about the frequency of ASC's in our culture.*

These studies investigating adults' sexual interest in children are a pioneering investigation by John Briere at The University of Southern California Medical School (*Child Abuse and Neglect*, 1989, and *Journal of Research in Personality*, 1992). Instead of starting with those who had been convicted of molesting children sexually, Briere first questioned a group of male college students. He felt they were closer to a typical group of people. In an anonymous questionnaire completed by 193 men, he found that 21% indicated they had at least some sexual attraction to children, 9% reported sexual fantasies about children, half of these men masturbated to their fantasies, and *7% indicated some likelihood of having sex with a child if they were guaranteed not to be discovered or punished.* The second study, conducted with women and men college students, supported the findings of the first.

Briere points out that if pedophilia is defined as overt sexual acts with children, probably at least 5% of his subjects are pedophiles. *If the definition is broadened to sexual attraction to children, then the pedophiles in his study increases to 20%.*

Briere is aware that his study must be underestimating the actual percentages because of the social undesirability of admitting these feelings. In addition, many men who have sexual interest in children are able to deceive themselves regarding the sexual nature of the interest—and the behaviors. The stories of recovering "offenders" told in Chapter 13 demonstrates how offenders are able to deny even to themselves that they are being sexual with children. On the contrary, these men saw themselves as protecting children from such people. Two men couldn't believe it themselves as they told me how they had been able to prevent themselves from seeing what they were doing when today it is so obvious. Briere's and others' research will have to contend with personal and cultural denial. Given the abhorrence toward oneself for having such thoughts or actions, I was amazed that Briere was able to elicit the responses he did.

WHAT EXACTLY *IS* SEXUAL ABUSE?

Most people, including most psychotherapists, view sexual abuse as physical acts of sexuality that resemble sex between adults. But this definition is so limited it doesn't do us much good when setting out to heal the abuse of children's sexuality, and to heal our culture's acceptance of covert sexual interactions. *Damage to children's sexuality comes from behaviors that society says are acceptable, in addition to the more obvious sexual violations.* For example, mothers who insist that their children be kept immaculately clean can communicate that genitals and anuses are disgusting, and can bring pain with intense washing. Parents can dedicate their lives to their children, spending too much time with them and giving them sexualized attention, and look like good parents in the eyes of family and friends. Taking a child as a surrogate spouse, even with no sexual contact, can create the same difficulties in adult life as overt sexual interaction. Mothers can bond sexually to their child in ways that go beyond healthy maternal bonding. Both parents might harm their children's views of their bodies and sexuality by pulling away from the child in order not to be aroused by him or her. This happens at any age, but perhaps most commonly at puberty, when the young person becomes more obviously sexual. We do our cultural healing a disservice when we view "them" as the problem instead of seeing that sexual damage is universal because it is built into our culture. We are all involved at some level. At the minimum, we all shame the sexuality of children and adults through our own discomfort with sexual things.

ADULTS WHO ARE SEXUAL WITH CHILDREN CAN RECOVER

It is possible to recover from all forms of transmitting sexual unhealth. The first step is to heal from the shame our culture has put on sexuality. Shame is a debilitating feeling of being defective for who we are, not what we do. Unlike guilt, which can be lessened by changing behavior, confessing, or finding out that we haven't violated anyone, shame cannot be eliminated without deliberate intervention. While talking one on one with a therapist, friend, or mate can help with shame created by specific sexual activities, such conversation can do little for the cultural sexual violations. This can be done only by forming groups to talk about normal, typical-looking sex in non-shaming ways, examining the rules our culture transmits that we cannot even see, and supporting each other in finding out what health looks like for each member. Shame is naturally reduced just by talking about the things we think of as shameful in a safe, supportive environment. When changing the effects of our culture, a supportive group of people is essential. *In order to undo the barrage of information presented all around us all our lives, we must create a new subculture where the rules have been changed to include talking about sex in a healthy way.* Even in situations where adults are not finding out that they have overtly been sexual with their children, but are "only" learning that their own sexuality is shamed by all those around us, the shame is strong, warding off understanding. Sexual shaming is a massive influence on all sorts of sexual activities and on our feelings about ourselves. In an environment of sexual shame, we have been forced to adapt to living with shame in order to be able to continue having sex. All of us have had our sexuality cross-wired in some fashion that prevents us from knowing healthy sexual energy. In my previous books, *Reclaiming Healthy Sexual Energy* (Health Communications, 1991) and *Discovering Sexuality That Will Satisfy You Both: When Couples Want Differing Amounts and Different Kinds of Sex* (The Printed Voice, 1993). I describe some of the ways we have been cross-wired, and describe methods of releasing shame.

SHAME INTERFERES WITH HEALING

Our culture places tremendous shame on those who are sexual with children, even though we know ASC's must number in the millions. If everyone who has had sexual feelings toward a child stood up to be counted, we would see neighbors, bosses, and family members. The numbers would be so staggering we would be unable to shame every one of them. We would have a visual picture of what this cultural illness looks like. We could no longer attribute it to a few perverted people who should be sent away from society. Instead, we would see that ministers and doctors and teachers, parents and siblings and grandparents, black people and white people and brown people, and people from all societal strata are included among the numbers who stand up. Rather than a tiny number, ASC's are all around us, made invisible by cultural shame that prevents them from acknowledging what they have done and asking for help.

As long as we cannot see who these people are, each of us must take on our sexual recovery as if we were the only ones doing it. Each of us alone questions the myths embedded in our culture, and thus in us, gradually pulling ourselves out of the sticky stuff that makes us feel like we belong. How much easier this would be if we had a clear picture of the truth.

ADULT SURVIVORS OF CHILD SEXUAL ABUSE MUST HEAL

Those of us who are recovering from the effects of adults' sexual activities when we were children have within us the programming to do what was done to us. Some survivors act on it, passing the effects on from generation to generation. Others work hard to make sure they are not sexual with their children. Sexual shame is passed on either way. The child who is touched sexually receives the shame of the adult and from his or her interpretation of the event. The child who is raised by parents and others who are working too hard to make sure the child is never touched inappropriately, communicate to the child that something is seriously wrong with sexuality.

The only route to preventing the passing on of sexual shame is recovery of our own sexual health. In order to do this, we must be open to knowing about our own feelings of wanting to be sexual with children, or our intense disgust or revulsion over such things and an overactive attempt to protect children. If we feel that shaming is appropriate for ASC's, and believe they are less than human, then we cut off our ability to examine our own sexual attitudes toward children.

Parents who become sexually aroused when a child gets on their lap have more difficulty telling this to a therapist than telling that they have hit their child. Everyone understands that parents feel like hitting children, and can have compassion if the parent feels remorse. But a parent, particularly a mother, who admits to being sexually aroused is shocking, and people, including therapists, have great difficulty understanding with compassion. But even if we have a compassionate therapist, our self-shaming attitudes still interfere.

If we can see that ASC's are human beings who have been sexually cross-wired in their own childhoods so they are reactive to children at some level, and that their shame about this is so intense that it makes it difficult to know about or to admit, then we have the possibility of looking at our own sexual feelings toward children (either expressed or prevented from expression) so that we can heal them. If we are unable to do this, then it will be difficult to resolve the effects of the things that were done to us.

As our history is told in the present, it opens doors to learning about what happened in the past. If we can accept our feelings, while making sure we don't act on them, we have a wealth of data with which to reclaim our shame-free selves. If, however, we feel nothing but condemnation for ASC's (very different from appropriate anger, even rage), then we will feel this also toward our own such desires, preventing us from seeing the possibility of a shame-free existence. It is OK to know that you have sexual feelings toward children, or that you have inadvertently shamed their sexual nature, or made comments that conveyed distaste for a child's sexuality. The more you are able to know about it, the less likely you will be to act on it. And as your shame drops, you will find out what healthy sexuality is, and these unhealthy varieties will diminish.

CHILDREN ARE NEVER RESPONSIBLE

While I am saying we must not shame people who are sexual with children, I want to be very clear that adults are fully responsible for their actions. Every one of us is responsible to know what we do, think, and feel, and then to take steps to change ourselves so that we are less harmful to children.

Even though a child may flirt, act seductively, initiate sexual contact, and even say sex with an adult is wanted, he or she is never ever responsible. The older person holds the power, and is the one who is responsible. It is possible to know that children are not responsible, and simultaneously know that adults should not be shamed or condemned or ostracized for their actions.

CHILDREN ARE NATURALLY SEXUAL

Sexuality is a natural part of being human, and begins even before birth. Vaginal lubrication, erections, and orgasms begin in the womb. Children will explore their vulvas and penises and testicles and enjoy the resulting sexual feelings. But in this culture, where we are blind to all but the most blatant sexual things, we don't respond to children's sexuality in ways that are useful to them as they grow through developmental periods that include learning lessons about sexuality. My colleague, a psychologist and new mother, pointed out to me the need to actively address childhood sexuality. Instead of merely reacting to events initiated by the child, we can be most helpful if we place sexuality and sexual functioning in the same category as other issues children need help with. We teach children how to count, how to read, how to tie their shoes, the names of body parts, the limits of the household, and brushing their teeth, but we don't calmly and comfortably bring up sexuality as a normal part of being human.

Our sexual shame and fear prevents us from naturally including the subject of sexuality in our parenting. When we as a culture don't know what children need in order to grow into sexual health and maturity, we set children up to be viewed as the "perpetrator" of sexual interaction. The child will then be shamed for her or his behavior. In fact, children are naturally flirtatious at certain ages, and additionally so if they have been sexualized by sexual interaction (see Chapter 11 for information on sexualized children).

WHY I AM WRITING THIS BOOK

I draw on my own experience in writing this book. As an incest survivor, and one who has lived in sexual fantasy and addiction, I have had to drop all the old rules about sex. In the process of doing my healing work, working with my clients, and writing my previous books, I have learned a lot about sexual shaming, and how damaging it is to healthy sexuality.

I began writing this book three years ago with passion and commitment, yet had no understanding of the role of these issues in my own life. I wrote that all of us who are survivors will have cross-wiring to children—but I didn't see that I meant myself too. The amount of shame that accompanies even thoughts of exchanging sexual energy with children, even for those of us who weren't overtly sexual with our children, is monumental. But I wasn't just ignoring my feelings. They were totally unavailable to me. I even told people that I wanted to know what happened when my son was small so that he will have full information for his healing. But I couldn't. The thoughts were blocked from access. As I look back, I can see that my desire to heal from something I couldn't name took the form of commitment to writing this book and getting it published. Even when publishers were shocked when my agent offered it for publication, and horrified that I was willing to say anything positive or compassionate about "those" people, I didn't waver in my knowing that somehow I would get this information out. My spirit pushed me along even when my defense mechanisms prevented me from consciously knowing what I was doing.

THE PURPOSE OF THIS BOOK

I chose to write this book so that readers will be able to step into the shoes of those who are sexual with children, or who think about being sexual with children, and find out what their lives are like. I am presenting many stories of ordinary people who were playing out their part in the generation to generation curse. These people aren't the hideous creatures, different from the rest of us, that are presented in the media.

I wanted to interview men and women and hear the details of their stories so that I could lift my own cultural attitudes and denial. I wanted to sit opposite men and women who had done those things that are so deeply condemned. I needed to know that my father really was the person he was perceived to be by his profession and circle of friends, and at the same time, he engaged in sexual contact with me. This was hard to grasp as long as I believed our cultural attitudes, and carried them inside of me.

As I talked with the people whose stories are presented here, my perceptions couldn't help changing. Even the homeless alcoholic, and the sexually-addicted pedophile who had sex with other women and men as well as his daughter, were real people. The work they have done to recover themselves has made them very accessible, and so I got to see real people surviving a curse that brings on social condemnation.

The best way to change your acculturated beliefs is to be in the room with me, hearing these people tell their stories. But this isn't possible because they won't tell them to very many people—only those who they are sure won't shame them. The intense shaming of their behaviors prevents them from showing themselves so you can see how many there are around you, and that for the most part they aren't "bad" people. As long as you can't see them and hear their stories, it will be difficult for you to change your perception. Therefore, I would like to invite you to go along with me in my explorations, and imagine you are in the room hearing firsthand what these people have to say.

You May Feel Arousal

As you read the stories of how ASC's were sexual with children, you may find that your own cross-wiring will result in sexual arousal. I would like to invite you to use your reactions as information about your history in a way that can help your recovery. If you give in to the shame and try to avoid it, then you will be inhibited from exploring. However, if the shame does arrive, I suggest that you breathe fully to allow it to flow through you and out. *You are not a bad person.* Detaching shame from sexuality, even cross-wired sexuality, is needed to heal ourselves, our families, and our culture.

You May Feel Revulsion

You may have adopted our culture's views of ASC's, and so find it hard to read their stories with compassion. If you feel revulsion, and breathe to allow it to flow through and out, you can free yourself from it. The result is that you will be better able to see that this is a cultural phenomenon, and not deserving of the strong reaction that has been programmed into you.

One purpose of the revulsion is to prevent yourself from discovering the possibility that you have cross-wiring that makes you respond sexually to children. The intense negative feeling will prevent you from acting on it, but it also shames you out of looking at it in a healing way.

Another reason you may feel revulsion is a reaction to the feeling of what it was like, or would be like, if you were the object of the behaviors described here.

Read This Book in Any Order

I discovered years ago that if I pick up a book, open it anywhere and read, my curiosity is piqued. Then I want to go back and read earlier sections if I don't understand what is written later. I feel more active in my learning. I would like it if you read this book in that manner—any way you want.

The chapter which follows is different from the others. I wanted to offer some background on how other cultures treated adults who are sexual with children. It includes historical information. The rest of the chapters tell the stories of people who are very like you and me. I invite you to read these chapters and have all your feelings along the way. While I was preparing these chapters I found myself having a variety of them: I raged at ASC's, felt their hurt and isolation, and experienced deep anger at a culture that prevents them from healing. It is only by reading and accepting their stories—and our own—that we as a culture can begin to heal.

Chapter 1

We Are Half Way Through a Cultural Shift

To show the need for a change in attitude toward adults who are sexual with children, I read the works of researchers to learn about the history of belief and disbelief about the prevalence of these behaviors. I invite you to share in my shock and anger about how this culturally-supported behavior has been condoned by some cultures and condemned by others. Never before in history has a major civilization faced up to the presence of adult sexuality with children, as ours is now. We are at the beginning of one of history's largest social revolutions.

WHERE DID IT ALL START?

Sexual interaction between adults and children has been going on for as long as history has been recorded—at least three thousand years. Over time, attitudes toward such interactions has swung from cultural acceptance (such as the ancient Greek and Roman cultures' sexual use of pre-pubertal boys) to cultural abhorrence, as we have at present. *But this is the only time in history that a cultural shift is in progress that will bring to light the entire picture of adult/child sex, and pave the way to discover how to access*

15

healthy sexuality. As long as these behaviors have been condoned or condemned, no culture has been able to find out what would happen if a child were raised in a healthy sexual environment. (Even children who aren't touched by adults while growing up will have their sexuality abused by living in a culture where such things are covertly sanctioned.) We have that chance now. The first step—naming the high frequency of child sexual abuse—is already happening.

In the past two decades, we have moved from medical textbooks telling us that only one in a million children are sexually abused, to knowing at least one in four or five are. But we have made little progress in accepting that the behavior of the person who was sexual with children is a symptom of our culture, not a sign of individual deviance and perversion. In order to change our culture, we have to take the next step. We have to know that we all have the inclination. Some have acted on it and others haven't. *This is not a matter of "them" and "us." It is a matter of a culture that has hidden a vastly common occurrence, and denied its existence—holding the adult entirely responsible instead of holding all of us responsible.*

Reactions to sexual activity with children, through history, have swung from pole to pole. We are now in a reactionary phase, against ASC's. But if we react with horror, we can't see the need for the ASC to recover, and we threaten to send the cultural awareness of sexual abuse back underground.

The articles I have been reading in professional journals provoke my anger, frustration, and hope. I am also frustrated that so much vital information is limited to journals that require going to a college library, and understanding the language in which they are written. I will review some of it here, and also encourage you to read the complete articles if the information interests you.

I found this first article, "Modern History of Child Sexual Abuse Awareness: Cycles of Discovery and Suppression," *(Child Abuse and Neglect,* Jan/Feb 1993) by Erna Olafson, David Corwin, and Roland Summit, particularly valuable. If you should want to read it, I recommend calling a college library. Reference librarians will often know of students who will search out articles, copy them, and mail them to you for a reasonable fee.

MODERN HISTORY OF CHILD SEXUAL ABUSE AWARENESS

Olafson, Corwin, and Summit, all associated with major universities, gathered together to write about our current social shift in understanding sex with children, placing it within the context of two centuries of belief. They describe the change we are going through as a great shift in world view, and point out how unsettling this is, even for those who have not been sexual with children.

Much of the authors' focus is on the psychiatric profession in Europe. They quote a writer in 1904 who describes a sickness of young girls and women, which takes the form of contriving false sexual charges against men. But just before the turn of the century, there was a very high percentage of prosecutions in England against those who had raped children. While the evidence of sexual abuse of children existed right before them, the people of that time were unable to see past their belief that mental illness caused women to make accusations.

Olafson, et al. go on to tell us that mental illness was seen as "isolated within the patient rather than embedded in a social context." Sexuality and mental illness were believed to be connected, but the connection was backward. "Perverted" sexual behavior in adult life was seen as the cause of mental illness, but it wasn't understood that sexual assaults during childhood and adult years brought about traumatic reactions expressed in sexual symptoms. I find it fascinating that in France, during this same time, doctors were saying that sex with children was common, and believed the children's reports, while a doctor in another European country (author of a book owned by Freud) believed that 60% to 80% of women's complaints of sexual abuse were false accusations based on attention seeking and "genital hallucinations."

Sigmund Freud, as he began developing psychoanalysis at the end of the nineteenth century in Austria, entered this scene, and attempted to make sense out of the reports he received from his adult patients claiming they had childhood sexual relations with their fathers. The story is well told in Alice Miller's book, *Thou Shalt Not Be Aware* (Meridian, 1986). Freud was for several years totally convinced that his patients were telling the truth, and then turned around and declared that their memories were only fantasies created as children. He became instrumental in the cultural suppression of the frequency of sexual abuse of children.

Many people angrily blame Freud for once again suppressing this cultural secret, but in truth he was only an instrument of the wishes of his culture. After delivering a paper near the end of the century to his medical colleagues on infantile sexuality and the relationship between current symptoms and childhood sexual assault, he was thoroughly criticized. Even his most staunch supporter and confidant, Wilhelm Fliess, objected to Freud's belief in his patients' stories. (Alice Miller tells us that Fliess's son, who was two when Freud abandoned his "seduction" theory, later retrieved memories of his father being sexual with him at that time. No wonder Fliess didn't want Freud to continue in this vein.)

One author (who was also read by Freud) presented a case study of a woman he diagnosed as "hysterical," who said that her father had been sexual with her. She was dismissed because her father was an "honorable man," and the charges she made were "extreme." The doctor so thoroughly disbelieved her that he had her committed to a mental institution, where, in that time, she received no help.

Another respected contemporary of Freud's, Charcot, diagnosed and took pictures of women in insane asylums, but didn't listen to their stories. The focus on diagnosis didn't include the causes of the symptoms even though his patients were trying to tell of incestuous experiences.

There were other people who did know. Janet, also Freud's contemporary, identified the defense mechanism of dissociation, the primary reaction to overwhelming experiences. But nothing further was done with his understandings until the Second World War, when research lead to the formulation of post-traumatic-stress reactions now well understood for those who fought in Vietnam. It was four more decades until the connection between stress in war and emotional symptoms was applied to stress in childhood and resulting symptoms in adult life.

Ferenczi, a disciple of Freud's, wrote about the role of sexual traumas in the symptoms of adult sexual "perversions" and personality fragmentation. He published his paper in spite of Freud's objection. After he died, Freud and psychoanalyst Jones, the major English interpreter of psychoanalytic works, agreed to censor this part of Ferenczi's ideas in the English versions. A letter from Jones to Freud showed that he believed Ferenczi would discredit psychoanalysis, and referred to Ferenczi's "mental condition." As in other times in history, those who see the truth are dismissed as insane. (This is similar to the refusal to believe that the world is round—an issue that had far less impact on those who disagree than does this controversy, and yet resulted in the assassination of its proponent.)

The authors end their paragraphs on Jones by telling us that he had been accused of sexual irregularities toward two young girls, and that he resigned from his job after a ten-year-old patient also accused him. We can see how Jones might have had a vested interest in seeing sexual behavior with children as not harming to them. If he believed Ferenczi, he would have to know that he was harming children too.

In defense of Freud, he was tackling this cultural taboo all by himself. Those of us who are now uncovering our own childhood abuses are unable to do so if we don't have the support of someone who believes us. I was in psychoanalysis for years in the 1970s. My body memories were ignored, and I had no way to know what had happened to me. It wasn't until I joined a group of people setting out to reclaim early sexual memories that I could begin to believe what I remembered. Freud had no one. Given this environment, where powerful professionals and common people alike wished to avoid the truth, there was no way to push forward to name the occurrence of the abuse of sexuality.

HISTORICAL PERSPECTIVES

Going back even further in history, Brett Kahr wrote a paper called "Historical Perspectives" that was printed in *The Journal of Psychohistory* in 1991, providing us with a more distant look at the history of sexual contact between children and adults. He begins with a review of current literature about the amount of sexual contact that goes on in the present.

Kahr cites the most frequently quoted study, conducted by Diana Russell in 1983. She found that of her sample of 930 women, 38% had been sexually abused before the age of eighteen. But this figure increased to 54% when she added abuses that didn't include physical touching. Kahr suggests that even these high figures are underestimates because they don't include subjects' experiences that aren't conscious. He points out that many women were sexual with adults when they were young children, and repressed the memories. This is supported by Russell's questions of her subjects regarding those early years. Very few had memories extending into early childhood. Yet, as Kahr points out, we know from reports made to CPS and the police that people are engaging sexually with very young children. Quoting another researcher (probably because Kahr doesn't want to be the authority on such a controversial subject) he states, "our best evidence shows that the *majority* of women in America today were sexually abused as girls."

An even more appalling finding was gathered by researchers in Berlin in 1988. By asking children directly, they found that 80% of school children had been sexually molested.

The more conservative research findings reflect lower rates, but even the lowest findings of 3% of boys and 18% of girls is still an enormous percentage of people. And yet we continue to think that only a small number of strange people are responsible for all these incidents!

Kahr turns to ancient Greek and Roman times, describing the many abuses of children, including the common and accepted use of pre-pubescent boys for anal sex. In Greece, the activity was very common, and contrary to sexual activity with children in the present, was socially acceptable and ritualized.

Plato and Aristotle both wrote about anal sex with boys—called pederasty. Plato believed that the boys should be shared among many men. Aristotle advocated sexual use of children, but, Kahr writes, may have been the first recorded writer to caution against sex between a man and his own son.

Ancient Roman sexual use of children was accepted, and integrated into the culture. One example was the establishment of a public holiday for child prostitutes.

Kahr explored Roman art and poetry, and came to the conclusion that girls were also victims of sexual abuse by adults, and women were sexual with children.

Moving on to ancient Egypt, incest prevailed at all levels of society, and brother-sister incest was particularly common. The ancient names for brother and sister were actually "lover" and "loved."

Among the ancient Hebrews, anyone who was sexual with a boy over nine was stoned to death, but anyone sexual with a boy younger was only whipped because the young boy was not seen as a sexual person.

These ancient conditions changed, and feelings of shame and guilt appeared as we moved into fanatical prudery in the medieval era. The Catholic Church was instrumental in trying to prevent the sexual abuse of children, even cautioning parents to dress their children so the parent wouldn't be tempted to be sexual with them. The intent seemed to be right, but shaming parents into changing their behavior only made their cross-wiring go underground. Sexual healing to prevent sexual abuse wasn't understood.

More recently, the Victorian era dictated the repression of sexuality, an influence we are only now eradicating. Yet during those years of supposed asexuality, an enormous amount of pornography was created. Some of it described sex between adults and children.

Kahr ends his article with a note of hope that I think may have been premature, written in 1991 before the backlash got underway. He writes, "...most people now appreciate that incest in the family and child abuse at large constitute grave dangers, and that both the abused and the abusers must be helped and supported. I am therefore quite optimistic about the emotional future of children in forthcoming decades, for though we have been trapped in our historical nightmare, I believe we are now almost completely wide awake." I share Kahr's hope, but the current backlash (described below) indicates that the old way of dealing with the sexual use of children isn't going to die easily.

KINSEY SUPPORTS ADULT SEXUAL INTERACTION WITH CHILDREN

Alfred Kinsey, the sex researcher, caused a stir in the middle of this century by talking openly about sex, and asking questions of many subjects to learn about this silent topic. While his work was very necessary in order to begin the movement we are in, he himself did not see most sexual activity between children and adults to be harmful.

The Kinsey Reports created major controversy when published in 1948 and 1953 (W. B. Saunders). The controversy revolved around the frequency of intercourse and the kinds of sex that were commonly engaged in, challenging beliefs of our country. But Kinsey had far more information that wasn't presented in the media. Questionnaires completed in the late 1940s and early 1950s, a time when people could hardly talk about sex, revealed that *one out of four of 1075 women reported that they had been approached sexually during childhood by a man.* Four out of five of these women said they had been frightened by the experience. This information was gathered at a time when no one suspected that sexual abuse was at all common. To the contrary, psychiatry text books still indicated that only one in a million people were sexually abused.

In spite of his own findings, Kinsey presented some of the same denial that still finds its way into today's views. Note that in the following quote he refers to children as "its," a manner of address that would never be used for adults. The term reflects the ownership of children that remains with us today, as well as genderlessness. In his 1953 report he said:

> It is difficult to understand why a child, except for its cultural conditioning, should be disturbed at having its genitalia touched, or disturbed at seeing the genitalia of other persons, or disturbed at even more specific sexual contacts. . . Some of the more experienced students of juvenile problems have come to believe that the emotional reactions of the parents, police officers, and other adults who discover that the child has had such contact, may disturb the child more seriously than the sexual contacts themselves. . . . .

BACKLASH

Lest you think that four decades have erased such views, take a look at an article published in 1991 entitled, "The Study of Intimacy in North America: Beyond Politics and Pedophilia" (*Journal of Homosexuality*). It was written by Gerald Jones, Ph.D., an affiliated scholar of the Institute for the Study of Women and Men in Society, at the University of Southern California. *Jones clearly states that some consenting sex between adults and children is not harmful.* He spends the pages of his article criticizing those who think otherwise, and distorting statistics to support his views. One example is his quote of a paper published in 1983—when child sexual abuse was only beginning to be frequently studied—that goes like this:

> A typical assumption of the child sexual abuse literature is that sexual contact with an adult is emotionally traumatic and causes damage that often extends well into adulthood. This is not at all an established conclusion in the empirical literature.

This abuse of the scientific method is used to make us believe that the lack of successful studies means that the observation of therapists isn't true. The truth is that in 1983, studies were only beginning to be conducted. Even now the entire subject is less than adequately addressed because there hasn't been enough time to do so.

Jones also suggests that child pornography may actually reduce sex with children by allowing the ASC to use it as a substitute outlet instead of requiring the real thing. This reflects a total lack of understanding of the process of recovering healthy sexuality, which involves giving up contact with children as well as anything that resembles such contact. He also overlooks the damage that is done to children during the making of child pornography.

Jones uses a term coined by child psychoanalyst Richard Gardner, author of *Sex Abuse Hysteria: Salem Witch Trials Revisited* (Creative Therapeutics, 1993). They both refer to the "child abuse industry," and *actually say they believe that people whose careers depend on child sexual abuse create and perpetuate the "industry" for profit.* Jones says the term is applied to the "collection of professionals who, one way or another, earn livelihoods from investigating, treating, prosecuting, or otherwise dealing with those involved in child abuse. In effect, they both profit from and influence public policy regarding child abuse." This is an amazing statement of his perception that thousands of professionals totally lack integrity, and the rest of us are duped into agreeing with them. These beliefs have a paranoid quality that makes me wonder what Dr. Jones is trying to hide.

Richard Gardner's book title demonstrates his feelings about the subject. While he says he believes that about 95% of accusations are true, his book is filled with scathing language applied to all professionals and feminists, telling us indirectly that he doesn't believe very many accusations are true. He uses his imagination to draw parallels with the Salem witch trials to demonstrate the false nature of child abuse accusations. He fails.

These men and other frightened people are grasping at any support they can find to prevent the cultural shift. Elizabeth Loftus has written books describing the difficulty people have remembering accurately, and has become the focus of the "false memory syndrome." Her writing is used by people who don't want to believe their accusers are telling the truth. They cite her research showing that people can be influenced in their perception. She works as a witness for the defense of people on trial for various famous crimes, invalidating the testimony of eye witnesses. While she is able to show that a person may not remember the color and make of a car, or the number of people present, a witness will not be convinced that they didn't see the accident. Even if memories of child sexual activity with adults aren't entirely accurate, the major parts of the experience and the fact that it happened are bound to be accurate. In addition, Loftus isn't aware of body or feeling memories that make up much of the beginning of memory of childhood abuses.

In spite of the intensity surrounding the question of accuracy of memory, I believe society's increased awareness of the size of this epidemic is too great to allow it to recede once again into repression. Too many books and too many trained therapists and too many recovering people are out there to let it happen again.

NOW WE CONDEMN THE "PERPETRATORS"

The cultural shift is underway now, and looks as if it isn't likely to be pushed back underground. But we are still a long way from seeing the whole picture. While we know that vast numbers, many millions actually, have been the object of sexual activity when they were children, we still do not have a clear picture of the people who were sexual with children.

Perhaps the feminist push to see the truth about our culture's institutionalized abuse of women, and seeing men as to blame, has carried over into this arena. The lack of equality of women was a culturally sanctioned norm, as is sexual energy with children. We couldn't see it very well until the women's movement forced us to challenge our denial.

It is becoming apparent that blaming men for women's lack of equality is in error. All of us created the system, and all of us passed it along from generation to generation. (Groups of women prevented passage of the Equal Rights Amendment in the late 1970s. If every woman had voted in favor of the amendment, it would have passed even if no men voted for it. As it was, with many many men in favor, the negative vote of enough women prevented its passage.) Either sex can change the system, as evidenced by the massive influence of the women's movement in the past two decades.

In the same way, we believe that most ASC's are men (a cultural myth that will come to light in time). Again, as with the women's movement, the "bad" people are the men who do these terrible things to little children. Until we can see that

these acts, along with discrimination against women, are perpetuated by all of us, we will have a difficult time establishing
a healthy culture that will allow each of us to be fully ourselves.

Chapter 2

Women Who Have Sexual Feelings for Children

Women. We are supposed to be pure, sweet beings who would never have sexual feelings toward children. In fact, until recently, we have been portrayed as sexless, having sex only to meet the needs of our man and to have children. Even then we were to feel embarrassed if the subject came up.

In this culture where sexual material is everywhere, we generally believe that we are sexually free. But the difficulty with talking openly about sex—which I see even in my office, where people come seeking help with their sexual problems—indicates that we aren't much freer than we were in the Victorian era. The major differences seem to be in how the media is allowed to stimulate us.

Yet we all have sexuality, and we aren't able to get rid of it entirely—even if our culture tells us to. ***Women who cannot fully claim a sexual relationship with their mate or themselves are likely to spill their sexuality over onto children.*** A woman can then think she isn't being sexual, but still give expression to this part of herself. In addition, women who grew up in sexually abusive or boundaryless homes will repeat the events that went on there, as products of that particular subculture.

29

As long as women can't talk about their feelings they will continue to unknowingly damage the sexuality of children. But our cultural abhorrence of mothers' sexual feelings toward children is so intense that few mothers will be able to step forward and examine themselves. We as a society must make room for this examination. Only then will mothers be able to look at themselves and change in ways that will stop the flow of sexualized relating between mothers and their children.

To gather information about this subject, I approached four women who had already acknowledged they had sexual feelings and were confused about how to physically relate with their children. I invited them to meet with me and talk about it.

These four women have been willing to address their shame and acknowledge they have sexualized feelings when with their children. Listening to them talk allowed me to know more about my own cross-wiring. Being with a group of women I deeply respect, and who I know deserve to be considered powerful, attractive, competent, morally courageous, and leaders, allows me to identify with them, and know the same is true for me.

As we gathered in my office for the first three-hour meeting, we were all nervous. I offered to begin because I wanted to shed my own shame as quickly as possible, and I also wanted to create a mirror for their experiences. But as I talked, the other women quickly wanted to talk too, responding to the ways they identified with my story. The three hours were filled with talk, each woman picking up as soon as another seemed about finished.

YOU MAY HAVE FEELINGS

The first draft of this chapter met with numerous responses from those who read it. Initially, I thought this information would be easy to read because no overt sexual activity is described. Instead, I had difficulty reading it myself. Some people felt shame when thinking women might feel sexual toward children. Others reacted to the idea that their mothers might have done what these women did. Women were shocked when they identified with the women, and saw that they too had such feelings. Shame followed.

The women in the group were startled to read what they had said. They told me I was perfectly accurate in my account, but they hadn't realized what they were revealing until they saw it in print. Several of us experienced arousal when reading about Deb and her granddaughter, a reaction we had not had when listening to Deb tell about her experience.

We met one more time, to discuss these reactions, and began with shame and fear, much as we experienced in the first meeting. But we were soon able to see that the shame was just one more task in front of us, and knew that we would get through it too. When the two-hour meeting ended, we agreed that we would meet every few months, or when one person needed a meeting, for however long it will take to eliminate this shame. We know it will take time, and we know we can do it.

If you find yourself feeling arousal, shame, horror, anger, or realization of what happened to you, please breathe, and know you are a good person regardless of what you have done or what was done to you.

THE FIRST MEETING

Three topics dominated our initial meeting. The first was our subject. We were there to talk about cross-wiring to children, whether in action, in looking, in thinking, or in feeling. As we talked we noticed that this subject was interlaced with memories emerging about the sexual activities with adults that took place in our childhoods. It became clear that the two are so linked that memories of one won't be likely to occur without memories of the other. This supported one of my developing beliefs: ***Those of us who are recovering from childhood damage to our sexuality are limited if we can't allow ourselves to also know that we carry cross-wiring to sexualize children.*** It may be the same cross-wiring that the adult who was sexual with us had. The five of us are willing to know what we have done, what we are doing, and what we are trying not to do in order to open all doors to recovery.

WOMEN'S ATTRACTION TO WOMEN

The third subject was our attraction to women, and how we disowned it. As we discussed this for forty-five minutes, I puzzled over it, wondering if we were trying to avoid the topic we were here to address—our attraction to children—but when I brought it up, it became clear there was another reason.

The attraction of heterosexual women to other women is also considered offensive by our culture, while that same culture inevitably cross-wires us to such attraction. We also receive the messages designed for men. We are told that women of certain shapes, facial configurations, and hair-styles are sexy. We are bombarded by the same display of sexual seductiveness and flirtatious sexual energy, yet because we are female, we aren't supposed to respond—just as we aren't supposed to respond to children. ***One of our cultural beliefs is that men will respond to female "sexiness" and women will not. In fact, we aren't different in this respect.*** The sexualization of women who are defined as worthy sex objects is not a natural, healthy use of sexual energy. Instead, it is cross-wiring for men. The poor sexual boundaries of our mothers and other female care-takers, followed by media display of "sexiness," have set us up to have the same reactions that men are trained to have. But we aren't allowed to have these reactions and feel normal. (Men are required to have these reactions to feel normal.)

As admissions of attraction to breasts and other body parts emerged in conversation, we could see that we needed to bring all areas of prohibition out into the open in order to relinquish all sexual shame. We cannot select one area alone, and leave the others untouched. We also noticed that it was easier to see the effects of our culture on our attraction to women than to children, so the comparison helped us break our denial of our culture's support for attraction to children.

PREVENTING SEXUAL RESPONSE

Much of the first three-hour meeting was spent talking about how we try to prevent ourselves from having "unacceptable" sexual feelings. Feeling revulsion so that we won't feel arousal is one maneuver we could all identify with. When this had to do with responses to other women rather than to children this was easier to see. Maggie spoke of her disgust when she saw young women in bikini bathing suits. When looking at their pubic area, she felt angry. As we talked she realized that she introduced these negative feelings in an unconscious maneuver to make sure she didn't respond with sexual awareness or feeling. Other women saw that they did too.

We thought then about how we felt when our mothers and other adults expressed this kind of distaste when we were teenagers. We could see how it affected our sexuality because when adults directed disgust toward us we believed something was wrong with our bodies. Even if nothing was said, facial expressions and other unspoken communications did the job. *Our bodies, particularly our sexual bodies, were mirrored back to us as the object of revulsion to people who didn't want to act on their sexual cross-wiring to us.* It implied that it was our fault, or our bodies' fault, that these strong negative feelings were elicited. We had no way to consciously know that our mothers and other women were sexually attracted to our bodies, and hated themselves for it. Now we are in their place, so unaccepting of our reactions that we prohibit them with hateful feelings toward those who stimulate them. Until we know how to change such feelings, we have had to choose feeling sexual toward other women, including the off-limit category of teen-age girls, or develop aversions so that we can't be aware we have such cross-wiring.

Pictures in women's magazines are one place we are allowed to look as long as we want, and to develop a sexual hum from the stimulation, as long as we don't know it is happening, or don't admit it to other women.

Shame came up as we discussed these reactions, but not as much as we felt when talking about how we prevent sexual responses to our children.

FEELING LIKE VICTIMS OF CHILDREN'S SEXUAL INTEREST

Maggie said she was able to be affectionate with her daughter until she reached three. Then she didn't want to hug her any longer. Not only did she not want to hug her, she found most physical contact repulsive. Maggie cried as she described how her body stiffened when her daughter approached her. She felt like a harmful, damaging parent for experiencing her as if she were a sexual perpetrator instead of loving her. Maggie knows she communicated to her daughter that she was repulsive, and that her genuine needs brought disgust.

Sylvia spoke about her feelings toward her seven-year-old. She said that she feels anxious and tense when the girl laces her fingers with Sylvia's when they are walking together. Sylvia is comfortable if she takes her daughter's hand to cross the street, or otherwise meet a physical need. But if she wants to be affectionate, Sylvia writhes inside.

As we continued to talk, we came to a realization. *Women feel like the victim of the child's sexual interest.* It is natural for children to experience sexual interest in parents, and for parents to set comfortable limits. But children who are eroticized by previous sexual contact with adults will have sexual interest that is stronger than developmentally appropriate. In addition, a parent who is cross-wired to respond to a child's sexual overtures will experience any initiation of sexual and non-sexual affection as a sexual come on, and may feel repulsed by their desire to respond. The child is rejected and taught that there is something wrong with her or his sexuality and body. This dynamic is well understood by therapists when it occurs with fathers and daughters. Another point is less understood. *Reacting to children's sexuality with repulsion takes place just as frequently between fathers and sons, mothers and daughters, and mothers and sons.* We are not as heterosexually dominant as our culture says. We are people, all in soft flesh, and we are capable of being stimulated by many configurations of body parts.

CHILDREN "SERVICE" PARENTS

I described my feelings of discomfort when my son rubbed my shoulders or otherwise brought me physical pleasure. I wouldn't let him because his touch brought up fear that I would be like my mother, who invited her children to take care of her need for physical contact.

My mother didn't like to sleep alone, and so when my father was out of town she said whoever got into their pajamas first could sleep in her bed. I always won. The deal was that whoever got to sleep with her scratched her back while she read for an hour or more. I was willing to do this for the physical closeness, closeness that seemed unintrusive because she wasn't doing anything to me.

My mother also paid my sister and me to massage her thighs after she read a theory that massage would remove fat. But in a short time I felt too uncomfortable with this arrangement. It was one thing to scratch her back, but another to rub her body while she lay on the bed.

While my mother wasn't overtly abusing me sexually, (in other words, wasn't eliciting direct sexual stimulation of either of us), my sexuality was being compromised. My natural physical boundaries weren't respected, and I had no room in our communication patterns to ask to have my need for touch met. Instead, her desire for physical ministration took precedence, and I was allowed to obtain some physical contact in exchange. This isn't how it is supposed to go. Instead, parents are there for the needs of their children, and are to meet their own needs somewhere else. In this way, a child is allowed to express her or his needs as they are developmentally appropriate, and have them responded to with respect. Sometimes a child needs to have parents set boundaries on the kind of contact they will have with the child, particularly sexual contact. When my mother asked me to touch her as if she were the child or the lover, it was clear that my needs were not the focus. I could expect that no loving boundaries would be set if I pursued further in a perhaps sexual way—she would either accept or be repulsed, neither of which was good for me.

I told the women about this background, and how I had observed myself doing the opposite with my son. I wanted to make sure he didn't do anything for me that was sensual so that I wouldn't do to him what had been done to me. This was an unconscious process because when it began I couldn't have said what had been done to me. All I knew was that when Austin became old enough to rub my shoulders, I froze at his touch. I felt massive confusion as I experienced it feeling good. I stiffened up, and wanted to tell him not to do that, yet I was unable to utter a word. I know this communicated that his touch was unwelcome, that his mother didn't want physical contact with him, and perhaps there was something wrong with him that brought on my reactions. His feelings about his touch had to be influenced by the reactions of the most important person in his young life. One rule regarding touch was that he could receive, but could not give.

When I finished with my story, Maggie was waiting to talk. She said she saw in herself the fear of touching harmfully, and so she didn't want to touch her children. She feels frozen when they approach, knowing that she puts out a good deal of sexual energy in the course of her sexual addiction to her husband, and occasionally to other men. She cried bitterly as she acknowledged that her children were deprived of their mother's loving touch, but at the same time, she spoke what the rest of us feel—it is impossible to know what is happening when we are in the middle of family interactions. It isn't possible to use our intellectual understanding to make sure children aren't hurt. The programming is so deeply imbedded that it operates even when we "understand" with our minds. Change only happens when we have explored our own pasts with our parents, and have had the feelings we couldn't have at the time. Then we change automatically with our children. *The challenge is to avoid feeling shame for our unhealthy relating with children, and for our inability to just stop.* Adults who are overtly sexual with children might be able to stop the behaviors, but can't decide to stop the thoughts. Isolation from children to make sure the adult doesn't act on the thoughts cannot be controlled either. I believe the change is automatic, as I will describe in the next chapter.

OUR MOTHERS DIDN'T KNOW THEY WERE SEXUAL WITH US

Rose's mother rubbed Vicks on ten-year-old Rose's chest when she was sick—an act that appeared loving. But when she rubbed over Rose's breasts, Rose knew there was something off about it. She didn't have words about sexual energy then, but did have associations with the shamefulness of sexual energy as well as the intuitive knowing that her boundaries were being violated. Even today she doesn't know what her mother was feeling or thinking, but she does know that a sexual violation was taking place.

Rose said that when she began the long process of recounting her past in Alcoholics Anonymous (AA) meetings and in therapy this memory was the most difficult to tell. The first time she told about it she almost threw up. Even her stories about repeated sexual abuse from an alcoholic neighbor did not bring on such despair. These feeling memories indicate that the experience with her mother was more painful and intrusive than the overt sexual attack by a drunk man many times her size.

We don't know the whole story about what went on in her mother's mind, but we know she didn't know she was being sexual with her daughter. If Rose were to confront her with the violations, I know she would be horrified that Rose thought such loving acts were sexual abuse. I know from my own experience, and the stories of other women, that we don't know. Our confusion stems from the ways we were objects of our parents' confusion, and their parents' confusion. We are blinded to all but the most obvious sexual contact because each of us received the spoken or silent message that this behavior is not sexual. As each of us felt obligated to believe the generation before us, we became unable to know that what we were doing was sexual. Thus we pass it on to our children with no conscious awareness of what we are doing.

Even if we go to great lengths to make sure we don't act on "it," we communicate shame to our children about their sexuality as they seek to express it. Parents who make their children dress in ways to prevent the parent from becoming aroused communicate that something is wrong with the child's body, and something is wrong with the child for triggering feelings that the adult views as intolerable.

WHEN MOTHERS DON'T WITHHOLD SEXUAL ENERGY

Rose has unknowingly been sexual with her children. Maggie gave Rose information from the time the two families ran into each other while camping. Maggie said that Rose acted as if she were sexually bonded to her eleven- and six-year-old sons, while she seemed to have no sexual bond with her husband. As Rose listened to the compassionate description, she cried openly. Hearing the truth, Rose received the first accurate mirror of sexual energy between parents and children, and felt the distress of knowing that she was harming her children's sexuality and their relationship with their father. Until her behavior was described, she had no way of knowing what she was doing. No one else around her noticed, or if they did, hadn't said anything. Without a mirror we can't be aware of what we are doing, and thus have no way to change.

Parents often ask me how they can know if they are violating their child's sexual energy, and I have to say that there is no way for me to tell them this. I would have to see the family in their home to provide a reflection. Until now, no family has invited me to do a session in their home for this purpose. It seems too painful to know.

Deb told us about her three-year-old granddaughter, whom she frequently takes care of. Recently the little girl was lying on the couch with her legs spread, rubbing her vulva. Deb said that she couldn't look at her because she knew if she did she would become aroused. As we talked about the arousal, she wasn't sure if it was because of attraction to little girls, or attachment to this one in particular, or if it was because any sexual scenes, even innocent ones, are arousing to her. This question made us realize that we live in a culture that withholds open, healthy conversation about sexuality, setting us up to be sexually responsive to sights that we might not choose to respond to. *When we can talk, we free ourselves of sexual shame and secrecy, which automatically allows us to access our healthy sexuality.* When this happens, we get to relinquish knee-jerk reactions to sexual stimuli, instead feeling sexual only when it serves us in a healthy way.

Whatever the reason, Deb and the rest of us were aware that her granddaughter received a communication about sexual energy from her grandmother's turning away. It doesn't take words to shame a behavior or feeling. Her young receptors are still tuned in to the reactions of others, and she uses this information to define her world. Deb helped her define self-stimulation as something that creates distress in adults. If all adults respond this way, she will have only one mirror—one that reflects her sexuality as at least strange, and at most shameful. She is being prepared to hide masturbation, or to give it up altogether, and this preparation will emerge more strongly when she reaches puberty and has no conscious memory of how she learned it.

Deb also talked about how she is drawn to children's body parts, but doesn't know if this is sexual or not. She talked about how cute young children's butts are, and their little round arms. We all agreed that we felt the same way, but couldn't separate healthy adoration from objectification. We will need to do more of our own healing from the way our culture has abused the sexuality of all of us before we can know.

RECOVERY BRINGS AWARENESS OF OUR CROSS-WIRING TO CHILDREN

Sylvia was filled with distress as she told us that as she moves along in her recovery from years of hidden sexuality with her father, she finds herself more aware of the ways she is sexually attracted to her children. She had assumed it would be the opposite. As a group we could see that all our experiences of sexuality had to emerge if we were to heal any one of them well, and so it made sense that she was having to become conscious of her attraction to them as she became conscious of her father's attraction to her. While Sylvia found all this painful, it provided some hope that she will be able to work through to the point of relinquishing the cross-wired response to her children. She is aware that the more she knows about it, the less likely she is to act on it.

While Sylvia knows that her work is in her children's best interest, she is left in the awkward position of not knowing how to relate with them about all of this. For example, her little daughter said she wanted to marry Sylvia when she grew up. Sylvia knows that the "right" answer is that mothers and daughters don't marry each other, and that she is married to her child's father. But Sylvia was aware that she really wanted to say that she wanted to marry her too. She felt that telling her child would be harmful because it couldn't happen, and the little girl might nurture the idea that she could sexually bond with her mother in a permanent, incestuous way. Sylvia mourned for her inability to be able to provide a straightforward, sexually healthy environment. We know that she cannot because her own childhood sexual experiences still influence her.

The group discussed another option that could provide the child with more sexual health than she might get from Sylvia's "right" response. The truth is that Sylvia likes the idea of marrying her daughter, and it is also true that she won't. I suggested that she could tell her daughter that while she had feelings of wanting that too, she knew it wasn't for the best, and so she wouldn't marry her. Sylvia might also say that she wanted to love her husband in such a way that she didn't have these feelings for her daughter, even though that wasn't happening. She could say that the best thing is for her daughter to fall in love with someone her own age when she grows up, someone outside of the family. In this way, Sylvia is telling her child the entire truth, including the unspoken feelings the child is able to pick up. And she is making it clear that while she has these feelings, they won't be acted on. Such a message can be infinitely reassuring, in contrast to children who watch their parents struggle with feelings of sexual attachment, sometimes blaming the child, and leaving the child confused, stuck with adopting the parent's sexual shame.

Maggie told about buying her daughter her first bra, and her fear that she was abusing her sexuality. Maggie's memory of humiliation when her mother touched her to see if the bra fit properly left her thinking that it would be harmful for her daughter, no matter what she did. In truth, Maggie couldn't help communicating distress to her daughter, and her daughter would unavoidably pick up some shame associated with breasts and bras.

In this situation, as in Sylvia's, telling the child about the parent's feelings in words they will understand can reduce or eliminate the negative effect. Maggie was able to allow her daughter to control the bra buying by deciding which ones she wanted to try on, and if she wanted to be alone in the dressing room. She chose to do it alone, and Maggie respected that.

While the bra-buying excursion went well, as Maggie could see when telling it, we know that her daughter picked up Maggie's feelings and doesn't have words to attach to her perceptions. It can be helpful if Maggie goes back to her and tells her about her own experience when she got her first bra, and about how she worried that she would recreate it. This will give the child words to match her experience, so she won't have to take on her mother's concealed shame. *We realized that we don't have to be perfect parents to prevent our cross-wiring from harming children's sexuality. We can help by telling the truth.* If our patterns won't let us do that, we can get someone else's help to tell the child what she or he needs to hear.

MEMORIES SURFACE

We met again a month later to continue our conversation. I was nervous all day prior to the evening meeting, and we all expressed our fear as we sat down together. We had been meeting for over a year to discuss sexuality, including the abuses each of us have experienced, and were well accustomed to the process. But when the subject was our sexual cross-wiring to children, the fear level vastly intensified.

As each of us reflected over what had gone on for us the past month, a theme emerged. Instead of being disturbed by what we did to children, we were reacting to uncovering more of what had been done to us. This suggests that one reason people avoid knowing about their cross-wiring is because it will elicit memories and feelings about what occurred during their own childhood. While the shame of knowing what we did and are doing is very painful, the pain of knowing what happened when we were helpless children can be worse.

A Mother's Grief

Deb talked about how she had sexualized the relationships with her children, who are now grown. Sobbing deeply she told us how she had become sexually aroused while her baby son was on her bed. He rolled onto the floor. She knew her sexual trance had caused her to be unaware of his needs, putting him in danger.

When he was older, she was sitting on the bathroom floor masturbating when she noticed him looking under the bathroom door. She didn't stop, or say anything to him. Again, her sexual trance prevented her from knowing his needs. While this scene may seem innocent, when parents are sexually bonded to their children scenes such as this create cross-wiring for children that will show up as they sexually mature. People who find themselves preferring to be stimulated by watching people be sexual, either in real life or pornographic services, may have a history of being aroused by observing a parent or other adult being sexual.

Maggie asked if Deb had been sexually abused as a child, wondering how she had learned to be sexual with her children if she hadn't been the object of it herself. But Deb has no memories or even patterns that suggest it. Instead, she lived in a family where her sister was the object of her father's adoring, sexualized attention. Deb was the outsider, the troublemaker who was disliked. Pushed to the outside, she sat on the fringe, wanting to be part of the family. Her loneliness and neglect prepared her to pay any price to avoid abandonment, including being sexual with adults because she intuited that sexual contact was necessary for the family system to function. Her preference was to be included, and pay the price of sexual violation rather than fill her role—being excluded and not sexualized. She yearned to have sexual contact with her father.

This history prepared her to create her own family with the same kind of sexualized bonding she had observed while growing up. Now she had the power to be the center of her family, with sexual energy glue binding her children to her. Her hope was that she could have the family she had been deprived of, but of course she had no model for how to do this in a healthy way.

Deb's story offers an example of how a person's sexuality can be damaged by what is going on in the family, even while not being sexually touched. The lack of sexual boundaries were part of the family behavior, and so they became part of Deb's view of what was normal. Her story sounds like that of many "offenders" as they say they just wanted to love the child, and be loved by him or her. Our culture has a hard time believing this is true, thinking that "these people" are just controlling rapists. In fact, many grew up associating sexual energy with family bonds, and so automatically create this kind of bond themselves. They are confused, however, by knowing it isn't right, and must be kept secret. Deb felt deep shame, guilt, and isolation for doing just what her family had done.

In the third meeting, I asked Deb if she would talk in more detail about these two interactions with her son. I was pleased to see that she had dropped much of the shame from telling it the week before, and could now give details in a way that allowed her to examine more completely what had gone on.

Deb began by telling us the history of Dwight's birth. She was nineteen. He had been conceived while she was preparing to divorce her husband, who was not Dwight's father. She had planned to go to another state during the end of her gestation and give the child up for adoption. But when he was born she realized she couldn't go through with it, and at the last minute kept him.

Her parents talked her into marrying the baby's father at the same time she was making a vow to never have sex again. She did have sex with him, but out of obligation. With these feelings about her husband, and the arrival of a baby who was open, inviting, and compliant, who loved her, and couldn't control her sexuality, she was programmed to bond with him in ways that belonged in a marriage.

As the group listened to her tell in more detail about the times she was sexually aroused in her son's presence, we saw that Deb's attitude about sex was more significant than her actions. She saw sex as so bad that she condemned herself for even being aroused when with him. *In truth, there is nothing wrong with finding one's sexual energy coming up when with a child.* We are sexual people and can feel sexual most any time. Deb had assumed that she had harmed him with it, and so wasn't able to ask herself the questions we could.

We found out that her arousal wasn't in response to him. It was something she could let herself feel when alone, and now discovered that it was also safe when in the presence of a baby. When he fell off the bed, she let that become evidence that sex was bad and harmful, something she had grown up believing. He was harmed by this situation, but not in the way she had envisioned. Her sexual arousal would not harm him if she were comfortable with it, knowing she wouldn't express it with him, and stayed present with his experience. Instead, she felt bad about it and stopped being aware of him because she assumed she was abusing him. The reaction to her arousal is what is harmful. *The damage came from being with a mother who emotionally isolated herself from her son when she felt sexual, teaching him that sexuality was shameful and harmful.*

We turned to Deb's second example, when Dwight looked under the bathroom door. We asked if she was more aroused by his looking, and she said no. If Deb had been sexually healthy, she might have stopped masturbating, opened the door, and told him that she was bringing herself good feelings. (In this culture this is an impossible scenario. We all feel too much shame.) Since she wasn't able to do this, he may have connected his curiosity with his mother's sexual energy and shame, preparing him to want to see sexual scenes in his adult years. In addition, Deb's bonding with him to the exclusion of her husband could have contributed to the cross-wiring created by watching his mother being sexual with herself. But ironically, Deb was feeling shame for events that aren't in themselves harmful to children.

TALKING BRINGS MEMORIES AND FEAR

Rose said that she had intense feelings for days after the first meeting. The rest of us nodded, affirming that the same had been true for us. Much of her pain came from seeing what she had been doing to her children. She also discovered more memories of what happened to her when she was little.

A neighbor, a man who was a friend of her family, abused her many times. She had only been able to recall the general facts, but now, as she cried on her way to work, specific memories emerged. For the first time she was able to see picture memories of his penis rubbing against her, and the dreadful feeling of being alone with this man. As a group, we knew that the memories are helpful because they give Rose more information to help her remove the effects of her past. But her pain was intense.

As the conversation continued, Maggie found herself wanting to avoid looking at us. She expressed a great amount of fear. With tears, she told again how she has no idea how to be with her children, especially as they reach puberty. As she pondered about how to talk to them about sex and what limits to put on their activities, she tearfully pointed out that she has no understanding of what is good for them.

I wanted to give her advice from reflections on my interactions with my son when he first had sex. But I could see that it would do no good. In spite of my own history of sexual abuse, some boundaries had become clear to me by the time he was a teenager. Decisions I made based on my intuitive knowing were good. At the same time, I was totally blind to other needs for boundaries, and so I either violated them, or deprived him of my presence by holding too far back. I knew this was what Maggie was experiencing, and there was no way to tell her what to do to solve her problems. Instead, remembering what happened to her, and removing the effects, is what will allow her to intuitively know what to do. In spite of this awareness, part of me wanted to say: the boundaries are obvious, just do it! My thoughts were reflecting the attitude of our culture—the belief that we can be told what to do, and then be able to do it. It isn't true. My "voices," based on unhealthy patterns created in my past, haven't been put to rest yet.

As Maggie continued to describe the despair that comes with permitting new memories to emerge, it became clear that this is what is needed in order to free ourselves to offer our children a healthy sexual environment. It made sense as we all talked about our current sexual boundaries with children that we were motivating ourselves to explore our pasts further. *Our shame for not relating in healthy ways with our children isn't as great as the fear of finding out what happened to us when we were children.* Those feelings from childhood felt more like life and death because we were dependent, and stuck with those we lived with. Now we can experience great pain over what we have done and are doing, but we are adults and know that we can live through it.

SEXUALIZED AFFECTION LOOKS LIKE LOVE

The subject moved again, and we made another important realization. *We grew up thinking that sexualized interaction was actually healthy loving.* Rose told us that when her children were born she grieved the loss of her husband because she believed she now had to focus all her attention on them. He grieved the loss of her too. Now, years later, she is seeing that she and her mate are the center of their lives, and their bond is the only one that should be sexual. The children are reacting to their changes by pushing in between them when they are relating lovingly. It seems threatening to them now because they are accustomed to the old ways. Rose is pleased that she is getting to begin an honest, loving relationship with her husband, knowing she isn't depriving her children by doing so. She said they were encouraged by family and friends to put the children first, noting how that pushes both parents to put sexual bonding energy toward their children.

Maggie talked about how she turned to her son when she divorced his father, and was between lovers. Looking back, she knows that he became the man in her life—a form of drug for her relationship addiction. Yet to the world she looked like a mother who really loved her son. Most people would "understand" that when she fell in love with a man there wouldn't be as much attention for her son. It wasn't seen that the energy she gave to her son, and then removed, was sexual in nature even though she wasn't having sex with him. When Maggie married her current husband, her son chose to live with his father,

reacting to the betrayals he experienced from her swings between him and men. We can only guess how her actions will
affect his adult sexual relationships as he tells this story through
his behavior.

WHEN TOUCH AND SEX ARE CONFUSED

***The association of sexuality and physical contact deprives us
of touching people we are close to.*** If we do touch, we may feel
sexual even when neither person desires it. If this happens then
we have a choice between touching and sexually violating, or
not touching and depriving both people. As we clear out old
patterns, we get to touch non-sexually, and have the deep
human pleasure of non-sexual bonding. This bonding is non-
exclusive, can happen with many people, and doesn't interfere
with relationships. It doesn't elicit healthy jealousy, the kind of
jealousy that signals a threat to a monogamous bond.

SOME POSITIVE CHANGES

In addition to the increased fear and despair, we also found
positive changes resulting from the first meeting. Sylvia told
about how her daughter asked her again to marry her. This time
Sylvia was aware that she didn't want to marry her daughter, and
could comfortably tell her she was married to her husband.
From discussion, and from feeling, she had become aware of the
appropriate boundary, and so was able to set it intuitively. If the
group had told her what to say, and she recited our answers, the
result would have been different. Her daughter would know
there was more, and Sylvia would have been relating from the
outside in. But with a real shift on the inside, she no longer
wanted what wasn't healthy for her child.

I also had a positive experience when I hugged my son.
Instead of a stiff, tight feeling, I was relaxed and open, knowing

I wasn't accidentally going to be sexual with him. As a result, I could really feel his body, and energy passed back and forth between us. I knew that I didn't have to hold back everything to make sure the sexual part was held back.

FINDING APPROPRIATE SEXUAL BOUNDARIES

As we settled into our chairs for our third meeting, I could see that all of us felt more comfortable with our subject.

The three-hour talk was dominated by our lack of knowing appropriate sexual boundaries with our children and all people. Some of us knew about some kinds of boundaries, but none of us knew about all kinds. It felt good to admit that we just don't know, and reduce the shame that comes from the belief that we must know. Now we were in a better place to learn.

As a therapist, my patterns tell me I must have all the answers. I don't. In my consultation group with three other therapists, we discuss ways that we don't set limits for our clients for the same reasons these women don't with their children. We have never been taught that we should, we don't have good models, and we are trained to be dutiful "helpers" however the other person defines that. While I had no training in graduate school, I was, at the same time, expected to already know what limits to set (much as the partner of the "sex offender" is expected to know what the mate is doing with the children).

When my colleague told us about a man who pulled his chair much closer to her while exhibiting sexual energy, I could see that her limit was to tell him to move his chair back. She wasn't able to. In that situation I might not have been able to either. She also couldn't comment when he told his wife in a couples' session that he wanted his wife's body to look like my colleague's. As we process examples like this every month, it becomes clear how we can see what the other therapist has a right to do, and should do to help their client, but for each of us who is presenting, it isn't at all easy to know. *We contend with a culture that encourages us to not see from the time we are born. Becoming parents and psychotherapists makes us realize how little we know.*

WE DON'T KNOW WHEN WE VIOLATE OUR CHILDREN

Rose expressed fully how frustrating it is to not know how she is violating her children's boundaries. But her shame about it is dropping, allowing her to experiment with talking to her children about sex. She told us that she read the chapter called "Growing Up In A Healthy Sexual Culture" from my book, *Discovering Sexuality That Will Satisfy You Both*, to her twelve-year-old son. (This chapter is also available on an audiotape read by me called *Healthy Sex: Real Life Stories of Bonding, Monogamous, Joyful, Shame-Free, Rule-Free Sex*, published by The Printed Voice.) Doing so sparked conversation that lasted over an hour. He asked questions of both Rose and her husband, and they thought of things that this open forum allowed them to tell him. The subject of sex is so off limits for healthy discussion that it is difficult for people to know what to tell children, and even if they know, to do it easily.

One of the subjects Rose brought up with her son was how she had bonded with him in ways that should be limited to his dad. She told him that she had been sexually abused by a neighbor when she was a child, and went on to talk about AIDS and safe sex. She found shame coming up when she was reading the chapter, but she was able to let it flow within her, and not hold back. She was pleased to say that she is feeling shame less and less. She knows now that telling him about sex doesn't abuse him. In contrast to the messages she grew up with, she knows that the only way she can provide a healthy sexual environment for her children is to be open about sex.

Rose ended her story by telling us that she visited her family with her son, and he casually mentioned that the neighbor had been sexual with her when she was little. Rose was horrified because she isn't comfortable discussing this with her parents. At the same time she could see that her son had no shame because she had provided a different environment for such discussions. It was working. Of course he thought that it would be the same with grandparents as it was at home. Even though it wasn't, he didn't feel shamed for bringing up a subject they wouldn't be comfortable with.

While Rose is learning how to be with her children differently, she is aware of how she hadn't known about boundaries until lately, and passed this lack of knowing on to them. She gets reports from the school that both her children don't respect the boundaries of other children, touching them when they aren't receptive. She understands now that her sons don't know because their mother didn't. And she didn't because her parents didn't.

Rose gave an example of her family's lack of boundaries. She has a cousin in his thirties who came up to her at a picnic, got very close, put his arm around her, and talked non-stop. This time Rose knew that he was intrusive, and that he didn't know she was displeased. She tried to move away but to no avail. While she wanted to tell him to get away from her, she was bound by family rules not to be rude. Finally she made a joke so she wouldn't embarrass him, telling him she needed her space.

As she reflected on this incident, she talked about how much she touches and kisses her children, and has difficulty differentiating between healthy loving and violation. I knew that her ability to ask herself the question with minimal shame was an accomplishment. Rose is stopping the cycle by changing her programming so her sons can change theirs.

Continuing to reflect, Rose told us about teaching her sons to wash under the foreskin on their penises. They haven't been circumcised, and she had heard that not washing well was a danger. Because of our cultural lack of understanding, she couldn't make the decision to leave her son's penises as they were without concern that she was damaging them. Now she thinks that she helped her oldest son wash far too long. She didn't do the same with her youngest. Once he was able to wash it, she let him do it, along with the rest of his body.

Rose recently stopped kissing her mother on the mouth. She is also refusing to let her mother pay for everything when they are together. While this feels good, she is grieving for the ending of a love relationship. Rose has grieved deeply for the fact that she has to question the relationships with her parents in order to do her healing. Now it was becoming apparent why. The loss of the sexualized bond with her mother is as painful as the loss of a long-term spouse. Sylvia pointed out that this separation from her mother, and discovering her own appropriate boundaries, is what will free Rose to know appropriate boundaries with her sons. Rose nodded sadly. The loss of the illusion of love with her parents will not be easy to face.

WHEN BOUNDARIES ARE TOO STRICT

Maggie talked about how her problem with her children was just the opposite of Rose's. Both women had observed each other when their families met while camping. Rose commented to Maggie that she wasn't affectionate with her children, and

Maggie told Rose that she was too physical with hers. Both were right, and neither knew what appropriate contact would look like.

Maggie had told us before about her fears while helping her daughter buy a bra, and her disinclination to kiss her even on the cheek from the time she was three. Her understanding of how children are harmed by lack of contact was deepening. Maggie looked stunned as she realized that children who aren't touched will feel as if something is wrong with their bodies, and with them. She also knew that understanding this won't make a difference. She can't make a decision to touch her children— the decision is made on an emotional, non-intellectual level. She still fears that she will do to them what was done to her, and this fear prevents her from touching them.

Sylvia pointed out to Maggie that when she felt an aversion to touching her daughter, she was "in memory." She suggested that Maggie make note of the ways she was afraid to touch her child, and at what ages, knowing that it holds information about what happened to her when she was little. Perhaps Maggie's body was violated beginning at age three. At present, Maggie only remembers sexual abuse during late childhood.

WHEN A PARENT CAN'T SET LIMITS

Sylvia is frustrated with her relationship with her older daughter, the one she doesn't want to hold hands with when out walking. Sylvia doesn't feel she has the right to limit interactions that feel sexual because she can't believe that an eight-year-old would have such feelings. Our culture doesn't make room for knowing that all children have sexual feelings, some more intense than others, and more intense at some ages than others. Sylvia assumes that her own childhood of sexual violation is making her uncomfortable, while her daughter's behavior is non-sexual. In truth, it is a combination. Her daughter has the right to approach her mother sexually, and to receive comfortably-set limits. This is how she will learn about physical and sexual boundaries. But Sylvia was required to let anyone sexualize with her when she was a grade school child, and not see it as wrong. That rule has remained in place.

Sylvia described her daughter sitting next to her on the couch, with her head against Sylvia's breast. Sylvia told her she couldn't do that. When her daughter asked why not, Sylvia evaded the truth and said it was because she had yogurt on her face. Her daughter wiped off the yogurt, and came back to try again. As we laughed, and then saw the seriousness of deceiving children, Sylvia could see that she had a right to say, "This is my body, and my breast, and I don't want you to touch it." Instead, Sylvia felt like the victim and her daughter the perpetrator. *By not having the right to set limits, she cast her daughter into the role of the one who gets to decide what will happen to her body, and then hated her for it.* As Sylvia becomes able to reclaim her body from anyone at all, then she will be able to set appropriate limits for her daughter, which will allow her daughter to grow up more comfortably, knowing appropriate body limits.

Rose believed she would hurt her children if she said no to contact with her body. While she can now see this isn't true, she isn't able to consistently act on it, still finding herself letting them be physical with her in ways that aren't comfortable. They learn that they can touch anyone any way they want, and they will grow up to believe they can be touched any way anyone else wants.

Sylvia and Rose's confusion is intensified by grief as their children are growing older and pulling away from physical contact. Sylvia's youngest daughter, age three, doesn't need the kind of physical contact she did as a younger child, and Sylvia is grieving. Her most valued contact was in this relationship because she is not able to feel safe interacting affectionately in her marriage. The sexual abuses from her childhood prevent her from feeling physically safe with her husband, although this is changing.

HOW DO WE KNOW WHAT LIMITS TO SET?

Rose was raised to believe that being a good mother means giving her children everything, which equals having no boundaries. Yet she feels violated by them if she doesn't set limits. When she feels violated, she gets angry, and her children pay the price. She shook her head as she said that honoring herself is good for her children. This is making sense to her, but when she is relating with her children, it is easy to forget.

Most of us associate affectionate touch with sex because our culture doesn't have models of non-sexual touch. Men aren't supposed to touch or hug each other because it might be seen as sexual, breaking one of our most cherished taboos. Women have more permission to touch, and also to have sexual energy with each other. But non-sexual touch is rare. (It is hard to find a body worker whose touch is without sexual or otherwise intrusive energy.) And when we do experience clean touch, it is difficult to know that it is. As a culture we are confused. The women in this group can admit it, and feel their discomfort.

Maggie looked at the reasons she is afraid she will violate her children with touch. As a child she believed her body was owned by her parents. She wasn't allowed privacy. Her father took pictures of her in her bra and underpants when she was a young teen while her mother was present. She was required to shower with him when she was fourteen, and sleep in the same bed when the two traveled together. His sexual violation of her seemed to be part of the package, little different from these other ways he owned her.

When Maggie walked in on her eight-year-old son putting his pants on she turned and walked out. Afraid she was like her father, she wanted to be sure she didn't abuse him. She feels the same way when her children walk into her bedroom when she isn't fully dressed—as if she has violated them with her body, and it is her fault. When the family was at a resort swimming pool her son told her that a boy was looking at her breasts. She felt guilty, and didn't wear her swim suit again that trip. She also knew that her son didn't see it as her fault, and actually said that the boy shouldn't do that. While Maggie can know this consciously, she abides by her old belief that any sexual attention she gets is her fault—a message from her childhood.

Deb, who knows her father didn't touch her sexually, also knows that he thought touch was sexual. He believed he owned her, and walked into her room without knocking. She experienced him as predatory, always watching, knowing, and showing up unexpectedly. This lack of boundaries in turn prevented Deb from knowing what her children needed from her.

We ended the meeting by talking about how old we were when we first masturbated. Of the five of us, only one did so as a young teen. The other four were over twenty. By not touching ourselves sexually, we were responding to the communication that our bodies were owned by others and were not for our pleasure. Any pleasure we had was assigned to a lover, not ourselves. This evidence of how we were cut off from our physical selves made it clear once more why we don't know what our children's bodies need.

Maggie provided us with a wonderful story in the next monthly women's group. Her daughter had begun to menstruate, and the experience was very different from Maggie's, and from that of all the other women. Maggie's husband picked the daughter up from a visit with her father. When she got in the car, she said, "Guess what, Richard!" When he said, "What!" she told him she had her first period. He exclaimed with delight for her. When they got home, she told Maggie, comfortably, with no embarrassment. Maggie and Richard had been able to present the subject in a way that allowed her to have normal feelings about it instead of the more common shame-laced experience of menstruation in this culture.

When Maggie asked her daughter if her stepmother had bought her pads she said no. She also said no when asked if she had told her dad. Maggie could see the difference between her family and one that has no recovery. We joyfully celebrated that her emotional cleansing is making a difference.

BONDING CONFUSION

Holding babies and children feels good to us. If it didn't, we wouldn't meet the child's needs. The warm, loving, sensuous feeling of holding a baby or a child communicates physical loving and safety. Energy is passed back and forth between the child and parent in the same way that sexual energy passes back and forth between bonding adults. This is necessary for the child, and appropriately pleasurable for the parent. If we have clear boundaries about our role as a parent, then we will exchange this energy only when it is right for the child. But if we think we have the right to meet our needs through the child, then we set up a situation where the child is required to use this powerful energy in ways that aren't good for the child.

Further confusion is created if the parent experiences the energy exchange as adult sexual energy. Then the bonding is monogamous, excluding the other parent and other children. Normal jealousy is aroused, creating chaos in the family.

I got to experience the difference one morning when I was lying in bed with my husband, Rex. My chest was on top of his, and I could feel my breasts and chest open with a soft, vibrating energy. As I paid attention to it, I knew that at this moment it wasn't monogamously bonding energy that was passing back and forth between us. It was the same kind of feeling I would have if holding a baby. I knew that it could be easily changed into the monogamously bonding kind. If it was time for us to use that energy, it would have shifted to include genital arousal and the urge to mold our bodies together to invite more intense sexual feelings. Because my parents weren't clear on the difference, it had been hard for me to learn. They couldn't model the difference for me.

A member of my men's group helped demonstrate the non-monogamous energy bond. After struggling with patterns from his relationship with his mother, he moved to a new emotional place. He looked at me in the way infants look at their parents. His face softened, becoming rather expressionless. His eyes were glued to my face. He said he was feeling sexual, but it wasn't an adult form of sexual interest. I saw that he was in a regressed state. He had moved back to his infant self, looking for the kind of experience he didn't get back then. He was open to a healing experience, a newborn now in a healthier family. I softly told him I wasn't going to be sexual with him, but I wanted to meet some of his child needs. For many minutes we looked into each other's eyes and spoke softly while the rest of the group looked on.

When the exchange had matured, the rest of the group spoke. One man said he didn't feel left out even though I was so focused on another "child" in the family. He felt loved too. Several others nodded their similar experience. He asked what

I had done. I knew the question was, what had we done. I was able to give this man love in a way that was not monogamously bonding, and the other men (except one) had completed enough healing from their childhood that they were able to share in this new family experience. They didn't project their past families onto this one, feeling deprived because one sibling got Mom's attention. We all got to see that it is possible for a new sibling to enter the family and for love to grow in quantity, rather than diminish. Several men talked about feeling love for the new "infant"—as I was—while they also absorbed the loving I was giving him. As my love was received, I felt alive and filled with love too.

One man's history remained with him. He wanted attention, and resented the fact that I focused so intensely on someone else. He is aware that his childhood was being projected into the room, and that he was unable to absorb the love that was flowing freely in many directions during those minutes. He could see from a distance that it was possible, enhancing his understanding of what can happen as he continues his healing.

I rejoiced in the experience of giving healthy loving to my client, and then seeing that my "family" has been able to grow into health and be able to share love too—not just what comes from me, but from each other, from themselves, and from observing loving expressed between two other family members.

My ability to be with my client in ways that allowed him to have this experience of non-monogamous, family love came from healing my own sexual energy. No clinical training could have helped me here if I hadn't done my own work. My clients couldn't have joined in the new family relating if they hadn't been challenging their own sexual histories too. It is more typical for members of groups to be angry when I focus intently on one member. I have seen that it is possible to obtain what our culture defines as impossible. We can love many people and be loved by the shared loving of others. But we can't do this by deciding to—contrary to the message of many songs and sayings, particularly those from the 1960s. We can do it by cleaning out the effects of our histories and our culture. When we do that, the results are automatic.

Chapter 3

Ignoring the Sexuality of Children Is Harmful Too

A dults who were sexually stimulated by older people when they were children will carry shame into their grown-up years. One cause of this shame is the fact that we end up with cross-wiring to have sexual energy stimulated by children even if we don't act on it. Most of us have it. We are drawn to incest, but if we see that it is incest, we either respond sexually or we are repelled by it.

Advertising calls on this fact by luring us in with ads that don't seem sexual, but draw our interest. Some very expensive ads exploit our sexual cross-wiring to children, demonstrating the power of the connection. One full-page ad from my collection of women's magazines advertised Calvin Klein perfume by showing us a woman in sexual/romantic bliss and little clothing clutching a young boy to her breast. The expression on his face shows fear and distaste.

While we look at and react to this picture, we aren't supposed to know what it is showing us. If you were to ask most people who aren't aware of how the media influences us, they would assert that this was a mother and son posed in a dramatic way, with no implications of incest. Those of us who have studied our cross-wiring know that, indeed, this is a picture of incest. Every time I get this picture out to look at it again, I am shocked by the information in it. It is a form of soft pornography, drawing on the cross-wiring of mothers and children—enough mothers to sell large amounts of perfume. Until we can know this, we can't recover from our own such cross-wiring.

I draw on my own experience to understand the role of this cross-wiring even for those of us who weren't overtly sexual with our children. A dominant feature of my recovery is addressing my blindness to sexual cross-wiring to some children's bodies.

I still have little information about relating with my son as a child, but more and more is emerging. I would like to tell you one story of how I brought more to consciousness. First, some background.

At least one adult was sexual with me when I was a child, perhaps more. I grew up thinking that sex between adults and children was a hideous thing, in part because of my own distress when it happened to me, and because of the reactions of people who, unconsciously or consciously, knew. My father must have considered himself abhorrent for his actions, and my mother hated both of us for it—without consciously knowing why. I believe his sex addiction stemmed in part from the shame of violating his values. I know my father didn't intentionally try to hurt me, and, if he had a choice, would have died before harming me. I have seen clients who were suicidal because they couldn't otherwise stop their addiction from harming innocent people, and I recognized his story in theirs.

One of the effects of his sexual activity with me is that I am cross-wired to sexual feelings for my offspring and for certain other children. Those of us who were stimulated sexually as children will have some form of reaction to children.

The irony is that the very shame that accompanies my cross-wiring prevents me from recovering from it, and thus eliminating sexualized attraction to some children. If I feel like a bad person, then I can't examine my attractions because it is too painful to admit it. Yet they must be examined in order to heal them. As a result, I have focused on the rights of all adults who have attraction to children, or who have acted on it, as deserving compassion and the right to recover. It is, ultimately, myself to whom I want to extend compassion so I can lovingly accept myself and recover. Writing this book with passion is one way I am working toward a new subculture so that I can diminish my shame in order to do the work.

MY RELATIONSHIP WITH MY SON

When my son was born twenty-three years ago, I had no idea that adults had been sexual with me. I was surprised when I had a fear that I might sexually abuse him. When he was about six weeks old I realized how frustrating it was to bathe him in the infant tub inside the bathtub. I had to reach over, stressing my back, and try to wash him with one hand while holding him with the other. The obvious solution was to take him into the bathtub with me so I could hold him on my lap and wash him with two hands. The moment these thoughts were completed a wave of fear grabbed me, and I was startled to find that it took the form of questioning if I would be sexual with him if I were naked while he was. It reminded me of my discomfort when a college roommate held her cat wearing only a bra, and enjoyed feeling the fur against her skin. I thought that must be a bad thing to do, and only years later was able to have that experience for myself.

I thought about it, and decided that it was possible to bathe with him without getting aroused, and so I proceeded to do so. The key was that I wasn't sexually aroused in my genitals. I know if I had been, I would have been overcome by shame and self-condemnation. I made a decision, without really being able to think about it consciously, that harm would come from sexual arousal brought about by stimulation of his body against mine, but that no harm was done if I had no genital feeling.

I didn't know that this isn't true. ***Sexual feelings can have no genital counterpart and still influence the sexuality of a child.*** Sexual energy alone can influence the relationship and the child's developing sexuality, as shown in the story of Monty and Trina in Chapter 7. My belief lead to great confusion when it came time to end bathing with Austin, and again when he became taller than me. When he was three I felt that bathing together should stop because he was getting too old—even though I had no understanding of why that age was relevant, or what harm would take place if we continued. I couldn't talk to anyone about it, including my therapist at the time, because I was unable to formulate questions regarding harm and safety for children. And the shame would have been too intense if I had done something "wrong."

Looking back, I am able to see that my decision to bottle feed Austin came from fear of sexually abusing him. I was able to say to friends that I wanted to keep my breasts for my relationship with my husband. I wasn't able to say that I was afraid I would be sexually stimulated by sucking, and didn't want to have a sexual relationship with my child. This was the case. I didn't want to recreate my own childhood.

At that time I was unable to formulate the thoughts because I couldn't have tolerated the shame that would accompany them. I now feel deprived of the experience of feeding my child from my body—deprived by the sexuality passed onto me from my father, as he passed it down through the generations. My intent (although unconscious) was to stop the cycle. I didn't understand that just stopping the behavior doesn't stop the cycle.

When Austin grew to my height, I found myself becoming unable to hug him. I wanted to be a loving mother, and be affectionate with my son, but it didn't feel right. Later examination allowed me to see that I had created an artificial boundary around my sexuality. I established a belief that I was only sexual with men who were taller than I was, which put a child off limits. This belief sustained me for the first eleven years, but once he became taller, I had to find other ways to make sure I wasn't sexually abusing him.

Years of awkward hugs went on until I was able to find a way to tell my own story and discover my cross-wiring. My good friend Jim and I used our relationship to work through some of our issues of sexual damage, although we weren't aware of this when it started.

WE ARE AWARE OF OTHERS' SEXUAL FEELINGS

Jim and I had been friends for many years, and had exchanged sexual energy in a way that we thought was affectionate, playful, and not serious when neither of us was in a relationship. More recently, as he launched into recovery from sexual addiction, I became a stand-in for his mother, who had employed sexual energy with him during childhood—perhaps as I had with my son. As we were talking about the most recent example of this, and working it through, he asked me why I wanted to do this work with him. I immediately began to cry, with no thoughts or words accompanying intense sadness. I wanted to tell him that I loved him, that I valued our friendship, and that I was delighted that he could use me as a stand-in for his mother in his recovery. But I knew this emotional reaction meant there was something more I didn't know about yet. I continued to cry for several minutes, resisting the impulse to explain it to him. I was surprised that no words emerged to show to me what this welling of feeling was about. It became clear in a different way.

As we continued to talk, Jim told me he had fears that I might be sexual with him, even though I was in a relationship with Rex. I responded as I do with clients. I reassured him that I wouldn't be. But as the words came out of my mouth, I realized that I wasn't telling the whole truth. I occasionally had strong sexual awareness of him, which I dealt with as I had with my son—I cut them off. I had even discussed this with Rex, but carried on the belief that Jim wouldn't know if I didn't tell him. He showed me the error of that belief by his reaction. He cried. Then he said, "All I need is to know."

His wispy expression let me see that he was talking to his mother as much as to me, but the truth of his statement captured me. The two of us had been carrying on relationships with our relatives as we related with each other, and as long as we were silent about it we couldn't stop. Also, his mother's denial and secrecy made him feel that something was wrong with him that caused her sexualized attraction. When I can tell him straight out that I am having sexual awareness of him, then he can see that this is just my feeling, even if he did something to trigger it, and that it isn't a sinful thing to happen.

He has been a stand-in for my son and for my father, but I hadn't been able to see that because I felt so wrong for having sexualized feelings toward him. These feelings of evil lifted as I talked with Jim and evaporated further when Rex joined us to be filled in on our conversation. Telling Rex, seeing his acceptance and understanding, I could bring the past out of my unconscious and into the non-shaming present. I could know that I wasn't harming Jim.

As long as I can't let myself tell my story with friends, and even with children, I can't fully believe I was sexually damaged when I was little. Until I do know, I can't fully recover. *Until this culture allows all people to access their cross-wiring to children so they can tell about it and remove it, we will*

perpetuate the sexual abuse of children. All of us cause it, and all of us must change to stop it.

THOSE WHO HAVE BEEN ABUSED CAN EXPECT ABUSE

Two weeks later Jim came to visit Rex and me. Almost immediately I saw that I was uncomfortable being close to him, and acknowledged that I had a feeling that can be called sexual. As I glanced from him to Rex and back, I saw the difference. I felt safe with Rex, safe with our sexuality. He has no characteristics of a perpetrator to me. Sexual energy flowing up and down feels present and solid and real. Then I glanced back to Jim, and became uncomfortable, tense, and on guard—an odd feeling to have with a friend who is willing to be entirely honest with me, and listen to me being honest with him.

I told Jim and Rex about my feelings, and began to explore them. The more I talked and thought, I realized that while Jim looked something like my son, he also resembled my father when I was a child. With the help of Jim's questioning, I could see that he resembled him in some ways, both physically and in his cross-wiring to addictive sex with men, but there was more.

Jim began to talk about his relationship with his mother when he was a grade schooler. During this time his parents' marriage was falling apart, and she lived for her relationship with Jim. He had to take care of her, and sexual energy pervaded the relationship. He had no words at the time, but he now knows that he expected her to be sexual with him to meet her needs for a sexually bonded relationship to replace the one she was losing. More than expected, he waited for it to happen. And now he waits for me to be sexual with him, as I wait for him to be sexual with me. His mother and my father bring sexual energy into a relationship where it doesn't belong.

In the morning I sat on a stool at the kitchen counter, and Jim came to sit on the one next to me. Responding to a jolt of fear, I yelled out, "No! Don't sit so close to me!" Rex walked over and stood between us to protect me from the person I was projecting onto Jim. That did the job. No one had seen there was a need for protection when I was little, and of course, no one acted on my behalf.

Jim yelled back. His feelings were hurt that I thought he was going to harm me, and he told me he was going to sit where he wanted. He became Jim to me again, and through further conversation we affirmed our relationship with tears of understanding that we are in a process of clearing ourselves of past, unexpressed hurts.

In reflecting over the day's events, I began to see that my father and my son were linked in my cross-wiring. It was my father who was sexual with me when he shouldn't be, but now, since he became taller than me, I am projecting the fear that someone will be wrongly sexual with me onto my son. I was seen as the one to blame when I responded sexually to my father throughout my childhood, and now I am seeing myself as the one with damaging sexual energy when with my son.

Some adults don't see themselves as the cause of all sexual interactions, however. This results in the confusing belief that the child willfully initiated sexual contact, and the adult was "only" responding. Therapists tend to see this as an excuse made by the person who is sexual with children so that he or she doesn't have to take responsibility. But it is more than that. To some adults who were, as children, used sexually by adults, anyone, including children, will be seen as the one who is initiating sex, and who is using the person for his or her own ends. These people truly feel like the object of the "perpetrator," whether the perpetrator is an adult, a child, or even an animal.

Those of us who are willing to take the entire responsibility (or blame) feel like terrible people for having sexual feelings toward anyone but appropriately designated sex objects. It is hard for us to understand that we were the object of inappropriate sexual stimulation, or disgust over our sexuality and physical needs, and because of that, we cannot see the needs of our children clearly. It is neither the child's fault nor our fault. *The appropriate responsibility we can assume as adults is to examine our sexual behavior and thoughts so we can recover from damage done to us.* This is the only way we can free our children from the generation to generation effect of cultural distortions of sexuality. This responsibility must be assumed on a societal level in order to prevent further abuse of children's sexuality.

TRUE EXPRESSION CAN DIMINISH SEXUAL FEELINGS

I thought about this last interaction with Jim and knew that I had to make some changes. I had held back what I was feeling, willing only to tell him when it was in the past. Doing this made it impossible to really be present, and so I saw that I had to tell him everything while it was happening. This has become easier for me in most arenas, but to do this with sexuality with someone who isn't my lover seemed almost too much to contemplate. We discussed it on the phone, and he was quite emphatic that this was indeed necessary. My holding back was increasing his trigger reactions, and he couldn't see me clearly. We discussed when we could pursue this, and made arrangements to meet in the town where he lived.

I arrived at the house he shared with another man, and we prepared to leave for a restaurant. I was already aware that I couldn't hold anything back and wanted to quickly leave his roommate with whom Jim had not shared the intimate nature of our work. Small talk was the last thing I had energy for.

I began in the car. I told him I was afraid he would be sexual with me. Almost immediately I was aware that my clitoris was becoming erect. I didn't feel aroused, exactly, because there was no emotional counterpart. Just a sensation that I recognized as sexual located only in my clitoris.

Now, I have never told a man who wasn't a lover that I was having a clitoris erection. But once the words were out of my mouth I felt freer. I laughed. And he laughed. As he pondered this, he said he had never thought about clitorises having erections like penises, but that of course they would.

By the time we got to the restaurant, I was quite delighted with myself. Once again I had learned that if I just say the truth, things become so much easier. Jim's willingness to hear everything allowed us to make use of our patterned "voices." I no longer felt like a child abuser. I could see that I had picked up some of his mother's attitudes toward Jim, and laced them in with my own toward my son.

As we sat at dinner, I realized that my clitoris alternated between no erection and then erection. I began telling Jim every time it became erect, and when the feeling intensified. I was aware that what I was doing violated our cultural rules about talking about sex. The only time we are allowed to mention a sexual body part, or say we are having signs of arousal, is when we are with a lover. In addition, this communication can only take place when partners are engaged in sex, or talking about becoming sexual. *This silence is a form of false boundary, an attempt to assure that we aren't accidentally sexual with anyone.* It doesn't work, as I experienced. Instead, it highlights the sexual issues that exist. They push out as the silence pushes back. Relinquishing the silence let the conflict subside, and allowed me to see. What I saw was that I wasn't going to sexually "abuse" Jim, and that I wouldn't have done so with my son.

As I described my clitoris' activity I was able to separate out my own feelings of being sexual with my "son," from what I had picked up from Jim about his mother, and was playing out in my body. As my shame and fear dropped to nothing, I asked him if I could "play" his mother, much as my clients and I do in therapy groups. He agreed, and I began to follow the information my clitoris and the rest of me was gathering. I expressed every feeling I had about wanting to own his body, to control him, and to have him take care of my needs. As we walked down the street, I approached him physically, invasively, and he reacted with disgust. I oozed sexual energy at him, expressing the feelings that his mother might have felt when he was the only man she had in her life. My shame was gone as I knew this wasn't me, but was the character of his mother I had picked up.

As I talked over the course of an hour or so, Jim was disturbed by the accuracy of what I said and did. But he also reacted strongly to his desire to leave his relationship with his mother intact, and was angry with me for tampering with his illusion. We met again the next night, and he told me that during his work day he alternated between believing everything I had said, and thinking I was a crazy woman out to destroy his relationship with his mother.

Any doubts I had about the sexualized nature of their relationship was eliminated when I overheard him on the phone. From the tone of his voice, I thought he was talking with his lover. When I entered the room as he hung up, he told me his mother said to say Hi. I was shocked and yet not surprised.

The next weekend I went to visit my son Austin, who lives in another state. When I saw him, I walked up and put my arms around him. It felt different than it had been for years. I was aware of the feel of his body, the softness of his chest in spite of the fact that he is young and works out. He molds easily, a sign of the body work of Rolfing he has had over the years. My body was very different too. Instead of feeling rigidly on guard, I could stay fully in my body, sending out my loving toward him. From this place of safety, and knowing I wasn't going to be sexual with him, I could sense what he was feeling in his body too. I had been deprived of this from the time he became taller than I was. I was aware of the gift both of us received from my work with Jim and with the women's group.

SENSUALITY AND SEXUALITY ARE DIFFERENT

Now that I had begun the work to remove the effects of my cross-wiring, it became easier to understand what it was about. I had connected affection and sensuality with sexuality. As with the sensual feeling of holding a cat next to my skin, I thought that the loving feeling of wanting to touch Jim and Austin must be wrong if it fit in "that" category. This connection is breaking up so that I can see sensuality as something quite wonderful and healthy to have with all people I am close to. Sexuality is limited to my relationship with Rex, but this doesn't mean that my genitals won't feel arousal of one kind or another when I am around other people. When it does, it doesn't mean that I want to be sexual with them, or that I will accidentally override my values and act out. If I am free to name the feelings, and not compelled to cut them off, I can't harm anyone.

AROUSAL DOESN'T AUTOMATICALLY MEAN SEXUAL ABUSE

My lessons showed up with a client, too. Kenneth wanted to learn about why pornography of certain types was so powerful that he hadn't been able to stop using it to act out. He knew it was related to his childhood and a story that still hadn't been told. So he arrived in my office with his latest collection, prepared to show it to me. We both knew that if he did this, I would be able to see more of his story, and then he would see too.

I had some concern that I might feel sexual arousal if he had pictures that matched my still present cross-wiring, but we agreed that we would both name anything we felt, and proceeded. In the first session, Kenneth spent most of the time expressing and feeling his shame and fear of what I would do to him if I saw how vile he was. At the same time he knew this wasn't true. By the end of the session we had looked at several pictures. I had no reaction beyond curiosity.

In the second session, we looked at many pictures, and I was becoming confidant that my cross-wiring was so resolved that I wouldn't react to any of them. But then he turned a page and I saw a scene that created intense cross-wired arousal. I knew I had to name it because if I didn't he would pick up my feeling and be confused about its origin and meaning. We stopped looking at the pictures, and returned to talking about what was going on.

The next day Kenneth arrived with his therapy group. When I went out to the waiting room to get them, he stood out to me as if he were radiating a bright light and everyone else was dim. I felt myself pull inward, becoming tense and agitated. As we all sat down, I knew I was moving into a state long familiar from my childhood—one that allowed me to cut off feelings and not know what I was doing or what others were doing. But I also knew that I couldn't sit in a therapy group as a therapist and continue to do this. I would be living a lie with these people I was helping to live more openly and in integrity. I knew all the way through me that I had to present the situation to them so their experience of me would match the truth.

I opened the subject. I asked Kenneth to talk about our session the day before as a backdrop to what I had to say. Then I told him and them that I felt as if I had sexually abused him by having sexual arousal in his presence. And, by holding this belief, I was now very removed from them all. Kenneth had already seen the change in me, and his patterns decided that he was the cause. His fear that I would find him disgusting now that I had seen his pornography made him interpret my changed mood as proof that he was right.

The group responded in positive ways. During the three months we had met, they had seen me as the "together" therapist who had no patterns. Nothing had come up for me to share previously, and so none, except for Kenneth—who I had seen for some time—had had a chance to see me reveal my own patterns. Instead of criticizing me, as my patterns expected, they were delighted, and felt closer to me. I was relieved to have spoken, and my agitation began to ease. I told Kenneth, who had sat next to me in the circle, that I needed to move my chair away from him, which I did. I told him this was because of my patterns, not anything about him. I named it as fear that I might act in ways that would harm him, which, if I did, would assure my patterns that indeed I was the terrible person I grew up thinking I was—the eroticized girl who was hated for it. The distance allowed me to feel relief, and to take in what was happening in the room.

As people took turns responding to what I was saying, and to what Kenneth had presented, I felt myself slowly thawing and returning to the present. Soon I wanted to move my chair a little closer to Kenneth. People's comments made it clear to me that I wasn't a horrible person for feeling sexual in the presence of a client (child). Instead, it was just a fact, and it was fascinating to them that I was willing to name it.

Then the subject turned to other issues, and the group went on as usual. My brain and feelings whirred away, this new, healthy situation changing old programming from my childhood. Soon I was able to return to my original place in the group, next to Kenneth, with no more fear that I might harm him. The remaining intensity faded, and he became once again the Kenneth I know. The discomfort has not returned.

Chapter 4

The Father Who Used His Daughter As a Lover

I received a call some time ago from Joyce, who was referred to me by her couples' counselor. I wasn't taking new clients at the time, and so I asked her about her needs in order to refer her to an appropriate therapist. She told me she had been working with her husband in therapy for many years, addressing his sexual activity with their daughter, and she felt that it was time for her to have her own individual therapy. As she told me some of their story, I saw that it could be a model of healing from this most difficult of issues. I told her I would like to talk to her husband about the book I was writing, and see if he would be open to having his story told. When Greg called me back, he said that he had read my first book, *Reclaiming Healthy Sexual Energy*, which his therapist recommended to him, and was deeply appreciative of my shame-free approach to sexual addiction. He was very pleased to share his story in the hope that those who needed the courage to confront their own sexual use of children might read it and know there is hope. We met for the first time soon after that.

Greg and Joyce live in a moderate-sized community near Seattle. Their grown daughter has moved to another city for her career. Now just the two of them, they take walks together, talk, and spend a large amount of time on their recovery processes. Greg thinks about his behaviors, and his history that lead him to sexual acting out, even while he works in his garden among the huge flowers he planted, cultivated, and fertilizes. He likes to propagate things from seed or cuttings. He discovered that working chicken manure into the soil in the fall produces seven foot dahlias, and lush vegetation. Splitting and stacking fire wood is therapeutic, as are walks in the woods. He and Joyce are bonded to their home and to each other.

As Greg told me the usual facts about himself, I saw that he was a normal-looking person, who would not be seen as abnormal by friends in the community or even family members. A college graduate, he went on to serve in Vietnam, where he was decorated several times. As a product of the 1960s, he tried drugs, but no longer uses them. His use of alcohol became addictive in his thirties, and now he doesn't drink. He is a pleasant-looking man, earnest and very, very genuine. His feelings show on his face, and his body language is entirely congruent. This man sitting opposite me did not match our culture's ideas of a person who would be sexual with children. On the contrary, his desire was always to grow up, get married and raise children in a healthy way.

RECLAIMING HEALTHY SEXUAL ENERGY

When I asked him about what his sex life is like now, he smiled gently as he spoke. He no longer has any sexual fantasies—neither socially acceptable nor unacceptable. He and his wife are learning how to be conscious of their interest in sex, checking to see if it is based on old patterns or real interest in bonding together. What he was describing is an example of what I now recognize as healthy sex—no mood altering, no leaving the partner emotionally, and no rule following. Instead, they have sex when they are feeling like they want to be together, and want to let their boundaries dissolve for a time. As with most people who try to explain what healthy sex is like, he had a hard time coming up with words. The experience is so different than what words can describe. I heard some of my own language being used, however—language I used in my first book. In the book I offered a list of questions to ask in order to differentiate between healthy and unhealthy use of sexual energy. Greg and Joyce have been using the items in order to remain conscious of their decision to be sexual and check for remaining possibilities of unhealthy motivation. They ask themselves if sex will open them up or close them in, if it is mutual or if only one wants it, and if it comes from the inside out.

Greg checks out what has been going on in his life to see if there are reasons he may want to medicate himself with sexual feelings. Often one of them will say they aren't comfortable having sex, and the other knows that if one doesn't, it isn't healthy for either of them. If Greg sees that he wants sex to medicate bad feelings, he says so. Sometimes, though, they have sex when it isn't healthy, but they talk about it afterwards, and get to learn about what was going on for them.

Greg told me they are deliberate about sex. He wears nightclothes to bed to make sure they don't have spontaneous sex in the middle of the night. He said they want to stay aware.

Greg has also had experiences of solitary sex that are quite wonderful. He told me about the time he was meditating after doing some breath work, and noticed some arousal. He said, "Well, that's interesting," and paid attention as more energy flowed into his pelvis. His penis became erect and he had a partial ejaculation. This happened with no sexual thoughts or fantasies.

He said this was really wonderful, and it frightened him too. He immediately wanted to ask his therapist if this was OK. On reflection, he decided that he was cycling through the developmental stage of a teenager who felt free to be sexual in healthy ways. I concurred.

Greg said he knew that if he had a dad he could talk to, he would say, "Hey, Dad, this is what happened, is this OK?" He also knew that the dad would say, "Yes, this is fine." I was touched by his expression. I knew that he turned to his therapist for this confirmation, but was also able to use himself as his father. I could see that this was a wonderful experience of an adolescent who had not been shamed for sexuality, and that this man was now able to have that after years of deeply shameful sexual activity. I was also touched by the fact that I didn't need to affirm it for him—he already had.

USING SEX TO AVOID FEELINGS

Greg discovered early in his life that sexual arousal was a pleasant drug to overcome feelings elicited by a severely abusive childhood. Long before puberty he found that touching his penis brought nice feelings, and once he reached puberty these feelings intensified greatly. His objective was to remain numb to any real feelings because they seemed impossible to bear. He grieves for his sister, who was a sex object for his father, and is in therapy for a multiple personality disorder. The trauma she suffered in the same home with Greg caused her to develop more than one personality so the trauma could be contained at least part of the time. While Greg has no conscious memory of his father's relationship with his sister, he must have perceived the abuses she was living through. As he told me about her, tears ran down his cheeks. Even though she was older, he feels heartbroken because he had been unable to protect her.

Greg's memories of the traumas he experienced are only beginning to surface. He knows, though, that they made life so unbearable that he turned to the intensity of sexual arousal to feel alive. He knows he was sexually abused by a male outside the family, but knows little about what happened within it.

In his teen years, Greg's addiction grew. He had intercourse for the first time at fifteen, and found this to be even more powerful than masturbation with fantasy. From this point, he sought girl friends to meet his need for sexual addiction. He broke up with them if they weren't sexual with him, and they broke up with him when he seemed preoccupied with sex. He states clearly now that he had no interest in the girls as people, only in what they could do for him. His life was so unbearable that he had lost the ability to have empathy for his lovers. This is a byproduct of his loss of compassion for himself.

Greg became deeply attached to Joyce when they were in high school. He knows now that it wasn't love, because he wasn't capable of it. He needed her as he had needed his mother, and she offered the reassurance of never leaving him, unlike his mother who had left him over and over again. Oddly, their relationship didn't feed his sexual addiction because she refused to engage in the kinds of sex that were necessary.

Greg's addict didn't stop demanding sexual fixes, though. He went out with other women just as he had when he wasn't engaged to Joyce, or married to her. He continually fed his addiction by looking lustfully at women in order to keep a continuous sexual buzz going. Early in their marriage he decided he wanted to get a divorce in order to be free to pursue his addiction more fully, and avoid the guilt that came with being unfaithful. But as he prepared to tell Joyce, she told him she was pregnant. He didn't leave.

ACTING OUT WITH A CHILD

Greg was unaware that he had any pedophile tendencies until his baby lived with him. When she was born, he knew he had no idea how to be a father. Frustrated and frightened, he turned his sexual attention to her.

I would like to ask you to pay attention to your feelings as I describe what Greg did with his daughter, Trish. If you are still an integrated part of our culture, you have been conditioned to feel anger and revulsion when knowing of sexual activity between a father and young daughter. You also have these feelings because your own cross-wiring seems abhorrent to you, and so evidence that others have acted on it will bring up your shame. You may also find yourself becoming aroused by the images. If you do, you may be trying to control them by anger and revulsion, or you may find your addict wanting to use the arousal addictively.

Whatever your story is, I want to invite you to be kind to yourself and let the feelings come. If you are aroused, know that it is because you were cross-wired as Greg was, although perhaps you don't act on it. Let it come and breathe through your shame so that you can release some of it. If you find that your addict wants to use the images, then please stop reading and call someone who is a support to you in your recovery. The information you can receive by discovering what brings on cross-wired arousal will be useful to you as you meet your responsibility to yourself, your family, and your culture to face the ways that you might be harmful to children. You are not at fault for having such cross-wiring. You weren't born that way. But you are the only one now who can take responsibility for changing what you were given. As you read, see if breathing fully helps. You are a good person.

When Greg's daughter was only an infant he rubbed her on his erect penis. He told her that she was made for him. When she was an older child he rubbed his penis between her legs, put his penis in her mouth, and put his mouth on her vulva.

When she was three she told her mother that she and Daddy had a secret. She described in her own language what they were doing. Greg yelled at her, saying she was lying and shamed her for making up such a story. He forced her into saying she was lying. She kept quiet another four years.

Greg told me that he felt deep remorse every time he was sexual with her. He believes this accounted for the low frequency of occurrences, because after he would act out with her, he would swear never to do it again. But eventually his need for a fix—to feed the monster, as he put it—was so intense that he would turn to her again.

I asked Greg what the remorse was like. Just being asked the question allowed him to bring the feeling to consciousness, where I could see it on his face. He described it as self-loathing, despair, feeling perverted, bent and twisted, and urgently trying to figure out how to never let this happen again. He said to himself that he had to stop before she got old enough to remember. From there he could give himself the common rationalization that she wouldn't remember and so wouldn't be hurt by it. Also, he told himself that he wasn't bringing her physical pain, and so she wasn't harmed. At the same time he knew it was wrong and felt deep shame and guilt for being sexual with his own daughter.

While Greg's guilt and remorse prevented him from acting out with Trish for a time, they fueled his tendency to act out his sexual addiction in other ways. He "needed" his drug to prevent himself from feeling this kind of intolerable pain.

The first time he "offended" her he went to a psychiatrist at his college, hoping to find a way to stop. During the first two sessions, he was working up courage to tell the man why he was there, when the psychiatrist said that he would be moving to another institution. He suggested that Greg go to the Veterans Administration (VA) hospital where he could get free help for as long as he wanted.

After this loss, Greg didn't seek help until he acted out with his daughter again. This time he went to the VA hospital. He walked in, and when the person at the registration desk asked if she could help him, he looked at her for a few seconds and walked out. Greg now questions what would have happened if he had entered therapy at that time, twenty years ago. I also wonder. In 1973, Child Protective Service units had existed for only a few years in some states. There were no requirements yet to report suspected or known child abuse, sexual or otherwise. If he had entered therapy, it was unlikely that he would have gotten a therapist who understood how to help him—it is difficult to find that even now. No writing had yet been done on the subject of sexual addiction—and wouldn't be for another decade.

TREATMENT WITHOUT SUPPORT

When Trish was eight she told him she didn't want to do it any more, and begged him not to. His fear that she would tell was so strong that he was able to stop. But she did tell.

Greg came home from a business trip to find that he was not allowed in his house. Joyce had reported him to CPS, and he was not allowed to be near his daughter. For one year he could have no contact with Trish. For many more months he could see her only in a counselor's office, and finally he was allowed to move back in. Trish was sent to see a counselor to help her with the effects, and continues to work on the them even in the present, twelve years later.

Greg was not prosecuted because the family didn't live in the same state in which the sexual activity had occurred. He was dealt with as if he were on probation, however, and did admit in an affidavit that Trish was telling the truth. He was required to be in therapy in order to work toward returning home. He continued even after that.

But the therapy was limited in scope. Dr. X, a clinical psychologist, told Greg there was no hope for him to change any more than his behavior. He would always want to have sex with children. As Greg told me this, he cried for the eight wasted years. Greg hated this diagnosis, but was ready to do what he could so that he wouldn't hurt his daughter, and so he could resume something of a normal family life.

I asked Greg if he had been tested with pictures of sexually stimulating materials with a strain gage on his penis, something often done to determine just what a person's cross-wiring is. He said no, he hadn't been tested at all except for an ink blot test and the MMPI, a 500-item true/false questionnaire. His therapy centered around reporting his desire to act out with Trish and perhaps other children, and monitoring his activities so that he could minimize that chance. He was less likely to think about being sexual with his daughter if he had to look Dr. X in the eye and say he didn't act out. He learned how to create boundaries to make sure he didn't have sexual urges toward her.

Greg continued to act out sexually the entire eight years. The subject of sex addiction never came up, apparently because Dr. X didn't understand that concept. He downplayed the possible role of Sex Addicts Anonymous (SAA) in helping Greg, saying that some people aren't comfortable with offenders being in the same room together talking about offending. Greg said, "I felt that I had made so many mistakes in my life that I just needed to trust in somebody so that's what I did. Whatever he said, I did."

Without the therapist's support and guidance, Greg was unable to become engaged in other therapeutic activities. At the same time, he continued to have sex with women until he reached a point of despair over his infidelity to Joyce, and stopped. But this was soon replaced by sex with men, a likely choice because it was easy to find men who wanted casual sex. None of this was asked about in therapy, and Greg didn't volunteer.

Greg told me that he didn't think of himself as a pedophile—a person who is specifically cross-wired to children, in contrast to those who are sexual with anyone who is convenient—because he was focused on sex with women for so many years, and then changed to interest with men. Yet he had sex with child prostitutes in Third World countries. He had been able to do this while seeing Dr. X without thinking to talk about it because he rationalized in typical addict fashion. He told himself they were very poor, and it was a way for them to get money—they wanted to do it so they could live more affluently. He made a decision that he wouldn't tell anyone about his other forms of acting out, believing he had to have sex with other people in order to relieve himself, or "feed the monster."

More recently, as Greg has been examining his history to search for clues to his behavioral choices, he sees that he is more of a pedophile than he had thought. He had chosen child prostitutes when adults were also available. It was more tolerable for him to think of himself as a sexual addict who reacted sexually to anything that he could use for a sexual fix. Now his understanding that he has strong cross-wiring to children (among others) both helps him know what he is dealing with in the present, and where to search for clues from the past. As he recovers from his pedophilia, he is more comfortable knowing how severe it was.

When Greg talked about why he didn't share his acting out with Dr. X, he had several reasons. One was that in the beginning he didn't want the truth to be known because he was afraid that he wouldn't ever be allowed to see his daughter. He painted a more positive picture to get back into his family. But he also deluded himself. He wanted to think that he was getting better even after receiving the sentence that change wasn't possible. He stopped drinking to remove any last assistance in acting out, and rationalized that his addiction was only between consenting adults. The Third World children were forgotten.

But another reason is important too. Greg didn't trust Dr. X. Dr. X conveyed mere tolerance for sex offenders, and a low opinion of them. He presented himself as a detached observer, not someone who was interested in Greg's recovery because, in fact, he didn't believe that recovery was possible.

REAL RECOVERY

This picture changed when Greg met Mitch Teufel, a psychotherapist who works with sex addicts. After reaching his lowest bottom, realizing that he was a major candidate for AIDS and impending death, he saw his wife's copy of *Out of the Shadows* (CompCare, 1983), recommended by her therapist. *Out of the Shadows* is a vital book written by Patrick Carnes, a psychologist who pioneered the field of sexual addiction. For the very first time, Greg learned there were people who believed that addicts, even pedophiles, could change, could mend themselves in such a way that they could, over time, give up their search for sexual drugs. After a few more weeks of terror, he finally drove through the snow to his first Sexaholics Anonymous (SA) meeting, and found home. Hearing about Mitch from other members, he made an appointment and began his real recovery process.

When I asked Greg how therapy was different with Mitch, he cited two things. First, Mitch believed that Greg could change. He didn't share Dr. X's belief that pedophiles are doomed for life with their curse, and are only able to control their behaviors. This hope, along with that offered by the Twelve Step program, opened a door that Greg had no idea was there. Once he knew that change was possible, he threw himself into it, facing the kind of intense pain that often brings suicidal thoughts.

The second reason is that he knew Mitch cared about him. Mitch respects Greg and others like him, understanding that he has been affected by his childhood and his culture in the ways that have been damaging to Greg as well as to those his addiction has used. Mitch doesn't believe there are two kinds of people—the offenders and the rest of us. Instead, he knows the truth. *All of us carry seeds of sexual cross-wiring, some legal and some not.*

Mitch knows from experience what it is like to act out sexually because he is himself a sex addict in recovery. He is able to reach out to those who want to take responsibility for their actions, and take steps to remove the influences that bring about devastating behaviors. Even though Mitch's acting out is not illegal, the feeling of being out of control and unable to stop the behaviors is very familiar to him. He knows that the first step of SA, admitting that one is powerless over the addiction, is the necessary first step toward recovery. He grasps the power of the addiction to make people violate their values. He knows how essential it is to have a community of peers who are also recovering from sexual addiction, people who can hear those truths that are still unacceptable to the average person. When Mitch nods in sessions with Greg, he is nodding from full appreciation of the anguish Greg is going through, both when his "addict" gets the better of him and when he faces the feelings that the "addict" had managed to override.

Mitch also knows that many people can't face the pain that comes with abandoning addiction. He deeply respects Greg for his willingness to give up his old coping methods, search through his despair-ridden childhood for causes, and tell painful truths to all the important people in his life. While this "formula" works vastly better than the control of behaviors he learned from Dr. X, it is not easy. Greg spends much time feeling disoriented and confused. When he works on large pieces of moving machinery in his job, he has to be careful not to access too much information. If he is "in memory," he could easily make fatal mistakes. But now he has an ally to see him through, a man he can trust to understand and stay involved no matter how painful it gets for either of them.

Greg looked at me with tears forming in his eyes, his face soft. He paused for a moment, and then said, "Mitch loves me." I nodded.

FEELING THE FEELINGS

Less than three years ago, Greg launched fully into a recovery process that has been filled with agony, terror, frustration, and shame, interspersed with hope. I have seen that people like Greg who have the most intense addictions, ones they will truly die from both psychically and physically, are able to undertake this massively painful process. Their lives were so filled with isolation and pain that the recovery process isn't any worse. Instead, it holds hope that pain can be healing. *People whose sexuality is only somewhat difficult will often choose to adjust, or change behaviors, which is easier and less painful than taking on full sexual recovery.* I like to work with addicts and sexual abuse survivors who suffer great pain because they don't have any choice in their approach to recovery. They aren't capable of going only part way, and are forced to do complete healing. Like Greg and Randel (see Chapter 16), these are the people who get to discover healthy sexuality as they give up the old destructive kinds.

Greg threw himself into his recovery. He attends SA meetings as often as he can. In addition, in the past several months he has joined a "Fourth Step" study group that works intensively on the fourth of the Twelve Steps. Members write detailed memories and relationships from the past, knowing they must deal with these things for recovery to move forward quickly.

Greg also does journal writing, particularly when he is traveling and cannot talk easily with his therapist or other group members. He writes letters to people who are important in his present and past life. In addition, Greg discovered a kind of breath work that involves listening to evocative music and filling the blood stream with oxygen by breathing continuously. This brings on an altered state that can allow a person to access primitive information that is prohibited by the conscious mind. Greg attended groups to learn how to use this method, and now does it on his own about once a month.

Through this variety of methods, Greg confronts himself almost constantly with information and feelings necessary to recovery. He has learned, and I have seen, that this assault on his addictive and abusive patterns is working. It means that he is in turmoil for long periods, and that pain wrenches him open over and over again. But when the choice is suffering pain with no purpose or, in Greg's case, death, it became possible to face a healing kind of anguish. Of course it requires a therapist who is able to truly be with him, and a group of other people who understand and accept him, offering support while he suffers. *These resources are necessary in order to keep the shame within manageable limits. Those who cannot do this recovery are inhibited by their shame—it seems worse than the isolation and pain they live with.*

I believe many people who hear about Greg's recovery, and what he has accomplished, would think he was finished. He leads a satisfying life, knows what he wants to do with his career, has a rich relationship with his wife, and a daughter who is doing her own recovery. He is in no danger of acting out sexually with children or anyone else. But Greg isn't satisfied. He intends to eradicate all cross-wired thoughts of sexual activity, and to continue finding out what are right ways for him to live. He is also curious to know why a person, himself in this case, would want to expose himself sexually to others and seek the humiliation that comes with it. At this point he still needs the help of a therapist and his Twelve Step group. He may make this a lifelong process because it is an enriching way to spend life.

HEALING REQUIRES TAKING RESPONSIBILITY

As we were about to conclude our interview, Greg said he had something more he wanted to say. He went on to tell me that as he explores the past and finds out what happened to him, he is afraid he might want to use it as an excuse, as a way to get off the hook. He wanted to caution me to make the point that we must take responsibility for what we do, and not pass that on to those in generations to come. He said:

> I take the view that there is a problem and I take responsibility for
> that. My first responsibility is to stop that behavior, and then to do

what I can for the victims, and then somewhere down the line it is OK to look for how I got cross-wired. It's been a big thing for me. I see people who are still in their stuff in meetings with wonderful excuses for why they did what they did.

His discomfort with telling me this, and suggesting how I approach the subject in this book, showed up, and he backed off. But I heard his message, and knew it was a vital one to include. My desire to focus on reducing the shame from these behaviors by seeing it as a cultural phenomenon pulled me away from naming the need for each person to take full responsibility for their behaviors. Greg is right. ***The only way a person can change him-or herself is to take full responsibility and use no information about their history or our culture as excuses.*** When each one of us can do this, we can see that the ASC whose house was burned down north of Seattle in 1993, and Greg, and every other person in this book, is not that different from you or me. ***Each of us was influenced by this culture, and every one of us perpetuates it even if we have no interest in being sexual with children.*** (See Chapter 17 for information on how our culture creates sexual damage to all children, and the role each of us can play to change the culture.)

I told Greg about the man I described in Chapter 12, "The Non-Recovering Pedophile", who was more concerned about what the state did to him than what he did to children, and who was not in recovery. This man agreed that he was a pedophile, but did not agree that the boys were harmed. He claimed he had been a father figure to them.

Greg became tearful, his face open and expressive of shock. He said, "It's not true. It's devastating, just devastating. I feel it in my chest. I can't imagine someone with information saying something like that, or feeling that way. It is devastating. It devastates lives. My daughter will never be the same. My sister will never be the same because of sexual abuse. I will never be the same because of it."

THE DAUGHTER'S RECOVERY

We ended the conversation by talking about his daughter. He told me that she had seen Mitch also. He said that Mitch helped her understand that he wasn't the good dad she wanted to see. She minimized the harm of his behaviors by saying that he never brought her physical pain, and so that meant he loved her. He believes her work with Mitch allowed her to move on and start her recovery process.

Trish made it clear to her lover that if they were going to have a relationship he will have to work on his stuff and they will work on their relationship issues because she wants a relationship like Joyce and Greg's.

He said, "She gets it that therapy is a working relationship rather than a sentence. She saw it before as, 'You did this to me and I am sentenced. I have to go to therapy and work through all this crap.' " No longer.

"I don't know where our relationship will go from here. My commitment is to support her in whatever she does. I acknowledge what happened did happen. As I get more information from my Fourth Step writing, I will write it down so she can know as much as I can tell her."

Greg continues to feel guilt over what he did to his daughter. At the same time, at only twenty-three, she is working on a healthy relationship and discovering what healthy sexuality is. Greg's recovery can pave the way for his child to have a richer life.

A SPIRITUAL POWER

I sent a copy of this chapter to Greg, asking for his comments to make sure I had reflected his story accurately. He wrote back, telling me some of the issues that he didn't feel were adequately addressed. He also let me see what it was like to read his own story. Here are some of the paragraphs from that letter:

> We received the manuscript on the 16th. Both Joyce and I spent that evening reading it. It presented us both with an opportunity to see how we currently do things. After reading this very sad account of our experiences, we went to bed and both felt a pull to be sexual with each other. We struggled with that energy for some time, finally dispelling it by reaffirming our commitment to listen carefully to the parts of us that were requesting abstinence from sexual expression at the time.
>
> The next morning as we talked about our feelings and felt the full force of the sadness and the shame, I began to have an erection. A light went on. We both began to make the connection between the intense pain we did not wish to experience as we read the evening before and the desire a short time later to be sexual. It was a powerful example of how addiction works to regulate the intensity of feelings of pain and shame.
>
> Reading my own story and learning more about Joyce's experience is very painful. Feeling the pain and the shame and allowing myself to stay with it and then move through it is painful. Seeing the almost immeasurable destructiveness of my actions presented clearly on paper before me without the benefit of any denial, is very painful. I tried to feel it, stay with it and then release it, knowing that to hold on to it is death to me. This pain is the pain of healing surgery, not the pain of disease. It is the good pain.

Greg went on to address some of the things he thought I hadn't included that he felt were vitally important. His hope is that at least one person who has been sexual with children will read this, and know there is the possibility of recovery.

Your writing does not seem to convey the feelings of utter despair and hopelessness that I experienced as the addiction ran its course. I had lost all dignity and all hope. I felt trapped, like there was no way out. Self-loathing lead to acting out which increased the feelings of being broken and unrepairable [sic]. That was how the cycle fed itself. Every good intention I had, every trick I tried, every decision I made to stop my addiction never helped. It seems important to say that from the seeds of my utter defeat was born the hope of a new life, that in the moment I truly knew myself, a wonderful gift was being offered to me. I want your readers to hear that in surrender they will find that path out of the darkness. That is my truth.

I was also struck by the lack of acknowledgment that a Power greater than us is the most significant reason that Joyce and I have the hope of a new and wonderful life. Anne, I am not a religious person. Quite the opposite. Nothing pulls my chain faster than someone pushing their particular beliefs on me. But I have to tell you that it was a spiritual power beyond my understanding that pulled me out of living hell and it is the same power that drives my recovery today. I could not have done any of this on my own. Believe me, I tried.

After completing my interviews with Greg, I asked his wife, Joyce, if I could spend an hour or so hearing the story from her experience. It soon became clear to me that her story deserved a full chapter. The partners of ASC's are as little understood as the ASC's themselves. Cultural belief says they were innocent victims of their mates' abuse of their children. Or they are seen as really knowing what happened and not stopping it. Neither of these pictures is accurate.

Chapter 5

The Other Parent Who Didn't Know

Cultural "wisdom" says we know important things that are happening to our children, and mothers who don't protect them are bad people. Mothers are mythological creatures who are supposedly able to intuit everything children need and then provide it. While it is true that children need mothers to be able to do this, we live in a culture that makes it absolutely impossible. Joyce loved Trish, and if she had been able to let herself know that Greg was being sexual with her from birth until she was eight, she would have taken steps to stop it.

HOW CAN WE NOT KNOW WHAT IS GOING ON?

Most parents are not able to read the signs that their child is having sexual contact with an adult. This is changing as information is being dispensed describing the symptoms, and bringing consciousness to many people. One effect of this mass presentation of information through the media is that survivors of childhood sexual contact are increasingly able to remember and talk. But they have more to gain and less to lose than the parent who didn't protect their child because they couldn't let themselves know. Guilt is a powerful preventative.

Therapists often guess that mothers need their husbands, their income, and identity, and so ignore what is happening, but in truth women who have their own identity and can provide adequate income don't believe their spouses are being sexual with the children either. It is even more difficult for a father to know that his wife is being sexual with a son or daughter. (Our culture absolutely denies, except in very rare cases, that women are capable of incest.) There are in fact many ways in which our culture prevents us from knowing the truth.

Growing up in a home with very poor sexual boundaries, Joyce couldn't know what was accurate. While she was able to stick with her intuition that wife-swapping, having sex in public, and other cross-wired sexual activities weren't healthy for her, she wasn't able to recognize some of the other signs that she and her husband didn't have healthy sex. Only now, having experienced rule-free, intimate, bonding sex, can she know that anything else is a cross-wired pattern. She and Greg remain ever vigilant to make sure they don't fall into the old ways.

When women are sexually bonded to their children, as Joyce was with Trish, they cannot perceive such bonding between husband and child as being sexual in nature. If the mother isn't overtly sexual with her child, then she assumes that her husband has the same boundaries she does. Since it is never talked about, she can't learn how he is different from her, nor how they are the same.

Women can't know the truth when they are told straight out that it is not true. When Joyce found out that Greg was having an affair that started within three months of their wedding, his denials prevented her from believing the friend who told her, and her intuition. When Greg attacked her, asking how she could believe this of him, his crafty "addict" gave her pause.

Our "addicts" are able to use intellectual reasoning—turning things around, and putting the other person on the defensive, as if it is their fault. Then it becomes necessary to prove the other is being unfaithful, or being sexual with children. In our culture, the "proof" that is required is actually seeing what happens, or having strong physical evidence. Given this burden, combined with a long family history and the effects of living in this society, it is impossible for most of us not to yield. In my therapy groups, it takes months before members are able to see when a person is "in their addict," and unable to think clearly. AA calls it "stinkin' thinkin'." Even with experience, the truth is not visible, and it often takes the mirror of another person to really believe that a pattern is being played out. In therapy groups more than one person will confront the person using these maneuvers, making it harder for him or her to continue believing their own deceptions.

Joyce spent years wondering if Greg was having an affair. She checked his wallet several times to see if he carried love notes, and searched for other evidence. But she found nothing. During this time he was having sex frequently outside their marriage. He was good at hiding his activities, and Joyce couldn't believe her intuition. Instead, she looked like the jealous wife—it was her problem. She reminded me of a woman I knew years ago who constantly worried that her husband was going to have an affair. She frequently cautioned him to be careful so he wouldn't fall into it unaware. But in spite of years of concern, she was devastated when she found out she was right. She said she always worried about it, but never actually thought he would do it. She could carry two incompatible beliefs.

Some therapists would consider Joyce's search for clues to be symptomatic of her "pathological jealousy" instead of symptomatic of her inability to believe herself. Two attempts at marriage counseling didn't yield allies for Joyce's suspicions. If we had a culture that believed in intuitive knowing, the therapists would have been able to perceive what was going on and intervene for her. But the therapists are members of this culture too, and easily taken in by the addict's deceptions. Greg stopped therapy both times before he had to reveal his addiction. Therapy wouldn't help as long as he was unable to tell what he was doing.

LIVING A LIE

I walked up the sidewalk to Joyce and Greg's house for my first interview with Joyce. The yard was richly green, and beautifully manicured, and the house perfectly cared for. Everything was in place, feeling warm and stable. Serene. Joyce's taste blended the rooms into a gentle work of art, offering a sense of order along with freedom and flexibility. I couldn't figure out just how she had accomplished the feeling the home provided. I asked Joyce if it always looked like this, and she said yes. She had come from a chaotic home with an alcoholic father who was very drunk much of the time, and she yearned for a home that was the opposite. While on the surface she has been able to create that, the relationships among family members has greatly resembled those of her childhood.

Shy and introverted as a child, Joyce found when she reached puberty that she was attractive to boys. She became popular. When she was twelve she went steady with Greg, who was then fourteen. He wanted to have intercourse, but she refused. When he didn't call for two weeks she called him, asking what was going on. He told her he was dating another girl, one who would have intercourse. She was hurt that another girl was willing to "put out" to get him, and it made her think she needed to do this too. But she gave his ring back, grieved, and forgot about him until they met again when she was fifteen.

Joyce and Greg dated again when she was a junior in high school. This time she had intercourse. It was clear that this was what he wanted, and she was willing to provide it in order to have him. To the rational mind, with an understanding of sex addiction, it is obvious that she made the decision to be the addict's drug in order to control him. She didn't have enough self-respect to be wanted for herself, and so she chose a man who would be dependable if he was provided with sex. He wanted a source for his addiction. Romance novels might suggest that she loved him so much she was willing to do what he needed, but this is further institutionalization of addiction. Both were set up to play their parts.

Joyce, and perhaps most women in our culture, felt that her primary value as a person and a woman was being a good sex object to her man. She also found outside-in value by being in a relationship with a man who was considered high on the scale of physical attractiveness. They both used each other to meet their needs to feel self-esteem from the outside in. Neither felt whole and satisfied with life, which is necessary in order to find a mate for the right reasons. Instead of trying to meet un-healthy needs left over from inadequate childhood, they would have been drawn to each other to add to the already present richness of life. Sex would have been introduced when they were ready to bond into a couple, and sexual energy used to speed up that process.

Joyce entered a relationship with Greg that was defined in part by her willingness to be attached to a man who wanted her for sex, not for intimacy. Yet she believed that he loved her. This first lie, created at the young age of fifteen, remained with her until she entered recovery.

The power of living a lie is massive. Joyce could not openly state that she was trading sex for ownership of a man. She couldn't even consciously know. When any of us live in such a lie, we have to make sure we don't see it so we don't have to take the next obvious steps. We can't delve deeply into anything of significance because it will threaten the lie. The result is people living superficial lives and having superficial conversations, both of which are rampant in our culture. If it is brought to their attention, it will evoke defensiveness because it is far more than a style of life or a subculture. It is a supposed solution, in the form of a mate, to all the deprivation of childhood.

This background of superficial relating to self, family, community, employment, and church creates an environment in which it becomes entirely possible to be unaware that one's mate is being sexual with one's child. A screen of illusion covers the truth, isolating people from one another. Much addiction serves the purpose of bringing people together for an approximation of intimacy. Without alcohol (or television or food or small talk or a variety of other pastimes) people have to be too real. While this feels much better than living in isolation, it also makes available the truths each person has worked hard not to know—truths that may seem too painful to face.

I am feeling defensive for Joyce. While she had the information available to intuit what was happening to her daughter, there was no way she could access it. This is not because Joyce was a frightened person, too incapable of confronting her husband. It isn't because Joyce was callous, not concerned about her daughter's welfare. It is because she lives in this culture, which does not understand healthy use of sexuality, and her views of sexual boundaries were badly distorted. Even her own interactions with her daughter reflected a lack of understanding of healthy boundaries that are necessary for a child to grow into a healthy, independent adult. Instead, Joyce experienced her relationship with Trish as a very loving one. She was more bonded to Trish than to Greg because her relationship with her daughter was constant and didn't pose the threat of betrayal. Joyce's way of dealing with her life with a sex addict was to replace him with a child—a common story in this culture.

As Joyce hid from knowing the truth about her husband, and her choice to marry a man who would betray her repeatedly, she was not able to see that her own relationship with her daughter was in part filling in for what she was missing. And she could not see that her baby was one of the "other women."

Joyce told me about her eagerness to have a partner who would make up for her miserable childhood, a further reason why she wanted someone who was addicted to her rather than someone who would truly enhance life. Greg asked her to marry him before he went to Vietnam, and she said yes. But having him gone deprived her of her drug—a man who wanted her all the time. She found a new drug, a man she agreed to marry, and broke off with Greg. He was devastated, but when he returned home he went to her house to convince her to marry him instead of the other man. She agreed. This story points out Joyce's desperation for salvation from the home she was living in, and from the empty life that accompanied it.

As Joyce told me about the dual engagement, she was shocked at her choices. She had gone off immediately to marry Greg, with her mother and sister accompanying them to Reno. She didn't tell her other fiancé until she got back. She hadn't thought about the effect it would have on him. He was waiting at her house when they returned, and, while Greg waited in the other room, she filled him in.

Joyce's relationship with her mother encouraged her choices. Her mother seemed to want to get rid of her, evidenced by her willingness support this situation. Joyce also remembered how her mother had let her date Greg when she was twelve, and let her go with him to drive-in movies. They had sexual activity, and could have had intercourse if she had done what Greg wanted. Her mother abandoned Joyce when she let her make choices she didn't have the maturity for.

Joyce wanted the perfect life of a wife and mother in a wonderful home. It now seemed possible to meet her needs from childhood in this new life. She was happy in her role and a life that seemed real for the first time. She thought everything was perfect, and so couldn't believe her friend when she said Greg had had an affair when they had been married only three months. The friend said Greg wanted sex with her too, but she preferred to be honest with Joyce. The one piece of honesty in her life had to be set aside in order to maintain the illusion that things were fine.

Joyce talked about the duality of a life that seemed perfect and at the same time seemed just like the alcoholic one she had left. She was so accustomed to chaos that it seemed normal. At least now she was the adult, not the dependent child.

It was painful living with a sex addict without being able to know it. She sometimes wanted to leave. But all our culture's attitudes prevented it. Joyce believed that you can't leave your husband, you have to make it work, and men just need sex. Then she got pregnant.

Joyce bonded with her baby before she was born, finding meaning in life that she didn't with Greg. Here was a person she could love and who would love her. She didn't think about Greg as much anymore. The issues that showed up in their relationship were abandoned, transferred to Trish.

Now Joyce knows that Greg began being sexual with Trish when she was days old. She had no information that this was happening, and still doesn't now. She could see no signs.

TRISH TRIES TO TELL

The first information came when Trish was about two and a half. She told Joyce that she and Daddy had a secret, that Daddy played house with her. When Joyce asked what that means, she said when Daddy takes her diapers off. Joyce knew something was wrong. This time information got through to her. She took him in the bedroom when he came home, and confronted him with Trish's comments. She wanted to know what happened. But then Greg did what her father and so many other people in her life had—he denied the truth and turned it back on her.

Greg was outraged. He said things like, "Do you think I would ever do things like that?" He said she was lying. Then he brought Trish into the room and asked her why she lied to her mother. Both Joyce and Trish felt something was wrong with them because he held the power in the family. Joyce had to have Greg's validation of her perceptions in order to believe herself, and so as a result, Trish did too. As her mother gave in to her father and was willing to see things his way, she had no validation of her reality.

When I think about a child so young being accused of lying, and her mother going along with it, it is hard to imagine this scene going the way it did. But that is because I am able to look at it intellectually, and seeing the truth is effortless. It is easy for Joyce, Greg and Trish (now twenty-three) to see it as well. But at the time, when Greg's "addict" was fighting for its life, and Joyce couldn't see that her own childhood had been crazy, it was possible for him to convince them both that he was innocent, and that the little child was the one doing something wrong. Joyce said that it didn't seem real, it couldn't have happened. Like the affair, this was incompatible with her other views of him. She said it made her feel like she was nuts when he said, "How could you think I could do something like that?"

Joyce had some sense that she should take action, but didn't know how. She thought of going to her mother, but knew that wasn't an option. She held her feelings inside.

Joyce has told this story many times, and by retelling it again she is relieving herself of the shame. But this was the first time I heard her tell it, and I could feel what it had been like for her. She needed to do something for her child, but with no emotional resources, and only a foggy understanding that something was wrong, she couldn't take the steps to the door or the phone and reach out. It was easier to believe Greg and let it go. She knows she communicated to Trish that she didn't believe her, that Daddy was just changing her diapers. Hearing this from both parents, it was no longer possible for Trish to reach out for help. Yet she did try again, five years later.

Joyce and Greg divorced when Trish was four. Joyce was not aware that he was having sex with other women. When he told her he wanted a divorce, she was astonished. She hadn't seen it coming.

Joyce had mixed feelings about it. Part of her wanted Greg to love and want her, and was against divorce. But the other part was relieved. She could let him go, and live alone with Trish. She thinks of those six months—the time the divorce lasted—as a period of supreme happiness. She no longer had to contend with the conflicts that emerged with Greg, and she had the loving relationship with Trish to sustain her. Joyce said she felt sane and together in her own life.

Greg wanted Joyce back once he had given her up. He again talked her into being with him, willing to pay what ever she demanded. They re-married six months after they divorced.

TRISH TELLS AGAIN

When Trish was eight, she again told Joyce that Greg was being sexual with her. She said that her grandfather, Joyce's stepfather, was too. Joyce was shocked. This time she knew it was true, and knew that it would be confronted. In retrospect, Joyce knows that it took hours or days for it to sink in as really true, and that during that time she communicated her doubt to Trish.

At first she was afraid to ask questions. She didn't want to know what had happened. But as hours passed, she was able to hear more and more until she could fully accept that in fact her husband was being sexual with her daughter. Greg was away on business, and when he returned she was ready to confront him. After telling the minister in their church what had happened, she arranged an appointment with him for Greg, knowing she would insist that he keep it.

As Joyce reached this point in her story, I realized that I hadn't been breathing well for some time. I was feeling numb, and knew that I couldn't listen to any more. We agreed to meet again in two weeks to finish the interview.

As I reflected, I wondered why I had that reaction. One reason is that my job was to collect information, not to focus on feelings, and so I had no arena to express mine. I couldn't imagine myself stopping Joyce in order to express anger or despair.

But I also knew that I could express these feelings even without talking to her about it. Even though Joyce was telling the story without feeling, I didn't have to hold mine back.

Upon further examination, I learned that I was reliving some of my own childhood. I also tried to tell when I was around two. I was given no help, and left alone to deal with the family secret that no one named. I had even less support than Trish because when I reached age eight, I thoroughly knew that I must not ever tell.

OUR CULTURE'S DOUBLE BIND

When I got home I was angry. I called people and talked about the fact that women are supposed to know when their children are being violated, while being raised in ways that prevent it. I could see clearly that we were in the impossible position of needing to be conscious to know what our children need, and at the same time, be feminine, ladylike and there for our men's needs.

Joyce's shame felt bitter to me. I know that her family system involved an alcoholic. Everyone danced around him. Intuition was not believed. But it is so much more than her family. Our entire culture supported her in believing her husband. If she loves him she is supposed to trust him. He has a right to complain to friends and family if she doesn't.

All of us are encouraged to develop blindness by living with people who don't tell us the truth. Rex and I discussed an example of this recently, when I mixed up some powdered milk for the first time in many years, and found it awful. It brought back memories of being told as a child that it was good, even though it was mixed half and half with "real" milk. Being told it was good while my taste buds said it wasn't made me believe that I couldn't assess such a simple thing as taste. The only conclusion that made sense was that I was defective for perceiving something differently from what the adults said was true. Thousands of such experiences taught me that my perception was off, and not to be trusted. If I refused to accept that I was wrong, which in some ways I did, then I had to contend with being different. I might honor my perception, but by doing so I set myself apart from the rest of my community.

I could identify with Joyce's experience of being told she was wrong and that her daughter had lied. I believe I might have responded the same way she did, even though my intellectual side says of course I would believe a child and take immediate action. But I know that I am still susceptible to believing a person's "addict" when they want to control me in some way.

Recently I was reflecting on my relationship with a sex addict client who tried several kinds of ploys to get me to not see who he was. First he calmly shamed me, and when I confronted that, he moved to aligning with me. That felt good at first, and it took me a few weeks to get onto it. Once I did, and stopped responding to his overtures, he felt angry and abandoned. He then engaged me with his wit, another attempt to manipulate me into liking him. When he finally ran out of things to try, he became himself and saw that I really liked him. While it is standard fare for psychotherapists to look past deceptions, even after sixteen years of experience I am still capable of being lured in with another person's definition of the truth. If I am still vulnerable, even while spending many working hours each week looking at my reactions, how could a person who had had no therapy and no understanding of addiction be expected to not believe an addict? When the addict is her husband, and she is supposed to trust him, it becomes impossible. My angry talking helped immensely, and I became calm enough to write the above. But I found myself nervous as I prepared to go again to Joyce's home to continue our conversation.

I began our second meeting by telling Joyce my own history, how I had been the child who had tried to tell, and how I knew both the plight of the child who isn't heard as well as the inability of the parent to hear. I also said that I needed to have my feelings as I listened so I could stay attentive.

JOYCE GETS REVENGE

Greg's meeting with the minister wasn't the end of his acting out. This is predictable to those who are recovering from sex addition. Simply being told you can't do it any more is ineffective.

Several months later he came to Joyce with a request that she condone further sex with Trish. He used his best intellectual arguments and addict manipulations to convince her that what he wanted was OK. He said that many other men do this with their daughters, and that he had a special relationship with her. Joyce said he was very convincing, but she knew the truth now and wasn't swayed. But she gave him permission anyway, knowing that she wouldn't back it up. He thanked her for this, and believed her.

Joyce immediately took Trish aside and told her that her father was going to ask her for sex again, and asked her if she wanted to do that. Trish said she didn't. Joyce told her that when he asked, Trish was to say no, and then come and tell her immediately.

As Joyce told me this story she felt shame. With her current understanding of children's needs, she knows that the best thing to do was to tell Greg no, he couldn't touch Trish, and report him to the authorities. They were living in a foreign country, and this was 1981, when there was little public understanding of sexual activity between adults and children, and so she had no one to turn to for real help. The minister advised her not to report him because in that country the penalties could be severe.

I can empathize with Joyce in this story too. Even though she couldn't manage the "addict" reasoning, she put her daughter in the position of doing so by forcing her to refuse the wishes and seduction of her father. It isn't a simple matter of saying no. He could be expected to use his well-honed methods of getting her to agree, including that her mother had said it was OK. While it is not right to put a child in such a position, Joyce felt as if Trish were capable of doing what she was not. Joyce couldn't imagine that even her eight-year-old daughter wouldn't see what he was doing—even though Joyce had been subject to his distortions for years.

As Joyce expected, Trish came to her in a few days and said that he had asked, and she had said no. Joyce was even more elated when Greg came to her too, saying how sad he was that Trish had turned him down. She rejoiced in her revenge. She didn't tell him she had anything to do with it. Instead, she expressed compassion.

As Joyce talked, her vengeful anger emerged. She said she realized that you don't tell an addict the truth, you outsmart them. She was more clever then he was, and got him at his game. Even now, over ten years later, she enjoyed telling me how she set him up. Now that she knew he would not be a person of integrity she was one step ahead of him. She knew that he was focused so much on his own needs that he wouldn't see the revenge coming. She created what looked like his addict's dream, and then threw a bomb into it. This story shows how enraged Joyce was after years of being controlled by an addict, and not being able to see what was going on. Now she had the power, she was in control. While this is not healthy either, it was an important transition to go through on her way to reclaiming herself.

CONTACTING CPS AT LAST

In spite of Joyce's increased understanding, she still had only part of the picture. It takes years to fully understand and assimilate information. When Joyce and Trish were back in the United States, and Greg was traveling, Trish mentioned that her dad had paid her money to be sexual. Joyce somehow thought she was saying this was still happening, and she had an intense reaction. She describes it as "the screen going blank." In shock, she knew that this was the final straw, and it was time to take more serious steps.

The next day Joyce called CPS to gather information. She didn't give her name, but just asked questions so she would know what she was faced with. She was told that Greg would probably be arrested, put out of the house and not allowed to be with Trish. Joyce spent the next twenty-four hours thinking about her life, and realizing it was time to risk it all. She felt ready to lose her husband, her house, her finances, and even her life to save her daughter. She realized she had to do this even if she lost Trish too. She believed that she and Greg were both poison for her, and Joyce couldn't tolerate it any more. She prayed while searching for the right solution. The next morning she called again, and set up an appointment to see a CPS worker.

During this first appointment Joyce learned that since they had been in another state or out of the country, this state couldn't prosecute Greg for what had happened in the past. But because Trish might be in danger, they would control what was happening in the present. She was told that Greg couldn't return to the home, and if he did, Trish would be removed. A therapist would have to be involved and give approval for Greg to return after significant changes had occurred. If they didn't seek therapy, Greg wouldn't be allowed to see his daughter until she was an adult. When Greg called to say he was boarding a plane to return, Joyce told him he couldn't come home. For the next year and a half he lived in a motel.

TRISH'S GRANDFATHER WAS SEXUAL WITH HER

When Trish originally told her mother that her father had been sexual with her, she also said that her grandfather, Joyce's stepfather, had too. Joyce had been overwhelmed by all this information, and it took months before she was able to see that steps needed to be taken here as well. Now that she was facing the collapse of her home life by reporting Greg, it was impossible to continue protecting her stepfather and her mother.

Joyce expressed shame at her choice of how to approach this next difficult task too. She dreaded telling her mother about her stepfather, and so she told Trish that she had to tell. Joyce knows now that she wasn't taking the appropriate mother role and protecting her daughter. Instead, she asked her daughter to take care of her needs. This is typical of an addictive, dysfunctional family, and something that Joyce was unable to see until she entered therapy.

Joyce knows now that the sexual contact had already put Trish and her grandmother at odds. Her grandfather allowed her to do things no one else could, and he wouldn't let his wife discipline her. He made it clear that she was special, which elicited his wife's legitimate jealousy. Trish had power because she could gain special favors to keep her grandfather's secret. In addition, their sexual bonding made her feel special and loved and so she wanted to be with her grandfather more than her grandmother, further increasing the jealousy. With this background, Joyce can now see that making Trish tell set her up to be blamed by her grandmother.

After her mother was on the phone, Joyce handed the receiver to Trish. The nine-year-old child said, "Grandma, Grandpa fucked me." When Joyce took the phone back, her mother asked if Trish knew what the word meant, and Joyce said yes. However, Joyce still doesn't know the extent of the sexual contact between Trish and her grandfather because she couldn't bring herself to ask.

Joyce glanced up at me as she talked. Seeing my face express my feelings, she said, "The story gets worse."

Her mother came to Joyce's house to talk further. She said she couldn't believe it, but at the same time, could believe it. He had been infatuated with girls in the neighborhood and with friends' children. He was also intensely jealous, expecting his wife to have an affair. He tried to catch her at it by monitoring the miles on her car, and following her.

Trish's grandfather was required to go through sex offender treatment, which included classes with other offenders, lie detector tests, and writing his sexual history. This process didn't offer hope to him, however. He became increasingly depressed. His wife was very angry, and planning to get a divorce. She had little to do with him. They weren't offered therapy that would have supported her in working with him to recover.

Joyce was helping her mother with a permanent when her mother said she had to go home. She was feeling uneasy about her husband, sensing that something was wrong. When she reached her house she found him dead. He had shot himself in the head. At sixty-three years old he died from his addiction.

Joyce told Trish, and, predictably, Trish thought that it was her disclosure that brought it about. This tragedy added one more trauma to an already devastated life.

Joyce continued her story of life with Greg out of the home. She arranged ways to see him during the year and a half. Occasionally Trish stayed overnight with her aunt, and Greg spent the night at home. Other times she met him in his room during the day when Trish was at school. They continued their sexual relationship, as well as frequent conversation.

CHANGING BEHAVIOR

All three went into therapy. Joyce was in a group for partners of sex offenders, and began attending Al-Anon meetings. Eventually Greg was invited into therapy with Joyce and Trish to determine if it was safe for him to spend time with Trish. At the first meeting, Greg was very emotional after not seeing his daughter for close to two years. She was now eleven. For many months the contacts were limited to supervised interaction, then to dinners out. Finally the question came up of Greg's return to the home. Joyce now realizes that again Trish was given the responsibility for making the decision, this time by her therapist. Her willingness to have him return was the crucial piece of information to make the decision.

The story doesn't end with Greg's return. The three of them had developed limits to make Trish safe from even covert sexual abuse. When they watched television, Joyce sat in the middle, at last protecting her daughter. Greg and Trish weren't alone together for long. Joyce worked in the house so that Trish could always come to her. When Joyce was working, Greg stayed in one part of the house so Trish could have the run of the rest of the house. Any changes in location had to go through

Joyce first. Therapy had helped them come up with limits that would allow Trish to feel safe and protected.

The trials weren't over yet. Joyce's developing awareness allowed her to realize that Greg was drinking more and more, and was acting like her father had when she was a child. Now knowing that these behaviors aren't normal, she confronted Greg with his belligerence when he drank. He told her if she didn't like it to get out. She told him she would. By now he knew she was capable of separating from him if she needed to, and so he suggested that he take a look at his drinking and see it if was a problem. By journal writing, he saw that he drank far more than he realized, and that he was an alcoholic. He stopped drinking and began attending AA meetings. As we know from Greg's story, his sex addiction was far more problematic to him. Alcohol, by comparison was very easy to give up. For him the two drugs weren't related, as they are with many sex addicts. His sexual addiction didn't depend on alcohol, and flourished even without the drug. Joyce remained unaware of his sexually addictive behaviors that went on while he was working in another state or another country.

As the family became reunited, Trish and Greg didn't get along very well. Their old sexualized relationship wasn't available, and so Greg didn't know how to be a parent. Trish expressed her anger at him by not cooperating with discipline, swearing at him and refusing to listen.

Joyce was angry with Greg as well. He didn't discover real recovery from sexual addiction until Trish was twenty, and so the three of them were trying to improve things while he was still acting out and feeling powerless to stop. Joyce now refused to hold back her anger as she had done all the years of her childhood and early marriage. She knew she wasn't the crazy one, as her father and then Greg had tried to convince her. She became more and more powerful, and recognized that she was in a relationship with an addict. She said that you can't expect an addict to be with you, they are with themselves. She was emancipating from the dysfunctional system.

Now that both are involved in recovery from sexual addiction and from co-addiction, she has support for her intuitive knowing. She attends S-Anon Twelve Step meetings for the partners of sexual addicts, and fires herself up to face the challenge. Now when Greg is in his "addict" she knows, and doesn't take anything he says or does seriously. She knows she cannot believe the "addict" while at the same time when Greg is himself, which happens more and more, she knows he is among the most trustworthy people alive. An addict in recovery learns how to be impeccably honest, and so they become deeply trustworthy. But to the extent that the "addict" continues to operate, the person will flip back and forth between the addict and honesty. While Greg can still move into his addict, Joyce no longer has to be entrapped by it. Now that she can see the difference, she can relate with Greg when he shows up, and not relate when the "addict" does.

Joyce is choosing to stay with Greg for a number of reasons. One is her continuing anger about what happened for so many years. She wants Greg to face it and make amends for the rest of his life. She said, "I will never not be angry about it. I want to stay angry about it. If I am here he will have to look at this every day of his life. He will never be scott free in my book. I don't want him to walk away from this." She said that if he chose a life that didn't include recovery, or walked away from his daughter, her revenge would be intense. Part of her would kill him with it, rip him apart. She tells his addict this when she knows he is listening in on her conversations with Greg.

At the same time, Joyce deeply appreciates the man who is emerging out from under the addict. She expressed her love for him, and talked about the incredible relationship they are creating. Together they are learning about healthy sex and how to avoid any other kind. They are learning how to love each other deeply and well. Joyce knows that she has to be equally as powerful as Greg's addict, in order for this to happen. His addict knows he cannot manipulate her any longer, and is giving up. She said she can be as big and ugly as he can, and that the destroyer in her would attack him if he ever touched another child or another woman. Her denial is gone, and she is allowing her "beast" out. Before she was "too nice," and couldn't attack even if she knew what was happening. Now she cherishes her beast who lies in wait.

Joyce also talked about joining with Greg to make the world a better place. They want to do this by telling their story, and removing other people's denial. Their willingness to tell me their stories is one way they are doing this. They want others to know what is possible for severe addicts and co-addicts who are willing to abandon old, damaging ways of being, face the pain, and find out what real life and love are like. Joyce listens to women's stories at S-Anon, and asks them if they want to hear her anger or hang up. They always say they want to hear it, and so she opens up about how harmful it is to be the sex drug of another person, and how the threat of loss has to be faced so that limits can be set. She says whatever comes out, such as, "He's using you, you're a needle in his arm, a fix. Do you want that? No? Then look at that. Let go of him. You are allowing it. You are abusing yourself and enabling him. Say no. No more." This is how Joyce lives.

REAL LOVE

I made one more trip to the comfortable home surrounded by manicured garden. Even though I thought I had plenty of information, my intuition told me to go once more when they were both there. As I walked in and sat down, I wanted to cry. My "voices" told me this was not appropriate, this was a professional context, I was here to listen to them. But I also knew that writing this book, and getting to meet people like Greg and Joyce, is for my own healing as well as to gather information to pass on to you. So I told them I was about to cry, looking at them there together in their living room. Joyce got some tissue, handed me some, and then said she would put it in the middle so we could all use it as they did in their Twelve Step meetings.

With this acceptance, I let the tears come. They poured, and with noise. I looked up to see Joyce dabbing at her eyes, and knew she was emotionally with me. At that moment I didn't know why sitting across from these two people was so touching, but as the next hour unfolded I learned.

Joyce and Greg were the parents I didn't have—the parents I could have had forty years ago if my mother had been able to see the evidence, the story I was trying to tell her about what was happening; if she had gone for help, and had my father arrested; if they saw there was no way to live with things as they were; if they were required to get help in order to have a family; and if there had been anyone who understood sexual addiction, incest, and the role of the partner, and so could help make a difference.

Then I might have sat across from two people who brought me into the world, and gotten to see real people. Instead I lived with people who had to develop superficial lives, who created rules to live by that were imposed on me too, who looked like respectable, valued members of our community. I grew up with no reflection of the horrors I lived through, thinking I was somehow defective. My mother was constantly jealous of my father, with no way to explain it because he never looked at another woman. She didn't consciously know that men were her competition. My father died from AIDS in his seventies, years before a natural death. Our family lived out a tragedy. Joyce and Greg are not.

As I looked at them, I grieved for my own family. And I knew that this was how it could have been. It was as if my parents were sitting in front of me. I knew that if they had been able to make things different, they would have. And this is how they would have looked. We could have cried together, having all our feelings as they emerged. We would have seen each other clearly, knowing the others' experience as well as our own. We wouldn't have been cut off from each other by massive secrets and the resulting isolation.

I was loved by Joyce and Greg and they were loved by me. Not love like the romantic illusions presented in the media, churches, and elsewhere, or the peace and love that is recycled at Christmas, but instead the love that comes only with absolute truth. This love emerged when Greg said he wasn't comfortable talking further about his activities with his daughter because his shame was becoming too strong, when our tears flowed whenever they wanted, unrestricted, and with our comfort in each other's feelings. Two hours in this room allowed me to feel connected and loved and with a complete right to be in the world—something I never ever felt in the home I grew up in.

I took in this new kind of love, and as it flowed into me it flushed out the old feelings that had been installed there by the shaming lies that accompanied every day and every minute of my childhood. The big lie was my father's sexual behaviors, including being sexual with me. The other lies included my badness for being an eroticized child, for being favored by my father, and my mother's hatred of me for that. She watched over me like a hawk, "overprotective," making sure I didn't use my powers in some bad (that is, sexual) way. And on and on. But now I could see that these two people, who had been very much like my parents before they discovered a recovery that really helped, have given up most of the lies they lived, and are intent on discovering and eradicating all of them. Their willingness to look, instead of working hard to prevent me from looking, is enough in itself. Their remaining lies are of no consequence to me. What matters is that I am allowed to speak the truth, even if it is painful. If it isn't time for them to look, they will tell me that. They won't convince me that I am harming them by looking and especially by speaking.

OUR HOPE FOR THE FUTURE

I also took in hope. This couple is moving from the sickest family system imaginable, with the most damaging consequences to all members, to becoming the healthiest family system I know of. They are a family working toward integrity, supporting the healing of each member in any way they can.

This is such a different love from the kind that is called "falling in love," the feeling that makes people think they should be together for the rest of their lives. Greg and Joyce's original attachment for each other was intense, but based on unhealthy needs. Their attachment is still intense, but now it is based on two real people clearly seeing the other partner for who she or he is.

I drove out of their driveway feeling like I had been crying steadily for an entire day. And I felt loved and connected, part of a community. This feeling is mine, whether or not I ever see them again. The love we gave to each other was complete.

Are these two people the scum of the earth? This is a man who used his little daughter sexually for eight years and might not have stopped if he hadn't been forced to. And this is a

woman who didn't know her daughter was going through this—
a mother who didn't protect her child, who thought it is always
right to believe an adult, never a child. Yes, they were sick.

And they are members of the new wave, the hope for our
culture. These are the people who were forced to change
because they were too sick. They are paving the way for the
movement toward emotional and spiritual health that is gathering momentum. They were lucky to have it bad enough that
they could not maintain any of the old, dysfunctional ways.
They are in a position to make the greatest change.

Chapter 6

A Man's "Covert" Relationship with His Daughter

Ted is a minister, dedicated to his work in a congregation with special needs for leadership. He was aware when he entered therapy that his profession left him lonely and isolated, as is often the case for members of the clergy. His social life and work life involve people who look to him for spiritual guidance— placing him in an authority position. He has few peers to whom he can turn to meet his own needs.

Ted moved to a large city so he could join SAA to deal with his compulsive sexual activities, which had been disturbing him for some time. He masturbated to fantasy, and engaged in voyeuristic activities when the opportunity arose. He was in a mild sexual trance most of the time, searching for a sight that might be arousing, and it intensified when he happened upon sexual stimulation. When heavily involved in his addiction, he used binoculars to search for women in a state of undress.

Ted had significantly reduced his addiction after two years in SAA, but when he read an article I wrote about cross-wiring he realized that he needed to explore this component of his sexuality. While the compulsion to use sexual energy addictively was diminishing, he still found himself wanting sexual activity other than loving sex with his wife.

Our first therapy session was almost over when Ted told me about the cross-wiring that disturbed him most of all. His daughter recently turned twelve, and was developing into a young woman. He found his interest in her changing from fatherly affection into romantic, sexualized "love." He knew that he would never touch her sexually, because his cross-wiring didn't involve physical contact with others. But he did know that he wanted to catch glimpses of her naked, and even the thought of doing so was sexually—and emotionally—arousing.

Ted had tiny mirrors that could be placed under the bathroom door to provide a limited image of a person inside. He found himself ready to put a mirror under the door when Jennifer was in the shower, but was shocked at what he was doing and stopped. After our first session he made a ceremony of destroying the mirrors.

Talking with me about his feelings for his daughter diminished the intensity of the obsession, providing great relief. *One effect of bringing secrets out in the open is that shame can drop, allowing a person to make choices about sexual feelings and activities that are more conscious.* Ted's obsessions also diminished as he began telling his own story—finding out what happened to his sexuality when he was growing up. As a result he began to have less need to act out the story with his own child.

COVERT SEX IS STILL DAMAGING

Ted doesn't speak sexually to Jennifer, and he doesn't touch her sexually. But he is harming her sexuality. Even though he doesn't speak to her of his feelings, or in any way control her for his sexual ends, he has sexual feelings for her. We humans know when this is happening, although often not consciously.

In addition to the sexual objectification, Ted also objectified Jennifer as a love object. He could no longer see her as the dependent daughter she had been for twelve years. Now he wanted to spend time with, spoil, and yearn for his adored princess. The fact that the relationship could never be expressed sexually was part of the power of the addiction. The voyeur, seeing his "partner" only from a distance, is not sexually excited by the person who is committed to him and available for sex. Ted described his feelings as "secret pining"—the same feelings he had when courting her mother many years before.

Ted's feelings had to be kept secret from his daughter in order to meet the requirement of his cross-wiring. He recreated his childhood experience—receiving a sexual invitation that he was not to recognize as such. His sexual arousal was coupled with the frustration of having no access to the person who offered the initial stimulation. Over the course of Ted's therapy, we learned that he would see his mother naked from a distance, a situation she created to arouse him. She may not have been conscious that she was inviting him to be sexual with her, but it is likely that she was engaging in the sexual experience of exhibitionism. When Ted, in his innocence as a child, moved to touch her sexually or otherwise express sexual energy, she shamed him for it. She didn't want sexual activity with him. As a result he became the counterpart of the exhibitionist—a voyeur, searching for a glimpse of her (and later, any naked woman). At the same time, he felt rejected by women, replaying the scenes with his mother.

Martha, Ted's wife, was also affected by his feelings for Jennifer. Until Ted told her about his attraction for their daughter, and his other cross-wiring, she had no conscious awareness. But once they were able to examine what had been going on, Martha could explore her own reactions. As Jennifer became a young woman, Martha had found herself jealous of her daughter's beauty and youth. She could see that she had tried to keep Ted and Jennifer apart as much as possible, and dressed her conservatively—all things she had not done with their older daughter, for whom Ted had no sexual feelings.

Jennifer was the apex of a triangle she had not chosen to be in. Her parents were not happily sexual with each other, and, to her mother and father, she became the reason. In the span of less than a year she went from being the delight of them both to being the sexual object of one and the jealous, resentful object of the other. As most children will, she assumed it was her fault. She intuitively knew that her maturing sexuality was the "cause." She was in an impossible position because even if she were prepared to "report" this to someone, she couldn't know what to report.

The only information Jennifer had to go on was her father's increased attention to her—something a daughter would be expected to enjoy. Yet she was uncomfortable with it because of her mother's resentment of this attention. Because her father went to work on his obsessions right away, the damage could be undone by her own therapy.

DAUGHTERS ARE CAUGHT IN THE MIDDLE

If Ted had acted on his obsessions, Jennifer might have had experiences similar to women I have worked with who came to me because they had great difficulty understanding why they didn't want to have sex with their husbands. They had no memory that an adult had been sexual with them as children, yet they still experienced an aversion to sex. Months of therapy—along with using guided imagery, learning to respect body memories as real memories, and telling and re-telling their experiences at puberty—finally allowed them to reclaim what had happened. The mothers of these women, in an attempt to protect them from the interest of men, sheltered and overprotected them, and tried to postpone their graduation to womanhood by not permitting them to wear makeup or fashionable clothes.

In order to maintain connection to their mothers, most of these women did as they were told. Others rebelled, and lived through tumultuous years fighting with their mothers, breaking the rules, and being punished. The fathers couldn't very well intervene because they were caught between attraction to the daughter for sexual drug fixes, and wanting the best for her. To take the daughter's side against the mother would further fuel the rift between mother and father, increasing the addict's distress and increasing his addiction. Most fathers stayed out of the picture, trying to engage in activities outside the home for as many hours as possible, and generally avoided the reality of the confusion they had brought about.

Our culture's views greatly increase this kind of damage to women's sexuality. First, the father cannot tell anyone what is happening to him. Only in recent years is there a place where an addict can reveal what is going on. Second, the father has been trained that a young woman's body is a sex object, and if he is a real man, he will look lustfully at female body parts, particularly in underwear and bathing suits.

At the beach recently I watched a young woman no older than fourteen walk toward me. She drew my attention because she looked as if she had stepped out of *Playboy* magazine, with large breasts, wearing a bikini. Laughing with a friend, she walked along the water line, no doubt the object of a great number of looks. I, a heterosexual woman, thought of sex when I saw her. The men on the beach did also. How is it possible for her father to look at her in her bikini and see only his little girl developing into a woman? He will also see a "sexy" woman, and perhaps attempt to inhibit sexual thoughts. The father will have difficulty differentiating his own daughter from the other young women he is "supposed to" look at. If he tries not to look, then the very prohibition is likely to intensify his curiosity and sexual arousal. A great number of fathers absent themselves from their daughters' lives in order to prevent thinking of them sexually and feeling the consequent shame and guilt.

Jennifer's situation was potentially more damaging than the typical young woman's because her father was also a sex addict. He sought out times he could obtain a sexual charge from the anticipation of seeing her partially unclothed.

FACING SHAME AND FEAR TO HEAL

Ted made rapid use of his therapy hours. Facing his shame and fear, he accepted my observations about the effect his romantic love was having on his daughter and his wife, and he experienced his feelings about it. As he let the shame wash out of him, he could think more clearly about his wishes for a satisfying love relationship that were made impossible by his cross-wiring. As Ted could see how his approach to finding romantic love was absurd, he could no longer maintain the attraction to his daughter.

Ted also worked on his own history, knowing that as he learned what had created the cross-wiring, he would be able to break it. His mother had been sexual with him when he was a baby, and had maintained a sexualized relationship with him throughout his life. An important clue came when he remembered that at thirteen he saw a picture of his mother when she was twelve, and found himself sexually attracted to her. The young women he later was attracted to, including his daughter, looked very much like his mother in this picture. He had been able to take his sexualized response to his mother and experience it in his own age range. However, not being able to work through the relationship with his mother, he had maintained an attraction to certain young women.

SOME ASC'S SEEM WORSE THAN OTHERS

The next chapter presents the experience of a woman who was sexually bonded with her daughter. I would like to invite you to make note of your reactions to Ted's story, and then to Trina's. Are you more negative about Ted's experience, or Trina's? Which do you think did the most damage? Do you react differently to the nature of their activities with the children? Does the age of the child make a difference? Do you want to excuse one more than the other? Your answers are information about your own story.

Chapter 7

When a Mother is "Only" Attracted to a Child

As is evident from the last chapter, we need to redefine what sexual abuse is. Most people, including most psychotherapists, view it as physical acts of sexuality that resemble sex between adults. But this definition is so limited, it doesn't do us much good when setting out to heal the abuse of children's sexuality, and to heal our culture's acceptance of covert sexual interactions. Trina and Monty are a couple whose story demonstrates the vast effects of sexualized interaction between a mother and daughter. They demonstrated how "covert" incest can be as devastating to a child's developing sexuality and perception of love relationships as the "overt" variety. The relationships offered her by both parents were contaminated, distorting her perception of sexual relating that she could have as an adult. These dynamics have been reversed, freeing their daughter Pam to love both parents equally, and giving her the opportunity to grow up knowing how to create a love relationship and family in a healthy way.

MONTY AND TRINA

I met Trina over a year ago when she came in for several therapy sessions. She had been feeling depressed, believing much of her lethargy resulted from her sexual relationship with her husband, a man who wanted sex all the time, and who had little awareness of Trina's feelings. I met Monty several months later when he came to my Healthy Sexual Energy class with Trina.

Both are professional people with a high income, who are well respected for their work. Monty's tendency toward work addiction, along with wanting to be the best at what ever he does, increases financial rewards. They have one child who is now three, with a second on the way. Both pregnancies were planned.

In the beginning, Monty was reluctant to address his sexual addiction, justifying his behaviors as no different from that of most men in our culture. But when he and Trina instituted a sexual moratorium he soon realized that he was addicted to sex with her as well as to sexual thoughts about other women. (Their story of sexual recovery is told in my second book, *Discovering Sexuality That Will Satisfy You Both: When Couples Want Differing Amounts and Different Kinds of Sex,* The Printed Voice, 1993. An example of their use of healthy sex is recorded on my audiotape, *Healthy Sex: Real Life Stories of Bonding, Monogamous, Joyful, Shame-Free, Rule-Free Sex.*)

Monty is in full recovery now, which includes sharing every addictive feeling with his wife and others who understand the nature of this recovery. And so as the two of them sat down with me to talk about their changes with their daughter, Pam, he told me that he found himself wanting to look at my breasts. I had learned in the men's group that this is his classic reaction to stress or feeling unsafe. I nodded, glad he was able to share this instead of being socially appropriate and keeping it to himself.

He tells so that the desire will stop, and so that he can see the real feeling that is being blocked.

MONTY IS JEALOUS

Monty began their story when they sat with me in my office for the interview. I already knew most of it, but wanted to focus exclusively on this experience, while giving them a chance to review the healing they have accomplished together.

Monty had asthma attacks while Trina was pregnant. He said he was scared to death of the baby coming. He couldn't breathe when going to Trina's doctor appointments and baby classes at the hospital. No longer the center of his wife's attention, his worst childhood fears were coming true. His "mother" was intent on someone else. Monty's "addict" wanted to control Trina, and have sex with her to make him feel safe. Now she was focused on a new being inside her, already attending to the baby even before it was born. Monty no longer received all her attention, which had been one of his reasons for marrying her.

Trina played lullaby tapes while she massaged her stomach, and, of course, the baby, with lotion. Monty was very jealous. He had, as a child, been enmeshed with his mother, and then had replaced his real mother with Trina; now he was going to lose this imagined source of safety. Trina took better care of herself while pregnant, and was less codependent with Monty. She was already bonding with Pam, replacing her unhealthy need for Monty. He reacted.

Monty's mother exchanged flirtatious sexual energy with Monty throughout his life, and into the present. Her sexualized adoration was a drug to him, and he often called her up when he needed a "fix," particularly if he thought he wasn't getting enough attention from Trina. He said a hit from mom made him feel giddy and wonderful. He liked to talk to his dad, but the sexual hit from her was best of all.

Through his therapy, he has become able to identify this addiction to his mother's sexualized attention, and now he rarely responds to it. Because of his lack of response, she is changing her behavior. But he feels a loss because she doesn't have anything more to offer him. She is either depressed and silent or intensely focused on him.

Monty also misses the "hits." While they were harmful to his marriage, and weren't real loving from his mother, they felt good, as all "drugs" do. Monty has seen the positive effects of giving up this drug, and is motivated to completely abstain from it. Occasionally he still finds himself responding.

Until recent months, he wanted this attention and didn't understand why Trina objected. He thought she had jealousy patterns, and wanted her to work on them. Through therapy he has come to see that his sexualized interactions with his mother were triggering appropriate jealousy in his mate. His sexual energy should have been going only to her. But, having experienced it his entire life, he didn't even know it was sexual.

Trina's Mom Was Sexual Too

Trina had a similar background. Her mother sexualized their relationship, and offered little affection that wasn't laced with sexual energy. Because this seemed normal, *Trina didn't know that sexualized affection for her baby daughter wasn't healthy, and that Monty had a right to object.* Both of them had come from such confusing childhoods that their feelings of healthy jealousy couldn't be sorted out from the patterned reactions they had developed in earlier years. When Pam was born, the craziness grew.

Monty's sexual addiction, focused in large part on his wife, intensified as his desperation increased. He wanted to control her, and sex seemed like a reasonable way to do this, given his background. In addition, Trina's sexual interest was diverted to her daughter, further frightening Monty. She dutifully gave him sex on a regular basis, however, until she read my book, *Reclaiming Healthy Sexual Energy*, and saw that she was feeding his sex addict.

TRINA BONDS SEXUALLY TO BABY PAM

We moved to the subject of Trina's sexual bonding to her infant. This was more painful to discuss because it brought up her remaining shame for what she had done. Of course she knew she was influenced by her mother's sexualized relating with her when she was a child, and reacting to not being happy meeting a sex addict's "needs." But nevertheless, her shame came up several times during the interview as Monty told her his memories. I had great compassion for her, knowing the myth in our culture that all "good" mothers love their children in healthy ways. I also knew about the intensity of maternal instincts. We are supposed to know how to parent our children perfectly, even though we have no good models.

The developing lopsided triangle was supported by what looked like Trina's overprotectiveness with Pam. If Monty did any caretaking Trina looked over his shoulder, criticizing. This angered Monty, making him less interested in discovering how to parent his daughter, as well as giving Pam the picture that her father wasn't an adequate caretaker. In his anger, Monty didn't want to take care of her when Trina was out, and usually refused. Trina responded to this by trying very hard to get him involved, not understanding that her behaviors contributed to his disinterest. She was constantly angry that he wasn't making himself part of things, and remembers seething frequently. They struggled constantly with no way to perceive the problem or how to solve it.

Monty didn't love his daughter. He felt great shame over this, further decreasing his interest in being involved. He knew she was afraid of him because of it, making him even more likely to withdraw. There were occasions, when he and Pam were alone, that they had a good time. But when the three were together, it was always trying.

Monty lit up warmly when he said how good it feels now to love her, and feel her love of him. It had been painful to know that his child was afraid of him, and rewarding to see that he and Trina have been able to make changes so that it is no longer true.

Pam was affected by her parents' dynamic. She acted as if her mother was the only one who could take care of her correctly because this is what her mother communicated. As a result, she ran to Trina whenever she had a need, and wouldn't go to Monty. This picture, common in our society, is usually blamed on incompetent men, while the long-suffering mother has to do it all. But perhaps more common is the situation Trina and Monty are now able to look at—the mother hovers over the children, making the father feel incompetent, and so he backs off, furthering the belief of mother and children and himself that he can't parent.

Since Trina and Monty have reversed this dynamic, and parent equally, Pam responds by going to both equally. We have gotten to see that when the mother can let go, and the father is able to discharge his feelings and become available to his daughter, the child's perception will change to match. She has been freed up to have two parents.

Monty and Trina told of a home movie they made that demonstrated Pam's reaction. Trina was filming, and Pam pursed up her lips to blow her a kiss. When Trina suggested that she kiss her Daddy, she turned and slapped him. As they talked about watching the movie recently, both grieved for the way it had been.

We are now able to see this triangle, that at first seems caused by a father who doesn't love children, because these two people have joined together to recover . The child's negative reaction to her father was created by his hatred of her because she was competition for his wife's affection—a drug that felt important to his survival. The change came about when Trina was able to see what she was doing, and begin the work of changing it. Monty is also freeing the family from this dynamic by learning how he is not really dependent on his wife to meet his need for affection.

Trina and Monty attribute the beginning of their explorations to a comment I made in the Healthy Sexual Energy class they took. I said that mothers can be sexually bonded to their children, both male and female. Even though I didn't go into detail or even give examples, they both knew I was talking about their relationships with their mothers, and Trina's relationship to their daughter. They began quickly to explore, having a new context to work within. The changes that took place were almost immediate. Trina and Monty began to observe what was happening, and to tell each other. They united in their exploration, which helped reduce the shame each felt as they became conscious of what they had been doing to their child.

One example took place in a restaurant when Trina's mother was with them. She gave Pam a French kiss, an act that was clearly sexual and harmful. Trina and Monty were shocked, but didn't feel they could be angry with her because this was completely within the family's definition of affection. After the kiss, Pam said she wanted to take her pants off. Trina and Monty were aware that she was sexually aroused, but both were immobilized by the dysfunctional family requirement to not name abuses.

Monty was seething, but was unable to say anything. He "checked out," emotionally leaving the scene. When thinking about it later he realized that he couldn't object because he had been violated the same way, and wasn't allowed to name it or refuse it. Trina felt abandoned by him when she needed him to work with her as a team to give her the strength to confront her mom. True to her patterns, she wanted to blame him for not giving her what she needed, when in truth it was her job to protect her daughter. She wasn't able to overcome the intensity of her reactions and say something.

As we talked about this example, Monty told Trina that Trina had done the same thing with Pam, and it had angered him. Her shame came up immediately, and she wanted to say that what she did wasn't what her mother did. She and Pam had what they called movie star kisses, leaving their mouths together for a time. Monty said she also touched tongues with Pam. Trina defensively explained that it wasn't sexual, even though all three of us could see that it was not appropriate behavior, and is something Trina no longer does.

If you find yourself having feelings about these sexualized interactions between mothers and daughters, let yourself have them and observe. You may be disgusted, amazed, or aroused. If you are aroused or disgusted, invite your body to tell you more of your own story.

CREATING CHANGE

Monty and Trina are constantly learning that raising their consciousness and having feelings that come with awareness is the most powerful way to create change. The episode with Trina's mother was just an example. Monty pointed out something to Trina that she hadn't known, she was able to see that he was right, and she felt the shame that came with it. The process isn't painless and smooth, of course.

She also reacted defensively to her shame, and took some time before she could see that Monty was right. Her anger and disgust at what her own mother did to her and to her daughter made it hard to know that she had done the same. Monty's firm, nonjudging approach was easier to hear than if he had shamed her, which would have added to her own shaming. When shame from the community accompanies the person's self-shaming, the combination is usually too great to be faced. Arrest, or fear of it, is usually necessary to force a person to get help and face their behaviors.

During the two hours in my office, Trina and Monty were able to take an objective view of the work they have been doing for a year. Their faces took turns lighting up as they remembered something. They were delighted to be able to tell the story to an outside person because they got to hear it themselves. I said very little as their story unfolded.

Monty talked more about his tendency to "check out" when forbidden sexual exchange is going on. He learned this by observing his father's reaction when his mother was being sexual with him—now he was the one who didn't want to see that his wife was sexual with his daughter. This maneuver that had once prevented him from having feelings is now available as a signal that something is going on. When he checks out with Pam and Trina, he tells Trina that she is being sexual with Pam. Sometimes he is wrong, because occasionally he has another reason to check out. In the beginning, Trina was upset when he was wrong, but now knows that all she has to do is check it out with herself, and tell him if he is right or wrong. It took them about six months to reach this point.

In the beginning, Monty had a hard time telling Trina, and she was filled with shame when he did. But she knew he was right, and he was her best mirror for how she was harmful to her daughter. Confrontations are less frequent now, as the overall change has taken hold. They are also becoming more fluid in the process.

WE DON'T KNOW
WHAT HEALTHY BOUNDARIES ARE

Becoming conscious of healthy sexual boundaries, and appropriate use of sexual energy, is difficult for people raised in homes where neither was modeled. The spoken or unspoken directives are taken in and assumed to be normal. It takes a great deal of examination to be able to change them. For example, Trina's mother criticized her for not being affectionate when Trina was revolted by her sexual hugs and kisses. She asked Trina what was wrong with her.

Trina's mother was so sexually demonstrative that Monty, along with all Trina's previous boyfriends, had sexual fantasies about her. She is full of energy, exuberant, and active. When she visits Pam she brings lots of things to do that intrigue a little girl, such as painting fingernails and making cookies, all laced with sexual energy. Pam loves it. It is hard for Trina to know that this is damaging because it looks like so much fun. Trina tried to bring Pam this same kind of "loving" and fun so she could be a good mother too.

When Trina believes that her mother is actually an innocently loving mother and grandmother, then Trina has to see herself the way her mother sees her—that she is defective for not liking her mother's hugs and kisses.

For Trina to fully know how to be with her daughter in healthy ways, she has to know how her mother was unhealthy with her. This means giving up the illusion of a loving mother who was filled with boundless affection for her, if only she could have figured out how to receive it. While the logical mind may think this is an easy thing to change, once she is on to it, in truth we can only be logical about other people's families. *Each of us has to grieve for the loss of the family we thought we had so that we can know the nature of the family we did have.*

Both Trina and Monty are seeing their mothers far more clearly, which is allowing them to change their relationship with each other and with Pam. However, talking to their mothers has not yet been possible. Monty realized that if he stopped responding to his mother's sexualized attention, she would have to stop giving it. She would no longer obtain any reward. Now that he has spent several months changing his behavior this is happening. But the idea of telling his mother that she is relating with him in a covertly sexual manner seems impossible. His reactions make sense because he would be speaking a language she is unlikely to comprehend. The only parents who are able to understand are those who realize there is something wrong with how they interact with their children, but haven't had a mirror to be able to see it.

Trina is setting limits about time Pam will spend with her grandmother, and is thus reducing the abusiveness. But while she won't let Pam stay all night with her, or allow other solitary contact, she hasn't been able to stop her mother from putting out sexual energy with Pam. The thought of telling her mother that she can no longer do that is overwhelming at this point. She will have to define what she means, which includes telling her mother that she also was sexual with Trina. This is a major confrontation, and it may take her some time to work up to it. Again, the people who have no choice are those who are arrested and required to go into treatment.

A HAPPY FAMILY

The "end" of the story is a beautiful one. Monty and Pam are loving and affectionate. He adores her because he is freed from the role of third wheel and of hating her for it. He feels he has the right to tell Trina whenever things aren't entirely clean in her relating with Pam, and to hear from her when he seems to be "in his addict."

Trina is healing her sexuality by refusing to have sex unless it feels healthy, no longer willing to be a sex addict's drug. By reclaiming her sexuality as her own, she can see when she is using it with her daughter, and can stop. She no longer comes in the room, giving Monty a casual "hi" while passionately embracing Pam. She knows it isn't healthy to intervene when Monty is interacting with Pam, and holds her tongue. As a result she has come to see that Monty is a good father, and Pam doesn't need protection from him.

Pam has been freed from her role as Mommy's special one, favored over Daddy. No longer required to favor Mommy in the same way, she can love her Daddy too. Now she has both parents, ones who will take responsibility for the family, allowing her to be the little girl she is.

Chapter 8

Falling "In Love" with a Young Person

A great number of ASC's "fall in love" with a young person. In contrast with our general belief that anyone who would be sexual with children must be cruel and uncaring, I have listened to histories of people who were passionately in love with a child in the same way romance addicts are "in love" with their lover, and would be shocked to learn they were violating a child. How we "love" depends on our childhood experiences.

As with typical love relationships, the romantic "love" of the ASC depends on his or her childhood cross-wiring. If ASC's grew up unable to have intimate exchanges, this will be seen in their relationships with children. Or, if ASC's grew up with a fear of loss, and translated that fear into an addiction to romance, then this addiction will also appear in relationship to a child. In contrast, people who were raised in ways that permitted intimate, perceptive, respectful relationships won't have sex with children because it will be clear that sex with a young person isn't part of a healthy relationship.

It is possible for an ASC to "love" a baby, as we have seen with Greg's bond to Trish. Following is the story of a man who romantically "loved" the child he damaged. Marc's story demonstrates how an adult can have an intense attachment for a young teenager of the same sex.

MARC'S PASSIONATE LOVE FOR CHRIS

I met Marc when he was completing his second year of court-ordered "sex offender" treatment. His therapist asked if anyone in his therapy group wanted to volunteer to tell me their story for this book, and I received a call from Marc. We met three times in my office where, at first with deep shame, he laid his story out. During the first visit he saw that I wasn't judging him as he expected to be judged by anyone who heard what he had done. By telling it to one more non-shaming person, Marc was able to remove more of the shame surrounding him. He also appreciated being able to have his story used in a way that might help other people. He made it clear to me that he was willing to do anything that could help with this project. He sent me copies of his writing to Chris, which he thought would never be read by another person. I could tell that he intuitively knew that sharing his story with me would assist in his healing from childhood, and from shame over the relationship with a young teenage boy.

Marc was married to Julie, and was helping raise her sons when they decided to take in two foster children. Chris, the oldest, was nine, abandoned by his parents and placed in a series of foster homes. He was a rough, tough kid who needed physical and emotional affection. Then in his tenth placement, he had little hope of loving parenting. Marc had no parental interest in the boy. In truth, Marc didn't like Chris, and avoided him. Julie was more interested in children, and had forced the decision to bring the boys into their home.

For many years Marc had been a sex addict, seeking impersonal sex with men to satisfy a deep desire to feel alive. Instead of satisfying it, each sexual act brought shame and loneliness, which he attempted to wipe out with another seduction. He occasionally had sex with seven or eight men in one night, demonstrating the desperate search for some kind of solution to his pain.

Marc's feelings were mostly locked inside, denied as they had been during his childhood. However, he was able to express some feelings in long letters and journals. He gave me copies of his writing to Chris, to his wife, and to himself. This writing offers a firsthand account during the years before, and during, Marc's relationship with Chris.

One journal entry, long before meeting Chris, addresses his experience as a sex addict—the horror of compulsively searching for a "fix" to replace devastating feelings. I have extracted sections that reflect Marc's self-condemnation.

It's so spooky to have to live with what's going on inside my head right now. People laugh and make jokes about it all the time, but you should have to try to live with it. I go off at night, haunting, seeking for that precious fluid of life. I always find it, but at whose expense? Mine and the other person's. It's an obsession with me, it never goes away. It is always there growing larger and larger, consuming my very life. It is out to destroy me. I'm evil, wicked, hateful, and spiteful. I have no business being alive. I can turn on you. I strike, I'm deadly. How can something as evil as I am ever have someone know I did that? They wouldn't want to be around me.

To have sex with a man for the main intention of creating a fantasy. When I have sex with someone, who I see in my mind is not the person I am with. It feels so good and wonderful, but at the same time it is very hard to deal with the guilt that goes along with it. The time, the lust, the passion, the most powerful driving force in my life. I sometimes wish it was love, I would love for it to be that, but it's not. It's the sex. It runs my life. God, I wish I could tell this to someone, but they would all think I was nuts. So they might be right. I wonder if I am. I couldn't imagine having to live with me.

At the time this was written, SAA was only four years old, and not well-known. There was no one to whom Marc could tell his story and begin the process of healing.

Marc includes evidence that he knows he has some goodness, but of course he questions it at the same time.

The only good thing in my life is my [ice] skating, and I really don't understand that. How can something of such grace and beauty come from someone as ugly and evil as I?

He goes on:

What would people think if they knew what my sex behavior was really like? I'm real sleazy and slimy and a mean and nasty person so I don't deserve to love anyone. I'm the things you could never tell your mother and the kind of person your mother told you to stay away from. Poor Mom, she would die if she ever knew. How could someone as evil as I am come from someone as loving as she is? She would never understand. Good does have to exist in this world and so does evil, but in the end evil will be overcome by good and then I will die. That will be such a release. When all this is done I do hope that some people will have a happy thought about me.

A year or so after Chris entered Marc's home, Chris intuitively perceived Marc's attraction to men. His own history with frustrating father figures, and sexual abuse in earlier years, programmed him to see how he could get the attention of his current "father" Marc. In a desperate attempt to get what little attention might be available, he conveyed a sexualized attraction for Marc. He did this by making sexual noises, leaning on

Marc and gently rubbing against him, and by admiring Marc's qualities. At the time Marc wasn't aware the child had perceived his homosexual leanings, or that he was playing on them. As long as Chris was a child, not yet going through changes of puberty that transformed his body into a young man, Marc didn't respond. He had no sexual interest in pre-pubescent children. But all this changed when Chris was thirteen.

Marc enjoyed wrestling matches on television then, and Chris was taking wrestling in school. One afternoon Chris joined Marc in front of the television, and, as was typical, snuggled up to Marc on the couch. As they watched the fighters and discussed what they were doing, they found themselves acting out some of the holds. Moving to the floor, they continued to bring their bodies together in ways prescribed by the sport. With shock, Marc looked at Chris's body as if for the first time. He suddenly found he had complete sexual awareness of this young man. From that point on he was constantly aware of sexual desire.

This turning point in their relationship brought many changes. The locus of power moved from Marc to Chris. Now that Chris had succeeded in gaining the sexual attention of Marc, he got to be the center of the relationship. This was exhilarating to the young man who hadn't been given his rightful place in a father-figure's life. For the first time Chris was in control and could demand and get exactly what he wanted. Life seemed greatly improved. Allowing Marc to have a sexualized relationship with him seemed like a small price to pay for having some power in his life at last.

Marc, too, felt more alive. His marriage had never satisfied his need for love because he isolated himself from Julie. After a childhood of rejection and neglect he had been unable to open himself to his wife's loving. Also, Marc required frequent casual sex with men to maintain a drugged state of equilibrium. But his fear prevented even an illusion of closeness. Unable to allow himself to receive attention, he focused on the pleasure of the men, obtaining his "fix" from meeting their sexual requirements. Affection had not played any role with these numerous partners.

Yet now Marc felt sexual with a boy who had been snuggling up to him, and for a long time had been putting his head on Marc's shoulder. Sex and love were combined. The result was overwhelming. For the first time he felt passionately in love, an experience he had thought was impossible. His own devastated childhood, filled with deprivation, abuse, and sibling incest, made it impossible for him to see that a love relationship with a thirteen-year-old boy was inappropriate. He didn't know that engaging him in such a way would prevent Chris from forming normal relationships with his peers. Marc didn't see that he was supporting Chris's harmful beliefs: one, that Chris would only be valued if he offered sexual attention, and two, that he could control his environment with his sexuality.

Marc's obsession with Chris made it impossible for him to know that the relationship actually consisted of mutual using. It took months of therapy before Marc could see Chris's needs at all—his obsessions overcame rational thinking. In time he could see that Chris really needed him to set limits on the sexual overtures, as well as refuse to receive his adolescent sexual energy. To counter a history that taught him the opposite, Chris needed to know he could be loved and petted in non-sexual ways, what we call "affection."

MARC'S CHILDHOOD

As Marc described his past to me, I could see the role his childhood played in his resulting relationship with Chris. First, his family did not have sexual boundaries. While he had no memories of sexual contact by either of his parents, he did remember sex with his siblings. One brother, seven years older than Marc, had sex with him in a forceful way that Marc did not like or want to continue. In contrast, when he was thirteen he began a gentle sexual relationship with a brother who was seven. This was the one relationship in childhood in which he could be loving and affectionate. *The six-year age difference allowed Marc to be in control, and thus invulnerable to hurt*—a stark contrast to the treatment he received from his parents.

His father, a superintendent of a school district, failed to nurture him. He was an alcoholic workaholic who controlled everyone around him. Marc's mother was a strict Catholic who did what she was told in order to survive her marriage. Marc doesn't believe that his parents were sexual with him, but he knows his sister was the object of adult sexual contact. We also know from his sexual activity with both brothers that incest was an accepted part of the family's covert rules.

Marc didn't receive loving attention from his passive, unhappy mother. She focused her attention on her husband's drinking and rejection of her, and had nothing left over for her children. They were left to fend for themselves, while she slept. Meals were erratic, and her emotions dominated family gatherings. The children couldn't object because they saw her as a family saint—the one who had the most difficult life of all. There was no way for them to know that children's needs have top priority.

Marc's brother, now in his later twenties, maintains that the sexual activity initiated by Marc when they were growing up was not harmful. He believes Marc provided him with the only love he received, and that without it he would have been even more deprived. While this may be true, the price he pays for having had this sexualized love, however tender, is damaged sexuality. He became eroticized by sexual stimulation that he didn't initiate and control—an experience different from the natural evolution of sexuality in children. He feels he entered the relationship of his own volition, but not only was he six years younger than Marc, he was also having orgasmic sex prior to puberty. (See Chapter 11, "Children Who Are Sexual With Children.")

Marc grew up to be a distrusting person. Therapy hasn't revealed the childhood abuses that diminished his trust in others. His relationship with a heterosexual male therapist has allowed him to develop trust for another person, and to believe that someone else has his best interests at heart. He sees his conviction for sexual communication with a minor, and required therapy, as blessings because he believes he may never have chosen to recover.

Distrust of people in positions of equal or greater power, and a childhood with no boundaries on sexual activity with people of any age or family relationship, set Marc up to respond to Chris in a sexual way. While his adult history didn't include an interest in minors, it still prepared him to respond to Chris's eroticized attention.

CHRIS'S STORY

Chris was programmed by past relationships in which he could use sexual power to meet his needs. Once again, seduction worked, reinforcing his damaged view of sex. Instead of receiving healthy love and respect from the adult male in his home, Chris learned that he could get an imitation of love by using sexual energy. Not only could he get attention, but he also discovered that this energy is so powerful to the ASC that he could use it to get many things he wouldn't otherwise have received. Over time he obtained a computer, a motorcycle, and many smaller items that weren't given to the other children. Yet the gifts couldn't make up for the deprivation of his real needs—for protection, for respect of his naturally developing sexuality, and for non-sexual affection.

Marc and Chris did not have sex. Their relationship con-sisted of sexualized communication, and Marc's "grooming" of Chris to eventually have sex. Over a period of three years the relationship intensified. Marc thought of Chris constantly. When he was at work he daydreamed of the boy and what they might do sexually. Marc lost interest in his other addictive activities, and gave up seducing men for casual encounters. He spent more time at home, attending to Chris.

Chris used the power to his advantage. He waited for Marc to come home from his swing shift job, and sat with his head on his shoulder as Marc unwound. Being the drug of another person was powerful because it made him indispensable. Chil-dren who have been deprived feel safer when they are needed. Of course Chris used the position he was given. As the child, Chris had no responsibility in the sexualized relationship. *It is entirely the adult's job to turn down the sexual energy and provide a safe, loving relationship for a dependent young person.* Marc didn't do this, which is why he is legally and ethically culpable for what happened.

When Marc didn't respond totally to the affection, Chris became more overtly sexual. On several occasions he got out of the shower, wrapped a towel around himself, and presented himself to Marc with an erection showing through the towel. These exchanges highlighted the sexual nature of their rela-tionship.

The two had long conversations over an 18-month period about the possibility of having sex. Marc made it clear that he would do nothing without Chris's permission. He had no interest in forcing the young person because that would not produce his "fix." Only a willing, loving exchange would meet the requirements of Marc's romantic obsession.

THE ILLUSION OF "ROMANCE"

As Marc suffered the sweet torture of wanting what he couldn't have, he was distracted from the reality of a boring existence. He no longer cared that his job held no purpose beyond bringing in an income. His feelings allowed a reprieve from the expensive and dangerous compulsion to find new sex partners. He couldn't see that he was incapable of a loving relationship with an equal. Marc's illusion of intimacy and closeness occupied him so totally that he felt as if he were alive for the first time.

In fact, he was no more alive than any person who uses romantic obsession as a reason for living. People with such cross-wiring usually have affairs in which one or both partners are married, have long-distance relationships, or create other circumstances to prevent them from coupling. This creates intense, longing feelings that can never be fulfilled—the romance addict's drug. While these relationships are harmful to those who create them, and to their partners, the damage is far greater when one person is a child.

Popular and country-western music play to the large numbers of adults who engage in such relationships. The songs focus on intense feelings toward those who can never be "had." It seems impossible for the singers to have healthy relationships, or to grieve for and release one that has ended. Instead, they nurture and prolong the pain—replacing the real emptiness of a life that accompanies lack of self-love.

Marc, from the influence of his empty, affectionless childhood, and the support of our culture, learned to use sexualized romantic involvement to create an illusion of meaning. In acting this out, he damaged the sexuality of a minor, setting him up to continue relating sexually as an alternative to healthy loving. He was unable to meet Chris's need to be refused sexually, and still be loved.

Romantic pain, and being in control—Marc's two relationship "needs"— were amply met. Marc's distrust of people left him unable to feel safe in an equal relationship—one where the others could think for themselves, and have the ability to come and go. Chris's age, and his status as the foster child, placed him in a position that didn't threaten Marc. Feeling safe from abandonment and harm, and fueled by a sexualized longing that couldn't be satisfied, Marc was totally captivated by his relationship with Chris.

How did Marc keep from seeing the damage he was doing to the boy? The defense mechanism of denial, so prevalent among addicts, can allow a person to suspend rational awareness. His addictive "need" was so intense that he couldn't consider doing the right things for Chris—just as most of those who are romantically "in love" can think only of their own needs.

Marc's "grooming" of Chris began with sexual looks and noises. When Chris cuddled up with him, Marc stroked his arms and back. These actions might have looked fatherly to an outside observer, but sexual energy was passing between them.

This contact met the needs of Marc's addiction for a few months, but, as with all addictions, he needed more of the drug to maintain his altered state. The second stage involved controlling Chris physically—restraining him from moving away once the two were cuddling. Chris's attempts to move away, and his distress over not being allowed to, fueled Marc's sexual arousal.

An additional emotional fix came from Marc's remorse and apology when Chris's distress level reached a sufficiently high pitch. (Similar interactions are typical of marriages in which the man is a controller and the woman his economic and social dependent.) After a few months of this stage, Marc needed another increase in drug level. The control-remorse cycle was intensified.

By the time Chris was fourteen, Marc began telling him that he had to have him sexually. He described in detail what they would do, and his arousal was heightened, as usual, by Chris's reluctance. Chris intuitively knew that he had power if he refused. While he couldn't know in a conscious way what was happening, he was able to discern that if he willingly had sex with Marc, his value would diminish. Instead, he could be a powerful drug by refusing sex. In addition, at his young age, the sexual pressure and control were frightening.

After a particularly distressing time when Marc pressed his erect penis against Chris's side, and held him tightly, Chris found himself angry. Now almost fifteen, and growing in height and strength, he fought back. Flinging his elbow into Marc's solar plexus, knocking the breath out of him, he ran to his room and slammed the door. Yelling viciously, he locked the door and sobbed loudly. Marc's reaction to this was immediate. His drug depended on a loving, though reluctant, partner, and this anger and rebellion brought him back into reality. He could see for a moment that he was forcing the boy to engage in ways that were not right, and he felt guilty. He stood outside Chris's door expressing his remorse with tears and promises to make it up to him. As Chris didn't respond, Marc felt more and more desperate. Finally, he offered to take him to the store to look at a computer he knew Chris wanted. After two more minutes of silence, Chris emerged with smiles and a hug for Marc.

THE DEMAND-REMORSE CYCLE

With the purchase of the computer, difficult to afford on Marc's salary, a new era of the relationship began—spending. The cycle started each time Marc felt the need for a fix. As he approached Chris with escalating requests and physical control, Chris reacted with increasing distress accompanied by threats to leave, or to report Marc's behavior. Marc's guilt and fear reached proportions he hadn't known were possible, and he entered a state of terror. At this point he would do anything not to lose Chris, and to avoid being reported. The next point in the cycle was the purchase of something Chris said he wanted. The end of the cycle came when Chris, enjoying his new toy and the "caring" that was expressed in the purchase, became the happy, affectionate boy that Marc desperately needed him to be.

The end of one cycle brought the seeds of the next. Marc spent money he didn't have. He felt controlled by this young person—the very feeling he wished to avoid. As his relief faded into the past, it was replaced by anger. Here he was again controlled by the whims of another, just as he had been in childhood. The money he saved for his own desires, and for financial safety, was drained by this person he so desperately needed. Marc found that his sexualized love was turning into sexualized hate, and this was expressed by escalating sexual demands and control—bringing on another round of fear and guilt, followed by making up.

This cycle came to a head when Chris was sixteen. Now a teenager who had a social life that included dates, he was engaging in activities that threatened Marc's hold on him. They fought frequently about his activities, Marc expressing his need to possess the young man. One particular evening, as Chris was preparing to go to a dance, Marc found himself jealous and angry. He couldn't believe Chris was leaving him for another person, preferring to spend time in activities that didn't include him. At the same time, he knew that it was natural for Chris, but his romantically drugged state couldn't tolerate it.

Since controlling another was one way Marc made himself feel safe, he set out to prove to himself that Chris was still in his control even though he was going out in the world in dangerous ways. Waiting in Chris's room while Chris showered, he looked him up and down as the young man walked into the room wrapped in a towel. Leaning back on the bed and smiling, he began to talk casually about the possibility of not letting Chris go to the dance. It sounded like teasing, but both knew it wasn't. He brought up the subject of his sexual attraction, and said he would let Chris go if he took off his towel and let Marc see him naked. Chris said no, he wouldn't, and threatened to report Marc if he continued to put pressure on him. Because this threat had been levied many times, Marc didn't believe he really would. In addition, his despair was particularly intense because Chris was pulling away as his interest in peers increased. This despair blinded him to the reality of Chris's threat.

Marc continued his quietly controlling demands, and Chris increased his angry rebellion. But the usual course of events didn't happen. At the point where Marc expected Chris to break down and beg him to back off, or actually do what was requested, Chris instead left the room. He returned to the bathroom and put his worn clothes back on. Storming out of the house, he screamed behind him, "I'm going to turn you in, you dirty fucker! You aren't going to get away with this any more. I have a life of my own, and I'm not staying around for this." He ran out of the house and rode his bike to his friend's. He called the social worker who was responsible for the foster home placement, and sobbed the truth into the phone. The next day an investigation began. Their relationship was over.

Immediately both the foster boys and Marc's sons were taken out of the home. The case worker contacted Marc's employer, who terminated his employment because he related with adolescents. While this was traumatic, his greatest pain came from the loss of his "lover," wrenched away from him. His reaction was as intense as the response of a husband whose wife has abruptly left him.

Marc's despair was so deep that he planned to end his life. He made a serious attempt and spent weeks in the hospital recuperating.

The lover relationship that Marc created with Chris was an attempt to make life meaningful. As with many addictions, sexual and romantic among them, *the objective is to bring on positive feelings to avoid the emptiness of life, and the feelings of self-hate and shame.* Marc's struggle between wanting to love, and feeling hopeless about life, is captured in his writing to Chris— letters he wrote but never sent. He put his thoughts and feelings on paper when he was aware that Chris was growing away from him, and that the relationship would soon end. Prior to the investigation and the suicide attempt, his thoughts of killing himself permeated the writing.

Chris did not receive the letter that Marc left on his computer long before he was reported, to be found if Marc killed himself.

Dear Chris,

I suppose it seems pretty weird that I am writing to you again but it seems that this is the only way I have to express myself without stepping on your toes. I hope to be able to create a journal that you will be able to get a hold of in the event that I am no longer around.

I wish I could figure out what it is with me and you. I had such a bad day today for no apparent reason. I wonder half the time if you know what it's like to go through a day feeling like you have a band around your waist pulling and squeezing so tight that you can hardly breathe. That's how I spend most of my days when you are not around.

After I get myself off to work it seems that the day starts to go down hill from there. It's so hard to concentrate, I find that my thoughts drift to you, wondering what you're doing, if you are up yet. Do you know how often I call to see what's going on at home? I call under the pretext to see what everyone is doing but I really call to see how your day is going. I wish that I could talk to you but I really don't have anything to say except how is your day going.

I know that if this letter ever gets to you that you will probably get the wrong idea like I am blaming you for what has happened to me, but I'm not, Chris. Something tells me you will feel a great deal of guilt and responsibility for it. I want to say right now that what I did I did of my own free choice and will. I knew a long time ago that I was not going to be around for that long a period of time. I always felt that I would go by my own hand and at my choosing. Know that I left with no hard feelings towards you at all. I left loving you as much as I always did. Know that I will always be there for you even after I am gone. If you ever need someone to talk to just talk to the air, I'll be there listening and somehow I will find a way to let you know that I was there.

Marc wanted Chris to see him as a good person who loved him. Blinded by his own despair, he didn't see sexual energy in their relationship as destructive to Chris. Continuing in his obsession, Marc writes:

All the people you have ever loved ended up treating you like shit. So you expect me to do the same. I was never quite sure of what you thought of me. I know it's the one thing I keep saying over and over but I hope someday you can believe it. The fact is that I truly did love you more than anything else in this world, I think that much must be pretty clear by now. I think that somehow in your eyes I must have been too much like your dad. God, I hope not. I'm nothing like him. I just wanted to love you too much and you couldn't deal with that. But you know I honestly thought that once you found out how I was feeling you would do something about it. I honestly did not think that you would let me die. Until the very end I always believed in you and me and that I was the person that you were supposed to be with. I want you to know that these last two years have been the best years of my life. I was never so happy as when I was with you.

Marc writes of his sexual abuse in his longest letter to Chris as he makes a case for their similarities.

My childhood, like yours, was no piece of cake. I don't think I suffered the physical abuse you did, but my life certainly contained enough sexual abuse that even now I cringe to think about it. I can't remember a time when it wasn't happening to me. My childhood, my teenage years, it was always there. You know the funny thing about it was that for probably twenty years or so I honestly could not remember a thing. And then one day I was watching a show on television on sexual abuse and seeing it was like opening a flood gate to me and all of a sudden I started to remember things. Most of them were not very pleasant, but they were there. Even to this day I don't hate him [Marc's older brother] for what he did to me. You know he never once told me that he loved me.

In the final weeks before the suicide attempt Marc wrote the following poignant love poem.

> *To hold you in my arms once tonight,*
> *your naked body pressed against mine.*
> *No words exchanged,*
> *the silence is the only thing heard in the room.*
> *Everything that needs to be said has been said,*
> *and it is only the silence that speaks.*
> *Three years of passion consumed in one moment.*
> *To hold, to touch, to love, and then finally to let go.*

> *Burned in my memory for the rest of my life,*
> *one can only hope it is enough to set me free.*
> *For what has been, for what is now,*
> *and for what the future will hold I thank you.*
> *I love you.*

Marc's addictive passion was never satisfied. He lost Chris first to the normal life of a teenager, and then to his removal from Marc's home. Marc was sentenced to one year probation, because no sexual activity was involved, and one year of "sex offender" treatment. His therapy has helped him abandon his addictive acting out, and open up to a positive sexual relationship with a man his age. He is frightened of intimate relationships, and it has been hard. At the time of the interviews he was dating a man who joined him in being together without sex. While Marc was able to be sexual in an entirely impersonal way, sex when conscious was terrifying.

In our last conversation, three years after his arrest, Marc's bond to Chris was not entirely broken. While the nature of the relationship was clearly obsessive, it was the only time Marc had felt something akin to being in love. This is hard to abandon, particularly when the real thing is laced with deep fear. Marc had not moved far enough along in his recovery to relinquish his pain, and be able to see fully that any sexualized relationship with Chris would be harmful to him.

Chapter 9

When Adults Are Sexual with Babies

When the subject of adults' sexual activities with
children comes up, sexuality with babies seems to draw
the most intense shock and disbelief. Our conscious minds
know this is absolutely outside the parameters of appropriate
behavior, and so it seems impossible to fathom. But those who
are sexual with babies rationalize it by seeing their behaviors as
different from sex with adults, belonging in a different realm.
So different that people can actually say they haven't been
sexual with a baby when an observer would know they had.
When we as a culture can talk openly about sex with babies,
then it will be harder for people to separate their behavior out
into a different world view. As this happens, it will become more
difficult to act on this kind of sexual desire.

I attended a men's sex offender therapy group (presented in
detail in Chapters 13 and 17) and heard these men describe
what they had done with children. They talked about how they
rationalized—and actually believed—that they weren't doing
anything wrong. They said things like, "the child liked it," "I
was loving him or her," and "they won't remember when they
get older." *Our culture supports this denial of the truth with a
global reaction of disgust.*

Most people can hardly stand to hear the details of what happens, which prevents them from incorporating these common behaviors into their perception of what goes on around us. As each of us can talk, we will provide a more accurate mirror of the behaviors that aren't healthy for children, and future generations won't be able to isolate sexual behaviors with babies in a way that allows them to not know what they are doing, or believe they are causing no harm.

When we do observe adults exchanging sexual energy with children, we have difficulty knowing this is what is happening because there isn't any overt sexual behavior. And when we do know that something is "off" we are prohibited by our culture from saying anything. If we do speak up, we can be told that we are misperceiving what is happening, and we can even be shamed for seeing something sexual when "it isn't there." Trina and Monty couldn't object when they saw Trina's mom give their daughter a French kiss! They knew she would dismiss their concern as absurd.

Fifteen years ago I was at the home of friends when I watched a father be sexual with his two-year-old daughter. Even then—when I believed such things only went on in rare cases, and certainly not in the home of people I socialized with—I knew something was wrong. I watched him hold her on his lap, stroke her and make noises that were clearly sexual. His wife didn't do anything, and my husband didn't observe anything. I would have felt absurd and totally out of line to bring it up. In addition, I couldn't have put words to what I was seeing because I couldn't say even to myself that it was sexual energy. All I knew was that it didn't seem right.

The daughter is now seventeen, and the parents are divorced. I know how to contact them and know that I could provide valuable information for all three people. But I haven't done it yet. It is frightening. I also know that it will be easier to contact the mother because she is more likely to agree with me. The father will be more difficult because I expect he will have the same reaction most people do when told they were being sexual with their child. But I am going to have to do it because otherwise I am teaching one set of values and living another—the very ones I grew up with.

As I ponder how I learned not to mention obvious signs of sexual arousal, I remember when I was a teen and my father got erections in his very brief bathing suit. I remember looking over at him when we were at a lake with family friends, and seeing this large bulge in his swim suit. I thought that he had a huge penis if it was this size when not erect. I only recently realized that it was erect. He was aroused and in a sexual trance. But nobody around us did anything differently. No one looked, or if they did, didn't indicate that something was different. I felt like I was the only one observing, and was alone with my information. I know my mother and the other adults thought that if they ignored it, I wouldn't notice. I know this because when I became a mother I believed I could ignore things and my son wouldn't notice it. My thinking was distorted by their thinking, and it is passed on from generation to generation.

If my father had been in recovery from sexual addiction, then ideally anyone in the group could have commented. And he could have said, yes, I am reacting to_____, naming his stimulus. If it had been me in my bikini, then I would have been supported by others who knew that this wasn't good for me. He would have been told, without shaming, not to look at me. I would not feel isolated by my solitary perception, and would be provided with a mirror of the truth. If his erection was not in response to me, but instead to another person, or to a fantasy, then I would know this truth as well.

But of course there was no recovery available for my father then. He didn't get caught in addictive activities by my mother until a couple of years after the first Twelve Step programs for recovering sex addicts were started. By then or soon after he had contracted AIDS.

Instead of the truth, I was presented with several adult faces that told me nothing, and left me alone with my perception. I also knew intuitively that I was not to ask questions. Penises and penis size were off limits for conversation, even though I was a teenager and approaching my first intercourse. I know that if I had said anything, the intense discomfort of the adults would have gotten me to stop talking. Their bodies would have taken on rigid postures as they withheld their reactions, wishing I would do the same.

With this kind of background, and lack of support by my husband, and perceived lack of belief by the man and his wife, the idea of saying anything to the man being sexual with his child couldn't even register in my brain. What could I say? What proof did I have? So I let another 15 years pass, and even now, writing a book on this subject, I am holding off contacting them.

As I remember that scene, and sexual comments he made about me as well, I know that he had no idea there was anything damaging about his sexuality. He didn't hide his interactions with his daughter, making it look like he was doing nothing wrong. And he got our agreement as we didn't indicate there was anything wrong either. I know he may have been more overtly sexual with her in private, and could have justified it as acceptable because of our lack of reaction in public.

My frustration is coming up as I write, trying to explain something that seems impossible to communicate. I know your own ability to rationalize and deny can prevent you from understanding, and from believing that it is possible to have sex with babies. I would like to ask you to think about times that you did something that you now know wasn't right, but at the time you rationalized it so that you thought it was. Having an affair, for example, or telling someone they weren't going to die when you knew they were. Lying to prevent a reaction you didn't want, or taking something that wasn't yours, and believing that it wasn't stealing, perhaps because everyone else does (such as taking office supplies from work). I'm sure you have an example of a time when you convinced yourself that what you were doing was all right, only to see later that it wasn't, that you were violating your values and other people. While the examples you have come up with may seem trivial compared to sex with babies, the principle of denial is the same.

As you read the following three examples, please let yourself have feelings so that you don't cut off understanding. Know that you may have been there yourself, and if you haven't, it is only because your boundaries weren't violated in the ways that prevented these people from understanding how they were harming babies. These three people are not different from us. They differ in that they know how they harmed babies in sexual and non-sexual ways. They have taken painful inner looks to know, and are facing recovery for themselves and for their children.

SHEILA AND HER BABY

Sheila had no idea she was damaging her six-year-old son's sexuality when he was a nursing infant. I believed her. She found herself aroused, and on a number of occasions, masturbated to orgasm while he breast fed. She separated her awareness of him from her arousal, and believed that by doing so she wasn't interacting sexually with him. He was getting his milk, and she, at the same time, was bringing herself an orgasm. It didn't seem different from answering the phone, and directing her attention away from the baby to a caller.

Sheila didn't know that her son would have a primitive awareness of her sexual arousal, and that it would stimulate his own sexuality in ways that aren't a result of his developmental needs. He might receive her body shame as if it were his, and he could associate food (the essence of life) with sexual arousal, preparing him for later addiction to sexual energy, or to food.

If you find yourself having reactions to the idea of a mother masturbating while breast feeding, please breathe, and pay attention to the feelings. The truth is that what she did was harmful. At the same time, there are many other forms of harm that we don't react to with such intense negative feelings because our culture doesn't condemn them.

For example, when mothers sneak out of a babysitter's home in an attempt to reduce their child's distress (distress that is natural from about six months to two years), the child is threatened with the abandonment of the most important person in his life. If this happens regularly, he or she will come to fear that the mother will disappear at any time, and might monitor her actions closely. This can be as harmful to the child's feelings of safety in the world as Sheila's masturbation while nursing, yet few people have a strong reaction to this second example. While children are harmed by sexual activity created for the adult's "needs," the harm doesn't seem to match the intensity of the disgusted reactions of those who hear about it. (Read Chapter 17 for more on this.)

Sheila didn't know her behavior wasn't OK for several reasons. One is that she was aroused by the sucking of her infant, a common and not necessarily unhealthy response. She didn't understand the difference between arousal in response to the child's needs and arousal to meet her own interests. The first is healthy, and one way a child learns about sexual energy of others along with appropriate boundaries. He or she learns they can do things that are sexually arousing to a parent, and not have the parent get carried away with wanting the child to meet their needs. They see that sexual arousal doesn't necessitate action, it is just a feeling, and can be contained within the person having it. This makes a child safe. If the parent shifts into meeting his or her own interests, the child is abandoned because he or she is no longer seen. This is frightening.

I fully understand why Sheila didn't know her behavior wasn't healthy for her son. I would have done the same if I hadn't had an intense desire to make absolutely sure what happened to me as a child didn't happen to my son. I was watchful, on guard, monitoring myself. I didn't breast feed. I couldn't state the reason at the time. I knew only that my breasts were sexual and I wasn't comfortable putting my nipples into a mouth for any other reason. Now I know that I was afraid I would do what Sheila had done.

Sheila discovered that she had been sexual with her son after discovering that her partner was sexual with him when he was a toddler. Although she has told the story several times before, her shame came up strongly when telling it one more time. She is vulnerable to the cultural abhorrence of mothers who violate their children, particularly when the violation is sexual. Men are expected to violate children. While men are harmed when seen this way, and their self-esteem is diminished, women aren't allowed any latitude from perfection.

ROB AND HIS BABY

Rob had been a sex addict from the time he was a teenager. Living on the edge of sexual trance had been a way of life. He was always ready to respond sexually until he entered recovery over three years ago. He searched for sexual fixes in many places, wishing to stay in his sexual trance state for as long as possible. So when his daughter was born, she became one more source of flesh he could use to stimulate himself.

If you are having emotional reactions to hearing about Rob, let yourself have them and observe. What he did is totally outside of our culturally sanctioned behaviors. You have been trained by others' reactions to be appalled. You may also be responding to your own cross-wiring to children, and wanting to prohibit your reaction with strong negative feelings. Or you may have had experiences similar to the baby's, and your own feeling "memory" is emerging. If you can allow yourself to have all your feelings, there may be information waiting to be expressed.

Rob didn't focus on children as his source of sexual arousal. He responded to any stimulation. When he got up at night with his daughter when she couldn't sleep, he rocked her in a rocking chair on his lap. Because she was on his penis, the motion stimulated his always ready sexual reactions, and he had erections. Sometimes he masturbated later, sometimes at the time, and occasionally he had an orgasm just from the stimulation of her body against him. Because he had many outlets for his addiction, including sex with his wife, he didn't make a habit of this kind of contact.

From Rob's point of view, he was just responding to a stimulation that happened to be there. He was in so much shame about his sexual activities that he couldn't see this was any worse. Going into a trance state, where logic cannot penetrate, he truly didn't think he was doing anything harmful to his daughter. The addictive trance is powerful in preventing people from knowing what may be obvious to anyone else. As with Sheila, he couldn't see that his behavior would have any lasting effects. She was under two, and wouldn't remember it when she grew up. He didn't hurt her, and the behaviors didn't look overtly sexual. These rationalizations work very well.

Rob knows now that his behavior was harmful to his daughter. He has been working for almost four years on his own sexual recovery, and can see his own damaging childhood where sexual boundaries were almost nonexistent. He doesn't know if someone rocked him and had orgasms when he was a baby, but he can see now that sexual energy is an integral part of communication between family members. He and his wife have difficulty going to family gatherings because they want to avoid the freely flowing flirtatious sexual energy. Rob knows that his family sees his sisters' flirtation with him as normal, even though they send him into an addictive trance. To aid his recovery, he has little contact with the family. His wife, who doesn't put out sexual energy, has always been uncomfortable with them. She was relieved when her husband was able to identify their behaviors, giving her a mirror for her perception.

Their daughter is now thirteen, and a sexual young person. They have told her that her father is a recovering sex addict, but haven't told her what happened when she was a baby. Even though they are in therapy, it is confusing to them to know what to tell and how to tell. They do know that it has effected her, and that she needs information in order to make sense out of her cross-wiring. But, as the women's stories in Chapter 3 point out, when we come from backgrounds with confusing, inaccurate rules about sexual exchange, it is very difficult to know how to help a child with sexuality.

GREG'S BABY GIRL

Greg's story has been told in Chapter 4. He was also a sex addict of major proportions, and could make no distinction between sex with his wife and sex with anyone else. He had already had sex with many women by the time Trish was born, and easily moved back and forth between his sex addict trance and his normal state. As with Marc, Greg fell in love with his daughter. In his addictive thinking, he believed she was there just for him, to take care of his needs as his mother and his wife had failed to do. A little child can be molded by a parent to look like they can take the place of the parent's parent. This is damaging even when the parent isn't sexual with the child, but is even more so when sexual energy is included.

Greg rationalized the same way the other two parents did. He didn't cause her pain, he didn't force her, he didn't restrain her. He seduced her. This made it look to him as if she were choosing of her own free will to be sexual with him, to be his lover. Of course it isn't possible for a child to make such a choice. She is dependent on her parents for her life, and sets out to learn what is required to be a member of the family. When the training begins in infancy, it becomes a natural part of life to the child.

Greg told me that he held Trish on his penis from the time she was very young, bringing him an erection and ejaculation. He was also aroused by stimulating her genitals with his mouth, and by her doing the same with his penis. He now knows how harmful this was to her, and her story confirms this. But at that time it seemed like the most natural thing in the world. He kept it a secret because he knew his wife would be jealous and angry. That is, until Trish convinced her mother Joyce what was going on when she was eight and Greg didn't want to stop. His distorted thinking is demonstrated by his attempt to convince his wife that it was all right for him to continue "loving" their daughter.

Babies record memory of intrusive sexual activity. Trish was affected, even though she wasn't able to talk or create picture memories. Her sexuality was stimulated in ways that were not consistent with her developmental tasks. She was harmed even in infancy. Greg knows this now, and is doing what he can to help her recover from the effects.

Chapter 10

Sibling Incest

S ibling incest, and other forms of sex between older and younger children, is very common, probably more common than that between adults and children. Most adults who are sexual with children began the behavior as teens, while many teens who are sexual with younger children don't continue that behavior when their adult value system engages.

WHY DO SIBLINGS HAVE SEX?

Sibling incest is common in families where sexual boundaries are muddy. When parents are sexual with some children, or where sexual energy flows even with no sexual contact, the children may express the boundaryless sexual energy among themselves. *Children who have been sexually stimulated experience more sexual arousal and desire to act on it than children whose sexuality is allowed to unfold naturally.* And children who have had adults be sexual with them may not remember it consciously, but will express the unconscious memory in behavior.

CONTROL BY OLDER SIBLINGS

Sibling relationships carry much of the authority-subordinate relating common to parent-child relationships. I have observed siblings in airports where parents leave them to play while waiting for planes or passengers. Older siblings, when they attend to the younger ones, are often controlling and dominating, passing the control they receive from their parents onto the younger children. They push to the limits the parent will allow, or the limit that the younger child will tolerate without throwing tantrums. Parents tire of constantly disciplining their children, and so allow the older children a great deal of control of the younger ones. As a result, the belief system of the younger children is that the older one has the right to control them. They have no mirrors for their right to be respected. This belief carries over to adult life in the same way that parent-child relationships do. The result is that younger siblings don't feel they can say no to an older sibling at times they wouldn't hesitate to say no to another person.

In the following example we can see how rigid control, passed from parent to child, is passed on to the younger sibling in a very distorted way. In Michael's case, the control of his little sister eventually evolved into sexual activity.

JULIE AND MICHAEL

Julie now in her early forties, originally came to therapy to work on her marriage and her career choices. During an early session, she told me that her brother was sexual with her for many years. He was three years older, and it had begun when she was about ten and ended when, at fourteen, she threatened to tell the whole family. I encouraged Julie to spend some therapy time working on the effects this had in her adult life, including in her marriage. She thought this was a good idea, but couldn't bring herself to go into any detail.

Two years later she returned, ready to work on the incest, and prepared to confront Michael in my office.

Julie was terrified before and during the first session. She expected him to deny that anything had gone on. Instead, he confirmed immediately that Julie was correct, and that he was glad the secret was out in the open. He expressed a great deal of emotion, including shame and relief.

Julie had asked me for the name of a therapist qualified to work with him, and was armed with her business card. Michael entered therapy willingly, and went to work on his shame and guilt for what he had done. Six months after this encounter, both Julie and Michael decided they were ready to work together, and they began bi-monthly meetings with Michael's therapist and me. Both had a great deal of fear of talking to each other. Michael had to check me out to see that I wasn't going to blame and condemn him for what he did to Julie. Julie needed to know that no one would minimize what she had been through.

After an initial period of adjustment, when each developed a sense of safety, Julie and Michael joined together to examine what had been going on in their childhoods that resulted in Michael becoming angry and controlling, as well as sexual, with Julie, and in Julie knowing that she would not get support from her parents if she told on him. Together they mapped out the family system that cast them into their roles, and took steps to change their parts in this system.

THE EFFECTS OF
SHAMING CHILDREN'S SEXUALITY

As Michael and Julie explored their memories, they talked passionately about a time that stands out in both of their minds. When Julie was about six and Michael nine, they were in the bathroom together when their parents were out of the house. Julie had been in the bathtub, and Michael was with her. They aren't sure of the details, but they both know they were being sexually curious with each other in a way that felt innocent.

Their parents walked in on them and exploded. Julie was pulled out of the bathroom and sent outside to wait until after Michael was punished. Michael's father spanked him and slapped his face hard—for the first and only time in Michael's life.

No explanation was given for the punishment. Their parents assumed they would know that what Michael had been doing was wrong. Julie, seen as the victim, wasn't directly punished, although she felt punished by being banished. She was terrified. She knew her brother was receiving the worst punishment ever given in their family, and she was not told what would happen next. Both children had already picked up their family's attitudes toward sexuality, and knew this was the worst offense.

Even though it didn't look like Julie was being punished, this memory is etched in her mind. It was one of the first things she talked with me about when we first met. As we talked about it again later, Julie could say more clearly that she was being punished by being sent away while Michael was scolded and hit. The very act that was to look protective—being protected from seeing her brother's punishment—in fact, enforced her aloneness and isolation, and the feeling of blame for causing problems.

The purpose of the punishment wasn't given at the time. Today their parents still claim they don't believe anything sexual was going on. Confusion remains about how they account for their intense response to finding their daughter in the bathtub and their son in the bathroom with her.

Michael and Julie were raised in the Catholic church and attended Catholic schools. This environment contributed to their belief that sexuality was the greatest evil, and the source of most punishment. They took turns telling stories about the nuns in school. One of Julie's examples was a girl who wore some mascara, and was screamed at by a nun who had taught both Michael and Julie. After public humiliation, the girl was made to stand up for the rest of the day. Michael showed no surprise. Instead, he told his own stories. (See Chapter 17 for more about how the Catholic subculture, and other religions, influence sexuality.)

The family shaming and cultural shaming of sexuality, coupled with the almost constantly dominating control of their mother, and passivity of their father, set Michael up to express vengeful rage on his little sister. In addition, it set her up to be unable to reach out for help. Beaten for sexual curiosity, and subordinated to his mother's whims, the most powerful form of retribution that Michael's unconscious mind could devise was sexual dominance over his mother's female child.

JULIE IS UNABLE TO ASK FOR HELP

Julie was unable to reach out for help for several reasons. She felt guilty for her own role in initial sex play with Michael, and also with neighboring children. All of them went along with acts they knew were totally forbidden by their parents. They played strip poker, frightened by knowing they could be caught if their parents returned. Because Julie had been involved in these early forbidden explorations, she didn't feel that she had a right to get help when Michael wanted to continue. And her parents had made her feel that she was somehow at fault for Michael's response. The victim felt responsible.

Julie also believed her parents wouldn't have helped. Her mother constantly told Julie what Julie thought and felt, or what she should think, feel, and do. None of her perceptions of Julie were accurate, which left Julie with the belief that no one in her life would believe the truth. If she wasn't believed about simple things like food preferences and feelings toward friends, how could she expect that she would be believed about receiving frightening, painful, and violating treatment from her brother?

Julie was told she was too sensitive, and that this accounted for the difficulty she experienced with the non-sexual violations she complained about. As she was told that she should be able to handle her brother's actions, it became impossible to think that she would receive compassion and help if she told the whole story. She was the one who was made to feel responsible, and, with no information to the contrary, she accepted that assignment. Julie told me she felt like she was failing because she hadn't been able to do what her mother said. If her mother told her to just tease Michael back, it implied that it should be possible. Yet Julie hadn't been able to. Deep feelings of inadequacy left her even less able to say that she had failed, and needed protection.

Julie was also confused about her own role. She was willing to play sexual games with Michael, but she didn't want to be forced to do so. To her child's mind, this difference couldn't register as significant because her life was dominated by being forced to do things by her parents, other relatives, and the school.

Julie had also been taught that authority isn't to be questioned. With this rule in place after countless deferrings to church figures, teachers, parents, and other relatives, Julie couldn't even think of objecting to the authority of a brother three years older, who was given this position by her parents when he was assigned the role of babysitter. Michael was handed the authority, and they both played the parts they had observed from the time they were babies.

MICHAEL WAS A VICTIM, TOO

Michael was violated by this set of dynamics as well. It was harmful for him to discharge rage on his sister. If Julie and Michael's parents had been sensitive to the needs of their children, they would have been able to hear what was happening to Julie, and then set safe boundaries for them both. Michael would have had help to express himself in ways that didn't create more shame and guilt and diminish his self-esteem.

It is also true that their parents couldn't have done anything differently. They were the products of their own childhoods and culture, and were reactive to evidence of sexuality in their children. Their inability to know what was going on with the children stemmed from growing up with no models of how to do this. Both wanted to be the best parents they could.

JULIE'S BETRAYAL

Julie began to talk in one session about her surprise that she wasn't able to be as angry with Michael as she had expected. But we discovered another reason Julie had difficulty accessing her feelings toward her brother's abuses. The two of them had felt bonded against their parents' control and redefinition of their beings. The siblings were able to support each other while neither was able to deal with the parents. Their initial sexual curiosity was part of their bond in revenge against the adults. They engaged in the most forbidden, off-limits activity imaginable, while condoning each other's behaviors. But Michael broke away from this bond. As he grew older, his need to thwart his mother's shaming control increased. Sex remained one way to do this, and electing his sister as the one to control both physically and sexually provided the strongest form of revenge.

Julie, on the other hand, lost her big brother, her one and only ally. She knew her parents wouldn't intervene, and she also knew that if she told, she would burn her bridge to Michael, and then be entirely alone. She said, "Then I'd have nothing." As Julie talked about this, she remembered that when she got her first dog, things changed for her. She bonded with the dog, and developed an intuitive relationship with him that allowed her to feel connected to another being. Soon after that she told Michael that he had to stop or she would tell the world what he was doing. She could afford to burn the bridge.

Resolving the betrayal will require grief as well as anger. It took Julie months of therapy to become comfortable expressing vulnerable feelings of grief in front of a family member. She built up patterns of hostile anger to cope with problems in her life because she felt this served her best when dealing with Michael. She understood intellectually that if she accesses her tender feelings she can heal more quickly, but it took time to act on it.

WHY MICHAEL DID NOT BECOME AN ASC

Michael's therapist and I asked ourselves how it came to be that Michael was sexual with his sister and cousins, and yet was not interested in being sexual with children as an adult. We saw the answer in Michael's focus on passing on the control and humiliation that was daily fare from his mother. He was powerless with her, but with younger children he could be the one in control. He could tease and humiliate. Now, as an adult, he is the powerful one with his children. While he still experienced a need to control, this didn't have to be expressed through total power over another with sexual energy for emphasis. He was able to see that sexual interaction with children didn't meet this need from childhood. Michael didn't go into the sexual trance that prevents reason from operating. If the sexual interaction with his sibling had taken the form of romantic or sexual bonding, as it did in Marc's reaction to Chris, he may have had more confusion in his interactions with his own children.

EVELYN AND JEFF

Evelyn came from an unusual home. Her parents were involved in a religious order that focused on teaching people around the world. When at "home," they lived in community with many hundreds of people creating a spiritually-based living and working arrangement. Evelyn's father was fairly high up in the ranks, and her mother held responsible positions that required specific skills. Groups of families ate together and shared living tasks, so Evelyn grew up as part of an extended family. She had two older brothers and a younger sister, in addition to numerous other children of all ages who came and went as their parents became involved in projects away from the home base.

Evelyn described her family as "normal" in a sexual sense. She and her mother loved each other, and as an adult, she had a friendly relationship with her father. Her parents carried on a civil marital relationship, although Evelyn did not observe much affection or intimacy between them. She believed this was normal from her observation of other families in the community. The "work" of the community seemed to take precedence. It was there that its members seemed to express their passion.

The leader of the order dictated that no one was to divorce. Marital difficulties were to be worked out in the context of spiritual teachings. Those who chose to divorce had to leave the order. (Evelyn only learned this information once she became an adult and married. Her mother filled her in on what had occurred during her early years.) Evelyn's parents chose to remain married because they wanted to retain their lifestyle.

Evelyn and her oldest brother were very close. They fought and hugged with equal intensity, and formed a bond that seemed to be absent in their relationships with their parents. When Evelyn was sixteen, and Jeff was twenty, they had sex. Evelyn was visiting Jeff at his apartment in another part of the city, and planned to spend the night. The evening was filled with drinking with several other people, who then went home. Evelyn planned to sleep in the same bed with Jeff as she had done occasionally throughout their lives. It was the only bed in the small apartment.

She climbed into the bed, in her nightgown, and reached over to hug him good night. When the hug seemed to be naturally over she let go, preparing to return to her side of the bed. But he didn't let go. Since this was her brother who loved her, she felt confused. If he wanted to continue hugging then it must be right. She was used to obeying him as she had obeyed her parents. Jeff began talking to her as he held her. He told her how important she had been to him all his life, and how he missed her now that he was out on his own. He stroked her hair and then her shoulders. Evelyn's inner state of confusion intensified, but she knew she couldn't think of pulling away because this was the most important relationship in her life. She couldn't end it. And she believed it would end if she didn't receive his affection. Besides, he was older and knew what was right. Nothing had happened before that her parents felt was out of the norm. If he was doing this, then by definition it had to be all right. Alcohol blurred her judgment.

JEFF MISDIRECTS HIS EMOTIONAL BOND

Jeff felt he was passionately in love with his little sister. He had loved her from the time she was born. Jeff and Evelyn's mother was emotionally absent, caught in her own obsessive thinking regarding her husband's sexual activities with other women. She loved her children, but didn't offer them the full mother-infant bond necessary for children to feel safe and loved, and from which they develop into independent people. Her children's physical needs were always met, and they could count on physical safety. But we humans need so much more.

While Jeff's situation didn't compare to the deprivation of war orphans, (who weren't held and played with and consequently died) he was indeed suffering from emotional deprivation. Consequently, when Evelyn delighted in his attention at a very young age, he misdirected the intense emotional bond he should have had with his mother. Evelyn bonded to her older brother for the same reason. Their mother was relieved that the two children were so close because it freed her from some of the frustration of meeting their emotional needs.

When Jeff reached puberty his feelings for Evelyn developed a strong sexual charge. He didn't act on it because he believed it was very wrong by the standards of his family. However, the loving relationship he shared with his sister now became the object for this added intensity of sexual energy. He developed an obsession for her, and countered it with an equally intense prohibition against acting on it. His sex addiction took the form of obsession and withholding, as well as complete attention to the person who was the object of his drug-like state.

Neither Jeff nor Evelyn understood that their "love" was fueled by his sexual obsession, because both had been raised in a home without clear sexual boundaries or an understanding of sexual energy. The sexualized loving exchanges both parents had with other people laid the groundwork for their belief that such feelings are a normal part of non-marital relating. Flirting and sexual tones that belong only with the parental relationship were going on all around them, and so they both felt their love was normal.

Jeff intended to have no overt sexual contact with Evelyn, but when she was sixteen and planning to spend the night in his bed, he worried. For days, he'd thought about what it would be like to make love to her. His sexual trance state increased, and alcohol shattered his resolve.

For over an hour or so Jeff steadily increased the contact, first kissing her on the neck and throat, then finally on the mouth. The mouth kissing was a turning point for both of them. Once she let him do that, she knew she had made the decision to be sexual. Deep kissing crossed over the line between the sexualized relating they had grown up seeing and overt sexual loving they knew belonged to couples. As she responded to his kiss, her confusion evaporated. It was like losing virginity—from that point on the prohibitions change. Evelyn made her decision. She entered into the sexual exchange, making love with Jeff.

The next morning Evelyn woke early, dressed and left while Jeff slept. She was in turmoil. On one hand she felt incredibly loved by this vital person in her life, and on the other she felt violated. She trusted him enough to sleep in the same bed, and he had introduced sex. But then she was flooded with feelings of guilt for not stopping him, and for even thinking it was OK to sleep together. These feelings were followed by fear of losing him. If she confronted him this would surely happen.

When she thought about telling her mother, she was filled with guilt and remorse. When she thought about being with Jeff again, she felt that she had nothing to feel guilty about. It had seemed so normal and right. Their relationship had always been close, and now they had added a new activity. By the time she reached her home, hours later, she had changed the focus of her thoughts, and could face her mother without any feelings about the night before. She resumed her teenage life, and put the experience into the recesses of her mind where it stayed until she entered therapy six years later.

Jeff woke to find her gone, and went into a state of intense despair. He wanted to marry her, but knew that wasn't possible. He was torn by his addiction to his sister and the deep shame that accompanied being sexual with her. For days he drifted through his college activities, unable to study, and thinking of suicide. Gradually he was able to push the memory from his mind, although not in the same way that adults can when being sexual with small children.

The sexual acts with small children are so out of the realm of anything that is discussed, shown on television or the subject of books that the adult has no mirror for the behavior. It is easier to repress the facts. Jeff, however, had been sexual with a woman who happened to be his sister. The experience wasn't much different from making love with a girl friend, and so he had mirrors that prevented repression. He had to live with his feelings, and avoid them by avoiding contact with Evelyn and his family. The siblings had no contact for three years.

When Evelyn reached nineteen, and was in college, she found that she had difficulty in her relationships with men. She wanted to pick fights with them after a couple of dates, and push them away. The ones who persisted received steadily increas-

ing attacks until she stopped seeing them so that she didn't
continue to be mean to them. The only men she saw for more
than two months were controlling and abusive. This allowed
her to feel safe that her abusive side couldn't emerge because
she knew they wouldn't allow it.

In the course of counseling, she remembered the experience with Jeff. With the skilled mirror of her counselor she
could see how she hadn't been able to allow herself to know
the violation that was occurring, and that she pushed it out of
her mind later. The counselor told her how her ability to not
see violation operated not just with Jeff, but with sexuality
throughout Evelyn's life. They began to explore the many
ways sexuality was violated in her early years and in the lives
of those around her.

HIDDEN SEXUAL RELATIONSHIPS

Through discussions with her mother, who was able to be
open and informative as she worked on her own recovery,
Evelyn learned about the myriad of things going on behind
closed doors in the supposedly sexually proper order. Affairs
were common and covertly accepted as long as they didn't
threaten physical disruption of families. In contrast to the
experience of children growing up together on a Kibbutz in
Israel, where spouses were rarely chosen from the sibling-like
relationships, this religious community was fraught with hidden sexual relating among the children. Jeff's initiation of sex
with Evelyn was merely an offshoot of typical activity for this
subculture. I can speculate that there are two reasons for this.
One is that adults stimulating children's sexuality results in the
children expressing sexuality outside their normally unfolding,
appropriate curiosity about sex. The second reason is that when

sexual boundaries are not clear, children will be confused about appropriate sexual partners. Outside-in sexual rules conflict with the covert behaviors going on all around them.

I have no further information about Jeff. I hope he has found therapy that will help him understand what he did, and why, so that he can drop the shame that must have been generated. His chances of getting a therapist who would minimize the implications of his actions are high. This approach would not help him, instead leaving him with his cross-wiring and lack of understanding of healthy sexual boundaries. Perhaps the fact that he has a sister and a mother who are willing to work with him can allow him to do the healing to free himself from shame.

Chapter 11

Children Who Are Sexual with Children

A s our society is becoming aware that adults are sexual with children, and that many people grow up affected by their childhood sexual experiences, the picture is broadening to include the sexuality of children. This culture believes that children aren't very sexual, and that the sexuality they do have is different from that experienced by adults. These beliefs have prevented parents, teachers, and psychotherapists from understanding that children actually have sex with other children.

Eliana Gil and Toni Kavanaugh Johnson wrote a book called *Sexualized Children: Assessment and Treatment of Sexualized Children and Children Who Molest* (Launch Press, 1993). While this book is written for mental health professionals, it avoids jargon and is very readable for the person who wants to know about this subject. I found that reading it helped put my own experiences of childhood sexuality into perspective. Their many examples offer a mirror for what I acted out during my pre-puberty years. I will draw on these authors' writing because I have no direct experience with children as clients or through interviews.

Gil and Johnson tell us that children are capable of arousal and orgasm from before birth. All children stimulate themselves from the time they are a few months old and able to explore their bodies. As they grow they will move toward active masturbation by rubbing genitals with their hands, or against a chair, stuffed animal, or bed. Children will also curiously explore each other's bodies.

The demarcation between normal curiosity, and sexuality that results from stimulation by an adult or other child, is difficult to make. Gil and Johnson try, but it will be decades before our cultural sexuality is healthy enough to fully know. Since virtually all children in our society have had their sexual boundaries crossed, and are subjected to sexual secrecy, none of us grow up able to adequately perceive when a child is being sexual on their own timetable, and when their sexuality has been stimulated by others. The authors are, however, able to describe clearly unnatural sexual activities that are symptoms of sexualization by adults, and they present us with the behaviors of children who "molest" other children. I will summarize some of their findings.

Sexualized children and children who molest engage in the full range of sexual behaviors experienced by adults. These include "vaginal penetration with fingers, penis, or other objects; oral copulation; fondling; genital contact without penetration; exposing genitals; intercourse; and French kissing" as well as "pervasive interest in sexuality; . . . touching the breasts or genitals of adults or other children; frequency of masturbation; sexual or romantic talk; swearing; the imitation of adult sexuality using props such as stuffed animals, dolls, or toys; writing or drawing things related to sex and sexuality; and sexual contact with animals."

The authors go on to talk about how children who molest confuse sexuality with other behaviors that aren't sexual, such as toilet activities. They also point out that children who molest choose children they know, usually a family member.

WHY DO CHILDREN "MOLEST" OTHER CHILDREN?

Until recently, mental health professionals didn't know that children were feeling sexual and acting out sexual behaviors except in rare circumstances, because our culture didn't allow us to be aware of sexuality where it doesn't "belong." Only as we become aware of the incidence of sexual abuse of children can we be open to knowing that children who were the objects of sexual activity will be far more sexual than children who are allowed to develop sexuality in a natural time frame.

With this culturally-induced blindness, we as a culture and as a mental health profession have not known what has been going on. How could we be able to think about the causes of something that we didn't know existed?

When it is obvious that a child is sexualized, adults will usually react with shock and disgust (unless they want to use the child's sexuality for their own arousal). Disgust implies that something is wrong with the child.

My mother told me that when I was seven I sat on the lap of a visitor. She had been very embarrassed, and said he was too. When she didn't explain why they had been uncomfortable, I asked her if I seemed sexual. With great discomfort, she told me yes.

The look on her face as she spoke was familiar from my entire childhood. Her expression and body language communicated that there was something wrong with me for exuding sexual energy. Being unable to question how this had come about, she could only see me as dirty and disgusting, someone who needed to be controlled so that I didn't get out of hand.

Because I now understand that sexualization results from sexual exchange with adults, I didn't feel shame as I watched her. I knew she had no other way to deal with this puzzling quality in her daughter. She wanted to eradicate my sexuality, and when she couldn't she was frightened for me as well as embarrassed to have others see her odd offspring.

My mother's attitude reflects one common in our culture. *It is believed that there is something wrong with a child who puts out sexual energy in such a manner that it can be seen by others.* Mine was too great to be denied. Since it is difficult to know why there is something "wrong" with some people, the difficulties are attributed to innate qualities that mysteriously show up. My mother, and most people, can't explain it. They are stuck with attributing it to some kind of "badness." As long as our culture doesn't see the connection between sexual energy directed toward a child, and the resulting sexualization of that child, then vague explanations based on badness or sinfulness are all that are possible. Now that we are beginning to see what is going on, children who put out sexual energy, whether they "molest" other children or not, can be seen as innocent victims of trauma, needing help to stop what they are doing. Perhaps as we see that children are deserving of this kind of attention and help we will be able to see that adults are too.

ELI EXPLORES HIS LITTLE SISTER'S BODY

Eli was a good friend during the time I began retrieving my early sexual memories. When either of us found that a memory had made it to awareness, we called each other to tell it. We soon learned how quickly shame would drop, allowing us to see the experience more fully. It led us back to other events in childhood as we gradually pieced together the story of how our sexuality was influenced.

During one of these times Eli talked about how he had looked at his little sister's naked body when his parents weren't around. She was about three and he was close to ten. He doesn't remember why she had her clothes off, but he remembers pulling her legs apart and looking at her genitals. She was uncomfortable with this, but didn't try to pull away from him.

This exchange could be explained as curiosity on Eli's part, satisfied by looking. But our culture made it far more. First, the very fact that Eli didn't know what a female child's genitals look like is the result of being shamed for looking. His mother had changed his sister's diaper countless times, times when Eli could have looked. But he had learned, in nonverbal ways, that he wasn't to do this. His curiosity about natural, human things had already been shamed. His sister could sense, as all people can, that he was feeling shame and the fear of being caught. These feelings were so strong that he could not see his sister's experience, and so she became an object to him. This distressed her, and contaminated her feelings about her body.

If Eli had grown up in a sexually comfortable family and society, he would have been able to learn about female genitals in ways that wouldn't violate himself or any one else. When children of similar ages can comfortably show their genitals to each other, the experience can be a healthy antidote to our culture's prohibitions. But if the experience is contaminated by shame or fear, then it can have the opposite effect—it can increase the shame of both people.

I Was Sexual with My Little Sister

My own experience seems even more innocent than Eli's, yet in retrospect I can see that it was symptomatic of the sexual contact I had with my father. When I was between two and three I was sexual with my sister who was twenty-one months younger. I have two clear memories, and a sense that there were far more. One sunny afternoon we were playing outside with no clothes on. I took some leaves off the ground and put them between the cheeks of her buttocks, where they stayed while she crawled on the lawn. I had strong sexual feelings while doing this, although I had no name for them. I didn't realize they were sexual until I was actively retrieving sexual memories.

Our mother came out of the house and saw what I had done. She picked my sister up and took her into the house to wash her, telling me I wasn't to do that again. I felt tremendous fear and shame, and realized that I mustn't do things like that if I could be caught. In retrospect, I know that most of my fear stemmed from the prohibition against telling what my father was doing to me. I expected to be annihilated if I did so, even if only through my actions. And here I was acting it out, and fearing that my mother could translate my behavior and know the truth.

The second memory was when we were somewhat older. I had strong sexual feelings as I told her to lie down on the bed. My memory is of the time she told me she didn't want to do that any more. Again, I felt shame for having sexual feelings and acting them out with her, particularly if she found it objectionable.

In contrast to normal sexual curiosity and discovery, I believe I was acting out an approximation of my father's sexual activities with me in order to tell the story. But the telling was impossible, of course. No one could, or wanted to, interpret their meaning.

Many children who have been the object of a parent's sexuality act it out with younger children. When parents see the signs, they do as my mother did—they tell the older child not to do it, but take no further steps to see what is going on. This is, of course, because until recent years no one knew anything about the experience of children when they were sexual with other children. Child experts, such as Gil and Johnson, are trying to define what is healthy and what is not. It isn't at all clear, and may not be for decades.

BABYSITTERS

When young people babysit for even younger people, they are given an opportunity to learn about the bodies of children in the course of changing diapers and giving baths. In addition, they are left alone to supervise children, providing an opportunity to act out the story of what happened to them. Some of these stories are sexual.

In my psychological practice with adults I have heard examples of activities occurring many years before. When the experience is years in the past, clients are able to see it in the perspective of their own damaged sexuality, and so their shame is not as consuming as it is for people who are acting in the present. In addition, the child they were sexual with is now grown—no longer an innocent victim in their eyes.

These memories may be conscious, but not thought about, or they may emerge out of repression after having been totally submerged. As with the retrieval of sexual memories, one day the person looks startled, and hesitates to speak. Their faces flush or blanch. Then slowly the story of what my client did with children unfolds.

KENNETH REMEMBERS THE LITTLE GIRL

Kenneth entered therapy for sex addiction that was so out of control it threatened his marriage and work. His pain and his desire to change were so intense that he went right to work on all issues that influenced his behaviors. As his addictive behaviors became manageable he was able to begin the deep work of retrieving the cross-wiring of his sexuality that brought him to his current sexual choices.

As Kenneth recovered, he was able to find out what healthy sexuality is, and rejoice in the new experience of sex as loving instead of as a drug. He discovered inside-out monogamy, and let go of expectations about what sex "acts" involve. He and his partner were able to invent their own sexual expression. Occasionally he returned to sexually acting out when he was particularly stressed. He also learned how to interrupt his addiction, and how to trace what had caused the episode. During these times he was filled with remorse for loss of the intimacy he was now capable of experiencing. This comparison strongly motivated him to continue the hard work of recovery.

As therapy progressed, Kenneth began to remember sexual abuse in his pre-school years. His father had put his penis in Kenneth's mouth, and, being in a sexual trance, had not seen the effect he was having on the three-year-old child. His own shame made him pull away from Kenneth after the sexual exchange, leaving Kenneth feeling abandoned in addition to sexually invaded.

As memories of his father's activities became believable to Kenneth, and were fleshed out in detail, he found another source of distress. His mother had sexualized him as well. When he was a young baby she used his sucking reflex to create arousal that went beyond the normal experience of nursing a baby. She also fondled his penis to quiet him, and felt sexual arousal when she did so.

About one year into his recovery, Kenneth was in my office talking about his brothers, questioning if they were also the objects of either parent's sexual activities. He stopped in mid-sentence, looking at me but not seeing me, and his breathing stopped. I waited, knowing something new was emerging. As he began to breathe again, he said, "Oh, no! I entirely forgot about this, although it seems like it was just yesterday." He went on to tell me that he had a memory of taking care of a girl about two years old when he was fourteen. She was the daughter of a neighbor and friend of the family, and he baby sat for her while her parents and his went out together. As she looked at him with trust he found her delightful. He couldn't remember how the thought came to him of being sexual with her, but the next thing he remembers is her sitting on his lap with her diaper off, and his penis out of his pants, and erect. He moved it between her legs, feeling his arousal grow.

As he slowly talked, an expression of deep grief crossed Kenneth's face. He looked at me with remorse. I could see that another aspect of the experience had come to him. Again he slowly began to speak. He told me that he could see the little girl's face. She was terrified. She looked up at him, her expression asking him not to hurt her and questioning why he was doing this, while her body remained rigidly immobile. He remembered this moment as powerfully gripping. He concentrated on her face, finding himself filled with a sense of unexplainable truth. A moment later he put her down on the floor and left the room—abandoning her the way his father had him.

In exploring Kenneth's memory, we realized he was telling the story of his own frightening sexual experiences with adults. The look on the baby's face was the only mirror he had for the look on his own face when he was around that age. He recognized it, and felt compelled to take it in and fill himself with it. Her feelings were more important than the sexual arousal he experienced from the stimulation of his penis. But of course, no one could see the story he was telling, and no one could help him bring it out into the world of reality—until he could tell it in another way, with me.

Months later Kenneth brought in a postscript to his story. When he confronted his father about his childhood experiences, the two of them talked for hours about many things that went on in Kenneth's childhood. In the course of such conversation, Kenneth's father told him that the family had a son, not a daughter. Kenneth was appalled that he could change his memory out of discomfort with the idea of being sexual with a child of the same sex. He still "remembers" the child as female. While Kenneth is heterosexual, and his addictive cross-wiring is heterosexual, he also needed to tell the story (through his actions) of the same gender-sexual interactions in his childhood.

Kenneth's story shows how it is possible to suppress memory of shameful activities undertaken even at fourteen—an age when we can't use the excuse of being too young to remember. He totally repressed the sex of the child, and prevented the memory of the events from arriving in his conscious mind. Learning about how adults had been sexual with him as a child, and learning over time that I would be a non-shaming audience, allowed him to retrieve the memories.

We explored the possibility of Kenneth's talking to the young man, now about nineteen, to offer him help with his own sexual recovery. Kenneth is terrified about doing this.

During conversation with his father, Kenneth gathered additional information that was useful in seeing his family's lack of sexual boundaries. His father had a long-term affair with the young boy's mother, all the while carrying on a family friendship. Both families were seen as model, church-going people whose children were examples of successful parenting. In later years Kenneth's father was also sexually suggestive with Kenneth's wife, Kathryn. She (also my client) fully believed he would have had sex with her if she responded to him.

We are encouraged to believe that this family is an unusual one. It isn't. When we consider that more than one out of every four women is touched sexually while growing up (and probably the same number of men), and that well over half of all men have sex with someone other than their mate (and probably a similar number of women), we can see that a large percentage of families do not have clear sexual boundaries. The lack of boundaries, and the denial of such lack of boundaries, results in supreme confusion of young people as they try to sort out their own sexuality.

KATHRYN IS APPROACHED SEXUALLY BY TWO LITTLE GIRLS

Kenneth's wife remembered a time when she was a teenager and baby-sitting girls who were about three and five. The five-year-old, with self-conscious giggles, said she wanted to show Kathryn something that felt good. She took off her underpants, spread her legs, and inserted a clothes pin into her vagina. She expressed her pleasure, and told Kathryn that she could do it, too. Kathryn, who also came from a childhood in which adults were sexual with her, found the experience arousing. She took the clothes pin and did as the girl suggested. The sister joined in, demanding that Kathryn do the same with her.

At the time Kathryn wasn't aware that anything out of the ordinary was occurring. Sex play between a teenager and two children wasn't outside of her experience, although she knew that none of them were to tell anyone. She had absorbed the rule that sexual activity among people of different ages and relationships was the norm. She associated great shame only with revealing it.

Kathryn now knows that these children were telling a story about what had already happened to their vaginas. Her lack of understanding at that time prevented her from helping them.

She knows if she were in the same situation today she would respond differently. First, she would lovingly tell them no, it wasn't right for her to put something in their vaginas. They could put their own fingers in and touch themselves, but no one else should do that. When they grew up and found a partner they really liked, then they could choose to invite that person to touch their vulvas.

Second, she would make a report to protective services, and ask them to take appropriate steps to protect these children from possible further sexual contact with adults or older children.

Kathryn felt less guilt than Kenneth because she didn't initiate the sexual activities. While both approaches are damaging to the child's sexual and emotional development, adults usually feel more guilty if they started it. As a result, it is common for sexual parents to communicate sexual interest indirectly, so that the child seems to be the one who initiates it. Some parents who are reported will say, in their defense, that the child asked for it. This may be their experience. But the adult is responsible for the activities. *It is the adult's responsibility to say no, and to create boundaries around appropriate sexual exchanges.* Sadly, few of us have good models for creating such helpful limits.

Chapter 12

The Non-Recovering Pedophile

This chapter is the most difficult for me to write because it addresses the person who refuses to see he or she has caused great damage to other human beings, and who isn't willing to make sure he or she will no longer do so. I admire Alice Miller for her ability to get inside Hitler's psyche with understanding in *For Your Own Good: Hidden Cruelty in Child-Rearing and the Roots of Violence* (Farrar, Strauss and Giroux, 1984). She, however, had the advantage of studying a man who is long since dead, and is no longer directly influencing lives. Not true for perhaps millions of people who continue to control children's bodies.

As I interviewed some of these people for this book, I became aware of why professionals who work with "sex offenders" find the job extremely taxing, and often burn out in a few years. I was only seeking information, with no responsibility to prevent these people from damaging others. Yet even this left me feeling discouraged and angry.

Bud fits the stereotype of sex offenders, the kind that accounts for much of the rage directed at them as a group. When we think only of this kind of person, it can be difficult to have much sympathy for them. I have to remind myself that he would have a greater chance of recovering if he were not carrying the shame of our culture. Letting himself know what he has done may feel intolerable.

BUD'S STORY

Bud contacted me after reading my article in a recovery magazine asking for stories for this book. He had been through the legal system, and so was willing to leave his name and number, since there could be no legal consequences from talking to me. Bud was a medical practitioner, and had his license revoked following his arrest and conviction. His attempts to have it reinstated, after he served his prison time, met with failure. I am glad. I would not want this man practicing his profession.

His style of interaction was typical of those people who, while admitting they indeed committed illegal acts, maintain no responsibility. During the interview he evaded my questions and focused instead on everything harmful that had been done to him—going to prison, having his license revoked, and so on. Not once during our conversations did he indicate in any way that he had harmed another person. He was so self-consumed he didn't appear to notice that I gave him no sympathy for his stories, and was angrily wishing to get him out of my office. This man is blind to the experience of others and incapable of perceiving the distress of his sexual objects. I know that while he was in jail, and during the year of required treatment after release, he was constantly confronted by counselors and perhaps by other ASC's. Yet he gave no sign of having heard any of it.

Bud gave me his history as if it were no more important than news stories about changes in the weather. He had sex with boys, minors, from his late teens on through adulthood. Perhaps Alice Miller's study of Hitler was easier because she gathered information from old documents. She didn't sit face to face with a man who told her he was serving a worthy cause by murdering and torturing millions of people. I sat across from one who expected me to listen with sympathy to how he had been wronged by the judicial system and the medical board.

Perhaps here lies the key. He has been wronged. But not by the legal system or by our culture's objection to adults using children for sexual ends. He was wronged by his own childhood that loaded so much shame on him that he is unable to handle the pain of knowing what he has done. Long before he thought of having sex with minors, he was told—by his parents and by the school system—that he was scum, worth less than any living human. If he is to be able to feel guilt for his current actions, he must also feel the shame he was raised with.

Perhaps if I were to read his story I would be able to see the damaged person underneath the blaming and irresponsibility. In the same way therapists work with adolescents who were traumatized in childhood, and now act out in anger-provoking ways, I must develop sympathy for the person who cannot yet tell me what happened to him. I know that people who come to me for therapy are asking me to point out what they are doing, and to lead them into the causes of their behavior so they can change. But not everyone wants help. Some people choose to replace aliveness with an artificially-induced energy through blaming others. Until such people can reduce the incapacitating shame that prevents them from taking a look at their own actions, they will continue to damage children and adults with their unconscious choices. My hope is that a book like this, and discussion of the need for recovery options, will begin a change in public perception that can yield help for people like Bud. Without it, we as a society are preventing them from knowing about the harm they inflict so they can prevent it.

A CHILDHOOD OF SHAMING

From information gathered over the course of three hours, I constructed the following story about Bud's childhood. He was raised by both parents, people who hated each other and showed it. Neither of them wanted a child, but his mother chose not to have an illegal abortion or give him up for adoption. From the beginning he was in the way, and his parents tossed him aside like a used napkin while they focused on their conflicts. Neither parent thought to abandon the marriage because it was exactly what each had come to expect as a result of their own childhoods. Instead, they acted out their distresses with each other, and with Bud.

Bud's mother hated sex because it reminded her of the sexual violence she received from her father. Hatred of her husband also made the idea of sex distasteful. He felt she owed it to him, however, and he regularly forced her. She had no recourse against this as long as she remained married to him because in the 1940s and 1950s marital rape was legal.

Since Bud's parents hated each other equally, they were both constantly enraged. It was natural to turn this rage on the helpless child who couldn't fight back. His mother also clutched him tightly to her as she attempted to meet her boundless need for affection. Bud felt suffocated by this, but until he became old enough to physically fight back, he tolerated her need for fusing with him. At the same time, his father hated him because he was weak and dependent, and because he received whatever "love" his mother had to give—causing Bud's father to feel deprived. Since his father sexualized anger, he routinely used Bud sexually, alternating his assault between his wife and son. Bud was literally trained to believe that he was his father's sex object and his mother's love object, and when they didn't want him that way, he was discarded.

This devastating childhood resulted in deep feelings of shame arising from the perception of himself as deserving intense rage and the ongoing violation of his body. When he was old enough to act out his reactions with unacceptable behavior, beginning in his preschool years, further shame was heaped on him. Once the schools were involved, and then the police, the shaming multiplied.

Bud compensated for his shame-dominated life by associating with other boys who were as shame-filled as he was, and they supported each other through the difficult teen years. An even more important compensation was Bud's intelligence, which didn't get lost amid the craziness of his life, as it does for many children. He was able to get good grades without trying, all through school, and thought it was amusing that this was valued. He believed he had conned schools into thinking he was smart, and he enjoyed continuing the con.

However, when he went to college and found that it was still easy, he decided to apply for medical school and obtain the highest credentials offered by our culture. His deep anger and intense competitive feelings combined with his intelligence to fuel the energy necessary to make it through the grueling process of becoming a doctor. He also nurtured an unconscious belief that if he could attain a respected position, somehow all his shame would go away.

It didn't. But he found instead a perpetual source of people to heap blame on, and who willingly let him control them. He became admired, but not liked, by his colleagues and patients.

Bud exercised control in sexual activities, too. He had no interest in women, finding them passive and weak. He became sexual with older boys even before puberty, and took an authoritative position with all his partners, regardless of age. As he moved into his teens he found he preferred pre-pubescent boys as partners, although he had sex with adult men as well. He acted out his father's control through seducing many boys by promising to be their father figure, and by giving them things. When he caused pain he apologized, but when he hugged them to him in supposed comfort, he was aware of feeling powerful enough to crush them in his arms.

Finally, he was reported by one young man who was not dependent on him, as most were. Bud was convicted and sent to prison. And now, two years after his release, he cannot see why his activities with these young men were worse than what was done to him by the legal system and the state medical licensing board. He cannot see that the seeds of his behavior and of his deep shame lie with his parents' treatment. He might be frightened of feeling responsible for what they did to him, or of finding out just how terrible it was to grow up. He may be on the verge of deep depression if he lets go of his blaming anger—blaming may be painful, but it approximates being alive.

Chapter 13

Treatment for Male "Sex Offenders"

Treatment for people who have been sexual with children is fairly new. In this chapter I will examine two approaches to treatment. Chapter 15 goes into more detail about behavior therapy for sex offenders. "Sex offender" is the term for people who have been sexual with children, have been reported, and then convicted. Once in the legal system, "offenders" go through treatment, although the type of treatment varies from community to community.

I first choose to have a look at one program run by psychologist Steven Zimberoff, Ph.D. I met Steve while interviewing the man I am calling Randel, whose story is told in Chapter 16. Randel's first therapy was of little help to him, and when he found his way to Steve's office, he felt blessed to have a therapist who understood his addiction. From there on he made rapid progress.

I met with Steve in his office for two hours to talk, and then returned in the afternoon to meet with one of his therapy groups which was attended by nine adjudicated sex offenders.

Non-shaming Therapy

Steve told me that he is the mental health professional who is contacted in his community when evaluation and possible treatment is required for a reported sexual offense. Steve interviews the person, does some basic psychological testing, reads the police report and other documents, and prepares a written report to the court. In addition, he obtains a polygraph from an outside source. Part of his report is a recommendation regarding the person's eligibility for treatment in the community instead of in prison. Only people who are arrested for the first time, and who seem able to use treatment, are eligible. The others automatically go to prison after being found guilty.

Steve distinguishes between "predatory" and "opportunistic" offenders. Those who search out children in their homes or parks or other public places are not good risks to have in the community when they are early in their recovery process. Acting out with children is too high a risk to permit them to stay out of prison. Those whose sexual acting out is in response to an opportunity—such as a vulnerable child in the home—can more easily avoid sexual activity with minors. In addition, strict limits are set on their contacts with children who might trigger sexual response. Most of the people in his group are allowed no contact with children. Some are allowed supervised contact.

Steve invites those people who seem to be likely candidates for treatment in the community to come to his therapy group immediately. This does not assure them the right to stay out of jail, but it does allow Steve to assess them further, and allows the person to get started immediately. Steve said that occasionally a lawyer will tell their clients not to go into the group because the information they reveal about past offenses could be used against them in their trial. Steve said it doesn't happen because the judge isn't allowed to use information based on old offenses that weren't tried. On the contrary, it gives the man a chance to show Steve that he is serious about treatment. Most of them are. The men as a whole are glad they were caught because they are forced to end behavior that has been bringing them deep shame, and which they know is harmful to the child. Being arrested prevents them from denying what they are doing, forces them to begin a change process, and allows them to reduce shameful existences.

When I asked Steve if he had any women in treatment he said no. Women who are reported and convicted in his community all go to prison. He says this is because only the most severe cases are reported, and so aren't amenable to treatment in the community. This makes sense to me. Women aren't seen as capable of being sexual with children, and so only cases that are clearly outside the bounds of our culture are reported. The children and the adults who could make a report do not expect to be believed when reporting a woman. I was told years ago about a case where a couple were being sexual with children in their day care home. The man was taken off to jail while the woman wasn't even arrested. Both had been sexual with the children and both had been reported.

Steve also told me that women are in denial more than the men, and so are less amenable to treatment. I think this is because it is so much more shameful for women to admit being sexual with children. We are indoctrinated with the image of the perfect mother or woman, and there is no room for this kind of behavior. For men, it is considered the worst crime, but it is not outside the definition of being a man. Men are considered abusers and women and children the abused. (You can read more about this in Chapter 14.)

Once the evaluation is complete, a probation officer makes a pre-sentence investigation which is used by the judge, along with Steve's report, to decide what to do. The person is sentenced, and then if it is possible to treat him in the community, the sentence is suspended as long as he is in treatment and does not act out again. If he re-offends, he will serve this sentence as well as any new ones. This method provides a good deal of motivation for men to stay involved in treatment and to combat their strong, culture-supported tendency to deny or minimize what they have done.

Therapy groups limited to those who have been sexual with children meet every other week. Each man is also seen individually once a week or once every other week. The community doesn't have SA meetings, a real draw back of living in a small town. However, while I was there one of the men requested information about how to begin an SA group. He had many years of experience in AA and so understands how Twelve Step programs work. There are enough people in Steve's groups alone to provide sufficient members, and perhaps sex addicts from the community will also be drawn to join.

The only structure to the group is that each member tells once again what he has done to children. Then each person can indicate how strongly he wishes to talk that day. Everyone is given a chance.

As Steve talked about how he views his clients, I appreciated his perceptions of them as human beings who have done culturally unacceptable acts. He doesn't shame them, or even call them sex offenders. He doesn't want to increase their shame with labels because he knows that shaming doesn't lead toward healing. On the contrary, it inhibits it. These men already feel so much shame about what they have done that any more is likely to make them act out again instead of take responsibility. While he doesn't call them offenders, he does expect them to say in plain English precisely and in detail what their offenses are.

In the group I attended I watched him re-state, or ask them to re-state, what they were saying so they truly acknowledged what they had done. For example, when one man said, "That's when it got started," Steve asked, "When what got started?" The client rephrased his statement by saying, "That's when I began molesting my stepdaughter." But when a man called himself a child molester, Steve asked him to rephrase that too. Steve pointed out that he wasn't a child molester. He had molested a child, and perhaps may again, but this is not who he is. He also disagreed with a man who said he had been good when not having thoughts about children. Steve told him he is a good person who has done bad things. He has not been good when going without fantasy, nor has he been bad when he has fantasy. Gradually Steve is changing their use of language in ways that will help change their perceptions of themselves.

When I asked Steve about his intense focus on this, he said that therapy based on trying to change people by shaming them is entirely inappropriate. Steve has found that ASC's have one characteristic in common. *They all grew up with shame, and have feelings of personal inadequacy.* This is not just in the area of sexuality, but in all areas of life. Most of his clients, even those who didn't feel inadequate in countless ways while growing up, identify with the movie *Revenge of the Nerds*.

I ended our conversation by asking him what he would guess is the proportion of people who are sexual with children. I knew it was an unfair question because there is no way to know. No research methods will get people to reveal what they are denying, especially not acts that totally violate their values, as well as put them at risk for arrest and prosecution. But I want to collect all the information I can in order to guess at what the figures might be when studies can be constructed. While Steve wouldn't take my bait and guess, he did provide some information. He said that his clients took a poll and discovered that they had an average of three victims. Steve had also read a study that supported this figure. From this information, and the results of several studies that reveal about 30% of women report having been touched inappropriately as children, we can make guesses. If each man were sexual with three of those 30%, then it would require that 10% of men were sexual with children. However, the predators, who may have far more victims, were not in these groups, which could lower the percentage. Leaning in the other direction, however, many women were touched inappropriately by more than one man, and many men touched only one child.

People in treatment are true pedophiles waiting for an opportunity to act out. They don't include all those who have sexual feelings for children, and who act in ways that wouldn't bring about report, arrest, and conviction.

When Steve told me that the men were willing to have me attend the group meeting, I was pleased. As the two hours passed, I realized I was seeing a scene rarely observed in this society—one I was very grateful to be part of.

A THERAPY GROUP FOR CONVICTED ASC'S

As the group convened in his basement group room, Steve collected fees, and then asked me to talk about why I was there. I explained that I was writing this book, emphasizing the need for a compassionate portrayal of people who are sexual with children. I wanted them to know I wasn't seeing them as the horrendous people our culture sees.

My first impression was of a room full of "good ol' boys," men laughing and joking around. They seemed so different from my men's group. I thought perhaps the difference was because I work in an upper middle class town, while Wenatchee is a farming community. But as they began to talk, I could see that each man was frightened by my presence and feeling great shame. Only when they didn't feel worse after telling their stories in my presence did the false joviality drop, and the very real men appear.

The first forty minutes consisted of the "confessions." Each man chose one other man to tell what he had done to children, and other unhealthy sexual acts. The listener became the next one to talk, until every man had disclosed. I sat there listening to the truly damaging things they had done to young people. Some faces were frozen and stiff, others were flushed. Each gasped for air and seemed to avoid looking in my direction.

The man who spoke last seemed most troubled by my presence. I wondered if I reminded him of anyone in his past, or if being a woman hearing his story was enough. He is on work release from the local jail. This means he is allowed to leave jail to go to his job and to therapy, but spends the rest of his time locked up. I didn't ask, but I assume this is so he cannot be around children until he is safe. He was proud to say that he had not had fantasies about children in the two weeks since the last group. Steve commented on his level of distress which let me see that my presence was having an effect. A big man, he looked like a friend from my past, and so I felt warmly toward him. His visible fear, which he did not attempt to hide, also allowed me to feel warmly toward him because he was so real.

As each man talked and felt his shame, I found myself hardly taking in the nature of their offenses. They all sounded very much the same. What I did hear was the way they had been able to deny that they were doing anything harmful. I asked them how they were able to violate their values, and they took turns explaining.

First, they said that they were the first to bad mouth child molesters. When they heard reports on television or the radio, they spoke strongly about how terrible it was, and that these guys should be hanged or castrated. One man spoke of telling his daughter, who was his victim, that child molesters were the worst people in the world, and should be killed. Yet he was able to do to her what he was condemning. Several more said that they condemned them too. They shook their heads and looked amazed when I asked if they could explain how they could do one thing and say another. One man said it's like dual personalities, except that you don't forget what the other personality has done. It is like being two different people. Another said it was like self-hypnosis, or being in a trance where, for the time he was doing it, he really didn't believe he was doing a bad thing.

Several men told me how they rationalized their behavior. One said he felt like a hero, bringing pleasure to the child. He believed she enjoyed it. He also believed he was protecting her from "perverts." When they were out together, he was watchful to make sure that no one could use her sexually. Other men nodded, indicating they had the same distorted thinking. Steve calls these "thinking errors," and the men have adopted his language.

Another man talked about putting lotion on the vulva of his daughter, but didn't realize it was abusive until Steve told him. Once it was pointed out, he could clearly see that this was not a benefit to the child, and was to serve him, but prior to talking about it he had been unable to assess his behavior as harmful.

Bathing was a common time for men to be sexual with children because they had an excuse to touch. One man explained his way of assuring himself that he wasn't doing anything wrong. He didn't lock the doors to his house, so someone could have walked in and found him. He believed if he was feeling OK with someone walking in, he must not be doing anything wrong. He had his clothes on and there was nothing to see.

I am very angry while writing this. Angry that many readers will condemn these men, believing they were lying in order to do things they knew were harmful to children, and that our society does not accept. I want each one of you to be in that room with me, seeing their faces, watching them learning how to become honest about their acts. I want you to see the face of the man who didn't realize he was abusing his daughter in the bathtub until he heard someone else share the same behavior and call it abuse. His face lit with surprise, and he blurted out that he did that too. His face and body agreed with his words when he said he just now realized it. He had hidden the nature of his behavior from himself as well as from others. He must talk to other people in order to understand what he has done and to learn alternatives. *Sexual secrecy in our culture prevents ASC's from seeing their need to recover.* They don't get needed mirroring of themselves as good people with bad behavior so they can accept themselves in order to heal. Yes, these men have "thinking errors," and have lied, but they are also victims of our culture's relationship to sexuality. (Please read more about the effects of our culture in Chapter 17.)

Some men rationalized their behavior by using the bathroom when a child was bathing. A child can't object because the adult can make a case for not being able to wait until the child is finished bathing. The adult can see it as coincidence when he later uses that image to masturbate to. (If you are having an emotional, or sexual, reaction to this imagery, pay attention to it. It somehow tells your story. If you use old methods to avoid it, such as vehement condemnation of the act or sexual fantasy, you will reinforce your reaction.) One man dressed his child in his undershirt for bed, knowing as she watched television and moved around it would hike up and he might be able to see her genitals.

A man said that he molested the youngest of his three daughters. The other two hadn't interested him in this way. He felt that he was being a good dad by looking for ringworm on her body when in truth he was receiving a sexual charge. As he told this story, even he was amazed that he had been able to believe that he wasn't abusing her, and, to the contrary, was actually being a good father. The unhealthy "need" to have sexual contact, or to see sexual scenes with children, is so strong that their minds go to great lengths to make it seem consistent with their views of themselves as good people. One purpose of therapy is to present ASC's with the truth so they have to see that what they are doing is harmful. Once they see that, many will automatically stop because they are no longer able to justify their behavior with "thinking errors." This is less true for the predatory pedophile, who is addicted to sexual contact with children, and will go into a sexual trance without having to rationalize it.

The group softened during the two hours I was there. They discovered that I didn't shame them, and that they didn't have to feel bad about themselves by seeing their behaviors through my eyes. As the softening went on, I got to see each man as a unique person, each with similar stories but with differences. The "good ol' boys" picture completely changed, and I saw a room full of human beings. With this backdrop I heard the last rationalization they discussed that day.

One of the men explained how he had connected sex and affection. Somehow in his childhood they were paired because little non-sexual affection was displayed. As a result he thought that when a child approached him for affection, she or he was really asking for sex. Several other men nodded, indicating they had the same connection. As they told this for my benefit, I could see the looks of amazement on their faces. After many months of being exposed to the truth in these therapy groups, they were astonished that their minds were capable of such an incorrect belief. Eventually their healing will require looking to their own childhoods to learn how this connection was given to them.

One way affection and sex become linked is when parents are only affectionate when being sexual with the child or siblings. Another is being parented by people who aren't affectionate with children, but who demonstrate sexual affection to spouses or lovers in the presence of the child.

The men also shared the things that were going well for them, and supported each other in their stories. They said they felt like a caring family. I could see it was true.

A man about fifty-five said that he had accomplished something that may not look significant to the others. He had taken two walks by himself without his wife along. As Steve pushed to get him to explain why this was significant, he got it out that his wife is protection when he is around other people in case they know what he has done. He says she is like a teddy bear, or a thumb. He can make himself feel safe and OK by looking at her, knowing that one person loves and accepts him. I didn't find out if people know about his behaviors, or if he just feared that they might. Either way, it makes the point that these men are condemned by our culture.

As the group disbanded, several men thanked me for coming, and said they would welcome me back in the future. They were thanking me when I was the one feeling grateful. But as they had to walk past me to get out of the room, I felt their fear arise again. Not only do they shame themselves for their behavior, and expect me to do the same, they are the most discriminated-against group of people in our culture. One man, who had agreed to be presented at a training for therapists working with sex offenders, later found a sign placed on the door of the pool hall. It said "Child raper, (his name) plays pool here." He carries the sign with him to remind himself of the seriousness of his behavior, as well as the seriousness of letting the information get in the hands of people who will use it against him.

I left Steve's feeling enriched, with a broader understanding of what it is like for a person who has been sexual with children when they have been reported and are in therapy. I could see the men were right when they emphatically and unanimously told me that being arrested was the best thing that happened to them. It might be excruciatingly painful, frightening, and potentially isolating, but it offered the only hope for a life with some reality and integrity.

ANOTHER APPROACH TO ASC TREATMENT

Jill Seipel is a colleague in Seattle who also specializes in helping people with sexual issues, although she no longer sees committed sex offenders. Before coming here, she worked in a university hospital with men who had been through the court system and were required to be in therapy. She saw people in individual therapy as well as in groups. Jill started a program for partners, initially working in groups, and later in individual therapy as well. She immediately learned they were hungering for help for their issues too. These women felt left out and excluded. Jill was able to see how necessary it was to look at the effects of ASC behavior on all the members of the family in order to help them restore their family. She pointed out how the pattern of isolation ASC's live with while acting out was repeated in therapy. Again they were isolated from the important people in their lives.

I asked Jill how she became involved in this difficult work, and she told me she got started during her internship while working on her master's degree in social work. Already an experienced counselor, she wanted a challenge that would stimulate further learning. But, in the beginning, this wasn't always pleasant.

Jill's first encounter with a person accused of being sexual with children was an assignment to evaluate a man who was very large and forbidding. He had been in prison, and was to be evaluated to see if it would be safe to have him in the community. This kind of task was not appropriately given to a new therapist in training who had as yet no experience with these issues. Jill still believed that offenders were frightening, dangerous people prior to her first session with this man, so she was already set up to be frightened. Then it turned out this person looked like a man who had tried to force her and her twin into his car when they were eight. When she saw him in the waiting room of the clinic, she went into an altered state and then into panic. She told herself she had to get out of there, she would walk out, leave the building, leave the area, fast. As she walked down the hall her supervisor happened to open her door and speak to her. She was startled by this contact with ordinary life, and it brought her back to reality.

Jill was experiencing a memory in the form of her current experience, which gave her an opportunity to discharge more of the distress from the childhood attempted assault. It also gave her a chance to take a look at how she carried our culture's views of ASC's, and to reduce her stereotypical beliefs. She was able to interview the man, do an evaluation, and see him as a person with a story instead of a boogie man from the past.

As Jill conducted the interview over the course of three meetings with him, she watched to make sure her personal reactions weren't influencing her decisions and recommendations. She believes they didn't. She remained uncomfortable with him because he was not truthful, minimizing his offenses and denying what he had done. He had no remorse or regret, and even implied that he had things set up to have access to victims once he was out of prison. He has been so damaged he was unable to make the shift from seeing his behaviors as necessary ways to meet his "needs," to understanding that what he has done is very harmful. Without acknowledging the harmful behavior, he cannot enter a healing process. Since protecting victims is the most important factor in these evaluations, she recommended that he not be paroled. He was returned to prison.

As Jill grew in experience, the director of the program felt that she had a natural ability for working with these people, although it took a while before Jill could know that was accurate. Jill was able to be direct and confrontive but compassionate and understanding at the same time. She was also able to interact with sex offenders without degrading them, as some counselors cannot avoid doing.

SHAME THERAPY

Jill and I talked about the fact that much so--called "treatment" of sex offenders is shame-based. Like a high school coach who yells at and shames athletes to get them to do better, our culture believes that more shame, not less, will remove unacceptable behaviors. ASC's and other sex addicts are prime examples of how ineffective shaming is. Instead, it actually promotes the very behaviors that it is meant to reduce. In sports, those who can meet the coach's expectations and demands are approved of. Those who can't, which are the vast majority, suffer from reduced self-esteem, anger toward those who succeed, and with a value system that requires they be number one to be valuable.

The men in my men's therapy group talked at length about how it is humiliating to be second. They agreed that it is better to not place at all. Jill told me about a man who was referred to her by his church counseling services after he completed offender treatment with a therapist who employs shaming, and who has no intuitive sense of his clients. The church's approach had also been unable to help him with his cross-wiring. They benignly told him to "put it in God's hands" in a manner that encouraged him to try to follow a rule rather than help him understand the nature of the recovery process. This advice brings more shame from failure when someone is as yet unable to take the first step of recovery.

Jill began by learning about who this man was, what his life felt like, and how she could have empathy for him through connections to her own life. She asks herself how this person got on this path in life. Jill knows that he or she didn't decide, "this is what I want to be when I grow up." She also talked about the need to look for the purpose of the behavior, how it was intended to help the person, even if it is not a healthy way to do so.

BEHAVIORAL APPROACH TO OFFENDER THERAPY

Jill believes a strict behavioral approach to therapy can be harmful because if the therapist looks only at the behavior, the individual is overlooked. She is angry with professionals who aren't curious about the person as a whole, and about the complexity of their lives. If they focus only on behavioral change, therapists can't see the healthy pieces of a person that have pushed to survive.

When seeing a new offender client, Jill didn't focus on the behavior initially, as is often the approach in offender treatment.

She didn't immediately read the court report or other information that contained the perspectives and evaluations of others, so that she wouldn't be prejudiced in her perception. She read the material only when she knew the person well enough that she wouldn't violate him or her with the information.

Jill continued to talk passionately about seeing the whole person and the need for empathy in order to help people heal. She pointed out that she could be sitting in their chair if she had their history. It's the luck of the draw. Each of us is no better and no worse, we are human beings. I cherished her willingness to place us all in the realm of being human, all of us subject to the same forces, differing only in how we manifest our distress.

TREATMENT FOR FAMILIES

I asked Jill what she learned about families by seeing all the members. She said that as she worked with offenders, and with their partners, she saw that therapy was limited if she couldn't meet with them together. By seeing both partners in a couples group, they were able to change their perceptions of the ASC as the offender and the partner and child as the victims. While the child is, of course, the victim, the partner and the ASC get to see that they are both victims and they are also, in some ways, both offenders. The children are able to see the ASC as a victim of his or her own history, broadening their perception of the person.

As all members of the family are able to look at each other's pain and issues, the healing of the child is enhanced. In contrast, clients of mine are denied the opportunity to heal when their parents aren't willing to be engaged in the therapy of their adult child, and instead blame the therapist for leading them astray, while denying that anything harmful occurred during the person's childhood. The chance to hear the truth, even though it is painful, and to perceive the whole picture, allows the person to make sense out of events, and makes it easier to put experiences in perspective. They feel loved by the parents in ways that weren't possible earlier in their lives. They don't have to settle for awkward relating, or absence of relating, that is often necessary for survivors who cannot enlist their family's involvement. Instead, they receive the most precious gift —hearing the truth, and having reality affirmed.

Family involvement also forced the offenders to see more clearly what their behaviors had done. As their child expressed held back feelings, the offenders' denial and minimization was attacked in powerfully effective ways. They got to see the harm they had caused, which is far more effective than hearing about it third-hand.

Jill told me that her team's program was criticized in Ohio for seeing offenders, mothers, and victims together. The court, Child Protective Services, and other clinics preferred to keep the offender away from the family. I was saddened to hear this, knowing the cost to the survivors' healing. It is an artificial way to control this "badness," a "badness" that is in our culture. It is not true that a few people who, if isolated from the rest of us, will no longer be able to bring harm. In contrast, sexual cross-wiring to children is built into our culture, and the broader the healing environment, the greater the healing for all.

I had one last question for Jill about how it was possible for mothers to not know what the fathers were doing to the children. From her experience working with whole families, she was able to explain that parents are usually equal in their lack of sexual boundaries. People with differences are unlikely to marry because a person with healthy sexual boundaries won't open themselves up to a person whose aren't. The mothers may not have been overtly sexual with children, but they weren't able to see the clues that the father was. She said the mothers crossed boundaries too, such as in the areas of bathing, dressing, chores, and school. By intruding into the child's areas, making decisions the child should be making, and generally not seeing the child's needs, the mother demonstrates that she isn't aware of what the child needs to be protected from. These violations also inform the child that there is no point in telling because she or he has no expectation that the mother will be different with this information than she is with many other areas of life.

This lack of clear sexual and other boundaries is another important reason why therapy with the family as a whole (as well as individual therapy and therapy groups with those like oneself) is valuable for entire healing. When I see the despair of my clients who cannot enlist their parents' cooperation, I believe it would have been desirable if the parent had been arrested for the behavior. This forces the parents who are able to work with their families to create new and better communities. The perception that being found out, arrested, and prosecuted is the worst thing that can happen is really not the case. It is often the only hope.

Chapter 14

Women "Offenders"

Women as well as men are sexual with children. This is hard for most of us to believe because it is not in the realm of our culture's perception of women. The myth is that women may be angry with their children, and some may hit them, but only very few are capable of using a child for sexual gratification. There are a number of reasons why we think that far more men than women are sexual with children.

SEX IS DEFINED AS MALE/FEMALE SEXUAL ACTS

First, sex is usually defined as acts typical of adult sex. Activities that are seen as sexual between an adult and a child are defined as the penetration of a penis into vagina, or oral-genital stimulation, or anal intercourse. Since women don't have penises, "having sex" with a child, particularly a girl child, is difficult for many to define.

Women have sex with babies by using the stimulus of sucking to arouse the mother while nursing. (While many women experience sexual arousal while nursing, this becomes harmful when it is invited by the mother for her pleasure rather than in response to meeting the baby's needs.) Other women rub babies on their bodies to bring sensuous, sexual pleasure. Touching genitals to relax a child, or for any reason other than cleaning or medicating them, is not healthy. Women can direct sexual energy toward their child, and express this through over-loving, such as smothering with kisses. The child's response cannot always be used as a measure of harm. Children may respond with delight because they welcome any attention. In addition the child may not know that the mother's enmeshing behavior isn't good for him or her. Even if the baby doesn't like it, it is hard for a child to turn down attention. When young children pull away or complain, they are usually criticized by the adult, or by others present. (Well, what's wrong with you today? Did you get out of the wrong side of bed? Oh, you don't love Mommy anymore?)

Other behaviors of women being sexual with children include having the child suck on the woman's clitoris, teaching the child to stroke the vulva and other body parts, rubbing the child on the woman's genitals, stroking the child in non-genital areas with arousal, exposing the woman's body to the child in sexual ways, making sexual sounds when being affectionate, and responding sexually when the child initiates sexual exchange. Women commonly see their sons as substitute mates, perceiving them as "my little man."

OUR CULTURE SAYS
WOMEN DON'T INITIATE SEX

A second reason it is difficult to understand that many women are sexual with children is that in our culture, women are not seen as people who initiate sex. Men "make love" to a woman and the woman responds. This has only recently changed after the sexual upheaval of the 1960s, which freed women to express desire for sex. But in spite of changes in magazine articles and popular belief, men making love to women is still the dominate view. This stereotype makes it difficult to see that a woman could initiate sexual activity with her child.

I have heard stories of male clients whose mothers eroticized them with sexual contact and sexualized interaction when they were very young. When the child discovered that the mother responded to sexual energy, then the child proceeded to initiate such interaction. In this way the mother maintained the role of the one who responded, and the child got attention he or she might not otherwise get from a mother who was depressed or who viewed sexualized interaction as the only valuable contact. These men are damaged by growing up believing they were responsible for sexual interaction with their mother. In addition, they are set up to addictively pursue sex with women, as they act out their childhood experience.

One client I will call Rick had a sexualized relationship with his mother from the time he was a baby. He knew he could always get her attention by rubbing against her breast. She breastfed him until he was four. He has clear picture memories of wanting to nurse to have her attention, and prolonging it by touching her breast in sexual ways. If he didn't go after her she had little attention for him, leaving him lonely and abandoned. He developed an intense interest in sexually arousing his mother in order to feel loved and safe. As he grew into a teenager and adult, this translated into intense pursuit of women as sexual partners. Even after two years of recovery, Rick will occasionally have fantasies of initiating sexual activity with his mother. He fully believes she would respond.

I believe his mother has no idea that responding to his breast stimulation was harmful to Rick. She and her husband came in to have a session with me, and stayed only ten minutes. The distress they felt because their son had said her behavior was abusive to him was intolerable. Some parents are in denial—

that is, on some level they know the truth, but don't let it become conscious—and so refuse to acknowledge what they have done. I believe Rick's mother really doesn't know. She doesn't have the information she needs to change her perception. If she were to drop her shame about having sexual feelings with children, and read a book like this one, she could embark on discovering how she was sexual with her son.

For her to do so would mean confronting her husband's sex addiction, and her decades of willingness to be his drug, possibly threatening their marriage. When told of her son's addiction to one-night stands and sex with prostitutes, as well as sex with his wife, she dismissed it as a "man thing." She saw no reason for him to be getting help for it, and sent me a note with her payment for the session saying that I was only in it for the money. Her fear of finding out the truth, as well as her great confusion over appropriate boundaries around sexuality, prevents her from healing.

I want to stress that living in this culture also prevents this healing. The amount of shame leveled at a man for such behavior is increased many times for a woman. Her family and community would be aghast if they knew. Nowhere among her acquaintances is there even one person who would say they know what she has been through, have empathy and understanding, and support her recovery. So far the only women who are able to do this are ones who have been arrested, usually put in jail, and required to interact with other women who have done the same. Finally, in an accepting community of peers, they are able to learn what they have done, and how their choices were shaped by their abusive childhoods. Rick's mother, now grandmother to adult children, is not likely to have the motivation necessary to confront her behaviors—and the shame accompanying them.

WOMEN ARE SEXUAL WITH CHILDREN TOO YOUNG TO REMEMBER

A third reason we think fewer women are sexual with children may be that women's sexual behaviors with children are most often limited to their very early years—years when retrieving picture memories is less likely. I have no evidence for this idea from research studies, but my experience working with male sex addicts has revealed that almost all of them have sexual confusion in their relationship with their mothers. Many are aware that these relationships include a sexual component. All therapists I have spoken with who work with sex addicts believe that almost all were sexually abused as children, and Pat Carnes's research described in *Don't Call It Love* (Bantam, 1991) found that over 80% of recovering sex addicts have been. Some men, like Monty and Rick, liked the sexual element in their relationship with their mothers even in adulthood until discovering how harmful it was.

Others, like another client, Steve, were revolted by this component. When Steve went to his mother's hotel room to pick her up for a session with him in my office, she took off her blouse to change. While in her bra, she asked him to open her suitcase for her. Steve, who was uncomfortable being with his mother in this state of undress, told her that he was staying in the next room until she put something on—then he would help her. She laughed, saying this was ridiculous, just come and do it. When she came into his line of sight, he handed her her jacket, asking again that she put something on. Again she refused. Finally, he stood with has back to her until she man-aged to open her suitcase herself, criticizing him for not helping.

Minutes later in my office, Steve brought it up. His mother dismissed it, saying he shouldn't feel that way, she was his mother. She said she wouldn't take off her blouse with someone who wasn't in the family, but because he was her son it was all right. He was thirty-two. Even when I intervened, she dismissed what I said too.

I believe that she has to maintain her perceptions because if she hears him now when he says he doesn't want her to act in certain ways, she may have to know that he expressed these same feelings as a child and that she ignored his legitimate reactions. She has created a value system that allows her to violate boundaries and believe she is in integrity. She can cite her beliefs as truth so she doesn't have to know she is affecting her children. In this way she avoids shame that would come with knowing that she has, indeed, violated his sexual boundaries.

Steve told me in his next session that he went with her to her hotel room after our meeting. At five o'clock in the afternoon, she took off her belt and her cuff links. While this doesn't look like something that might violate the boundaries of an adult son, she communicated to Steve that she could do what she wanted and would not limit her undressing in respect for his feelings. His only option was to leave, which he did.

I would like to be able to tell you the stories of women like Steve's and Rick's mothers, but I haven't been able to figure out how to do that. They cannot tell me about themselves in ways that would make sense of their behaviors with their sons, because to do so would require speaking freely and having feelings. This is too threatening because intolerable shame awaits. Alice Miller solved this dilemma by studying the art of famous people and deciphering the stories they didn't know they were telling in *The Untouched Key: Tracing Childhood Trauma in Creativity and Destructiveness* (Doubleday, 1990). But the mothers of my clients haven't produced something I can use—

except for the symptoms my clients have in response to their mother's treatment.

CARETAKING CAN MASK SEXUAL ENERGY

Women who have been raised with poor physical and sexual boundaries can believe their sexualized behaviors are part of normal caretaking. Bathing, loving children's bodies, and the natural need for skin to skin contact can be sexualized without the mother's awareness. This is easier with a dependent young child than with an older one because babies don't seem like people. Babies seem to be of a different order because they don't look like us, they are totally needy, and they haven't suppressed their natural feelings yet. The rules that determine how parents will be with older children and adults can be easily disengaged with these little beings that a mother spends much time alone with.

If a woman's mother and grandmothers and aunts all cuddled and snuggled children with sexual energy, she can only think this is normal. As she was required to interpret sexualized affection as love, she lost her ability to perceive it as harmful. *As each person gives up knowing she was violated, she gives up being able to perceive when she is violating.* This is why we must, as a culture, become conscious of when sexual energy is present. As we all do this, we will free mothers to know how to be with their children in healthy ways.

It is hard for a mother to know when she is being sexual with her child if she came from a childhood where boundaries weren't clear. When the infant looks deeply into the eyes of its parent, bonds to her or him, and develops awareness of the self as a community member, the feelings that accompany such looking are a form of sexual energy. It is similar to adults who look deeply into each others' eyes when they are bonding sexually into a couple. *It is also different in that it isn't monogamous—others can join in and many can bond into family.*

If a mother was raised with clear sexual boundaries, she will know that the feeling is intense for the baby and for herself, but that it isn't the same as when she and her mate look at each other. She will know that the baby is serving her or his needs, and she is there to help the process. But when she grew up with parents who weren't clear with her, she won't be able to know this, and may feel invited to use the child's adoration as a replacement for the loving that is appropriate between her and her partner.

I want to stress that this form of sexual interaction with children is unconscious. Not only does the mother not know, her culture tells her that she is being a good mother when she dotes on her child with intensity. Fathers feel jealous of the monogamously bonding energy between their wives and children, as they should, but they are programmed by our culture to think that something is wrong with them for having this feeling. Instead, they should be supported for knowing that the adult monogamous bond is broken. (I wonder how many men's decisions to have affairs come from intuitive awareness that the monogamous bonds with their wives are broken, even though they cannot put this into words.)

As our culture changes, and we become able to recognize when sexualized interactions are occurring, we as a society will be able to assist each individual with the quest to know when boundaries are clear and when they are not. First we must be able to drop our shame about ways we are not clear with children, knowing our limitations are culturally determined. Then we can begin our renewed education about how we can be healthy with children.

MOTHERS CAN ABUSE CHILDREN WHEN NOT SEXUALLY AROUSED

Therapist Jill Seipel worked with several women offenders, only one of whom was able to stay in therapy for several months. The mother had been reported for bathing her eight-year-old son at an age when he was fully capable of doing that for himself. Not only did she bath him, she scrubbed him thoroughly, including his genitals and anus, and then powdered his entire body. She was compulsively clean in all areas of her life, including her own body, house, and car. A survivor of child abuse from her own childhood, she compulsively worked to create a contamination-free environment.

As Jill worked with this woman, she received no indication that the mother felt sexual when she washed her son. The mother denied that she had sexually abused him throughout therapy, believing that sexual abuse meant sexual acts accompanied by sexual feelings, which she did not have. At the same time, this boy's sexuality was affected. His privacy wasn't respected, and his body, including the sexual parts, was being violated.

Without therapy, these experiences could manifest in a number of ways when he grows to adulthood. He might react with revulsion when a woman touches his genitals. He may not be able to have sex with women. He may have to entirely control his sexual activities in order to avoid replaying his early bathing. Or he might become a sex addict, and turn his childhood experiences into fuel for his addiction, perhaps wanting his lovers to rub his body and genitals vigorously to enhance cross-wired arousal. Or, if severely damaged, he might become a rapist, punishing and controlling stand-ins for the woman who scrubbed his body while never seeing the person residing within it.

This mother needed treatment that included group therapy with other women like herself. In this context, she would have a chance to learn about normal and appropriate boundaries between a mother and her developing children. She would do this by talking about her own childhood, learning about what she needed and how she didn't receive it. As she became aware of her need for respectful boundaries, she would automatically become aware of her son's needs. She could know why her behavior violated his body and his sexuality.

Our Perception Changes

Anne Banning wrote an article called "Mother-Son Incest: Confronting a Prejudice" (*Child Abuse and Neglect*, 1989) describing many of the reasons for the difficulty perceiving women as able to be sexual with children. She provides an excellent example, which I will present here, of how we can see the identical situation as abusive or innocent depending on the gender of the child and of the adult.

A four-year-old boy in Australia was brought to treatment because he was playing a game with girls in his preschool called, "Check a bum," which entailed putting his finger or a stick into girls' vaginas. His mother said this was a common game for children, and she was more worried about the preschool's alarmed reaction than she was about the behavior. The mother had wanted a son, and after having him, gave up a promiscuous life style to focus on him, treating him like an adult male partner and the center of her life. She left his father when he was nine months old.

The mother described her son as highly sexed, wanting to fondle her breasts, see her body when she bathed, and give her tongue kisses. He had male dolls attack female dolls by putting a bayonet between their legs. Drawing a line on a piece of paper, he said it was a vagina and that it smells.

His mother said that both she and her mother kissed his penis when he was a baby to soothe him. She also made a game of chasing him naked, catching him, biting his bottom, saying I'll eat your bottom. Her mother had played this game with her as a child. When the interviewer commented on her difficulty knowing appropriate boundaries, the mother said, with surprise, "I felt his body was mine."

Banning tells us that this case was not reported as sexual abuse, and thus would not have been figured in the statistics for mother-son sexual contact.

The author then changes the gender of the family, inviting us to see how our perception changes.

Imagine a girl in preschool who is playing sexual games with the boys, touching their penises, a game called "check a bum." When her father is called in and asked about it, he says he isn't concerned about the game, all children play it, and he is more concerned about the reaction of the preschool. When asked about the girl's home life, he said how important she was to him, and that he had given up his promiscuous life style in order to be with her. She was like an adult female partner, and the center of his life. He had left her mother when she was nine months old.

The father said his daughter was highly sexed, wanting to see him nude, playing with his penis, and giving him tongue kisses. Drawing a line, she said it was a penis, and it smells. She played with dolls, pushing a bayonet between the legs of the girl dolls.

He said that he and his father both kissed her vagina when she was a baby to soothe her, and they played a game where the father chased her naked, caught her and bit her bottom saying he would eat her bottom. When the interviewer commented on his difficulty knowing appropriate boundaries, the father said, with surprise, "I felt her body was mine."

I have been working with male and female incest survivors, and I have talked with both men and women who have sexual feelings toward children, yet I had different reactions to this scene based on the gender of the family members. The truth is that both children are being abused in identical ways, and the effects in their adult lives will be of similar magnitude. But my perceptions don't match the reality. The sexualized boy doesn't seem out of the ordinary. My distorted thinking could go so far as to say that this is typical development for boys' sexuality, something that no one questions. But when the sex is changed, I have no doubt that what the father is doing is very damaging to the daughter, and she is trying to tell the story of what happened with her own behavior. If this situation were presented to me in a class I teach on healthy sexuality, I might find myself less concerned if the child were a boy with a mother than a girl with a father. In the latter case, I would feel compelled to make an immediate report to Child Protective Services, and assure the person who presented the case to me that this was serious and must not be overlooked. Knowing I still have this bias, I often reverse the genders in my mind in order to see how I would react so that I can be sure to offer appropriate protection.

Banning's example is evidence that there are far more women being sexual with their children, and with other children, than we suspect. Until researchers like John Briere begin the long process of questioning normal samples of women with children about how they interact with them, we won't have hard data.

This example given by Banning makes another point, as well. Young boys are known to engage in sex play more frequently than girls. It is considered part of typical male behavior.

Yet if sexual behavior is a result of sexual violation by adults, as it is known to be in girls, this suggests that more boys than girls have their sexuality damaged at young ages. Before we can appreciate this possibility, we have to change our cultural perceptions of differences in the meaning of sexual contact for girls and boys.

THERAPY FOR WOMEN OFFENDERS

The subject of therapy for women who have been sexual with children is very new, even newer than that for men. Until the past few years, writers said that those few women who were sexual with children were psychotic, or otherwise impaired, and didn't consider it necessary to create therapy to meet their needs until 1984 when two psychologists, Noel Larson, Ph. D., and Sally Maison, Ph. D., did so in Minnesota. Those few who were believed to be sexual with children were usually put in prison, rarely trusted to remain in the community.

Jill Seipel's experience working with women offenders contributed to her decision to stop offering court-ordered therapy. None of the women assigned to her were able to make use of therapy because they saw Jill as an extension of the system. She was. Jill gave one example of a male offender who was working well in therapy, was not a danger to his children, and who could be treated appropriately out of jail. Yet one year after she began working with him and his family, she was required to testify in court. Even though she spoke in his favor, and against a prison sentence, he was taken from the home and put in jail. Jill's women offender clients knew this was always possible for them too, and so were not able to develop the trust necessary to begin healing.

Jill spoke sadly about how she attempted to create a safe environment by telling them what she already knew about their situation, withholding nothing from the women, but she couldn't diminish the very real danger of revealing their activities with children. Jill could not prevent them from being sent to prison or having their children removed from the home.

When I asked Jill what she thought needed to change, she said firmly that punishment and help cannot be mixed. The court system in the two states in which she worked before coming to Seattle were consistently damaging to sex offenders, and frustrating to those who tried to help them. She said that Steve Zimberoff's program in Wenatchee seems to be the exception rather than the rule. Steve has a good working relationship with the court, and his clients seem to be well served. Perhaps this is possible when a humanistic therapist interacts with the court in a community small enough to be influenced by his attitudes. Steve is not punitive. Instead, his focus is determining if a person can be treated out of prison, and if he is an immediate danger if left in the community. With this backdrop, the men he assesses know they have everything to gain by becoming involved in therapy. If they cannot, then they will go to prison. This provides a very different motivation than that provided for Jill's clients.

Jill added that while these issues are true for both genders, it is even more confusing for women offenders. The attitudes of those involved in treatment and in the judicial system are even more reactive when dealing with women being sexual with children. As Jill talked, I found myself feeling disoriented and confused in a choppy, jerky sort of way. Jill affirmed that she felt the same, in contrast to our conversations about therapy for male offenders. *The culturally-created emotional reactivity to women being sexual with children prevents courts, therapy centers, and therapists from understanding the needs of the community, the family, and the ASC.*

PRISON-BASED TREATMENT FOR WOMEN OFFENDERS

Noel Larson, Ph. D., and Sally Maison, Ph. D., created a treatment program in a prison that housed an increasing number of women who had committed sexual crimes. The psychologists received a grant to create a program, and to study its effectiveness. They prepared a manual for use in other prison programs to fill in a very empty gap. (This manual can be purchased from Dr. Larson in St. Paul, Minnesota.) Their therapy began with two hours of group therapy weekly, supplemented by couples, family, and family-of-origin therapy. This was followed by an intensive, two-day sexual learning seminar, a weekly support group, a post-release group for parole follow up, ten-week sex education groups, intensive, two-day treatment marathons, and prison staff training.

Their approach is based on a family systems view of therapy, a more holistic approach than behavior modification task-oriented treatment. The authors state, "While taking responsibility for the crime is clearly reinforced, and recidivism (re-offending) is of ongoing concern to treatment staff, the inmate's own victimization experiences in childhood frequently become an important area of concentration. *Resolving early victimization, the arena in which perpetrators learn to offend, is of critical importance to this treatment model."*

I was pleased and relieved to hear this because it matches my own experience with sex addicts—those who have been sexual with children and those who haven't. Larson and Maison's outpatient program is for women who have been incarcerated for a sexual crime, those who have committed a sexual crime but were not incarcerated, and women who are afraid they might commit a sexual crime in the future. These researcher-clinicians created a program that anticipates the future wave of need that will appear when we let ourselves see that women, perhaps as frequently as men, are sexual with children. Their manual was published in 1987.

As I read the stories of women who shared their painful histories and current lives in their therapy groups, I was touched by the manner of the therapists. They had compassion for the women they were helping. Seeing them as human beings who had grown up in devastating childhoods, they sought to know the inner experience of each one. This humanistic view is beautifully conveyed in their dedication of the manual:

> To the women in our sex offender group, who allowed us to intrude into their lives and their souls, letting us go beyond the layers of toughness covering unspeakable hurts, so we could know the damaged, terrified little girls within: thanks for helping us learn.

Chapter 15

"Behavior Modification" Treatment of Sex Offenders

Treatment for people who have been sexual with children is fairly new. The behavioral school of psychotherapy has devised one kind of therapy, coming out of the Masters and Johnson behavioral approaches to sexual "dysfunction," and other behavior modification techniques. Sex therapy has been dominated by behaviorism, and so the treatment of sex offenders naturally evolved from it.

Behaviorism examines the reinforcers of behaviors (for instance, good grades reinforce studying, and eating takes away hunger so we eat when hungry), and the creation of new characteristics for a behavior by repeatedly experiencing it in the presence of something else (such as Pavlov's dog experiments. Pavlov rang a bell every time he fed dogs, and soon they salivated when the bell was rung when food wasn't present). These principles can be applied to any behaviors, and therapy methods using them have emerged over the past three decades.

While "behavior modification," as the therapy approach is called, can be useful to change behavior, it can also violate a person's integrity. The therapy often becomes mechanical, focusing on only one aspect of a person's being. The physical, emotional, and spiritual facets are not addressed, nor is the person's history.

A stern, punitive approach to sex offenders has emerged from this school—supported, of course, by our punitive culture. It makes sense to me that this has happened because as long as socially unacceptable behaviors are the only focus, the therapist cannot feel very positive toward his task and subject. Behaviorism doesn't invite a spiritual connection between therapist and client, and it ignores childhood experiences that have caused present symptoms. Instead, the focus is changing offenders' sexual behavior through a variety of techniques.

Many of these techniques are harmful to the human being. Instead of allowing the person to heal from their past and from the effects of their adult activities with children, the individual is seen as the problem with no cultural context in which to place the behaviors. This approach adds shame, as the person is objectified much as they objectified their victims. The feeling of shame is allowed to decrease only if the unacceptable behaviors change. While this might create motivation to do the tasks prescribed by the therapist, it doesn't allow an inside-out relinquishing of the shame that is built into the person's view of themselves—a change that will result in letting go of the desire to have sex with children. This approach seems guaranteed to create either resistant, rebellious clients (much as teens who aren't respected will thwart authority) or compliant, obedient people who will express their aggression in indirect ways.

In contrast, the approach that views these behaviors as addictions, sees them in the context of a culture that gave men and women permission to do them, and begins by reducing shame so the person can take responsibility for changing. This approach doesn't diminish the fact that the behaviors are wrong, and must be stopped, or that the only one who can do this is the ASC. But the change process is deeper, and respects the whole person.

I have heard many stories of people who spent time in behavior therapy for sexual "deviance" before making their way to programs based on addiction or other humanitarian approaches. They consistently abhorred the first treatment, and highly valued the alternative they eventually found.

I have selected one person's story to tell you, a story that is hard for traditional behaviorists to discount for several reasons. Rob was not reported for child sexual abuse, he chose therapy because he wanted to change his sexual behaviors. When he left the behaviorist he found another therapist to work with, and over the course of three-and-a-half years he has made great progress. He cannot be dismissed as a person who just doesn't want to change, or who isn't willing to tolerate the painful process to do so. He has changed, and he has tolerated tremendous pain. He also had enough self-respect to refuse to continue in a treatment that made him feel more shame, where the therapist didn't engage with him as a human being, and didn't listen attentively to the issues he wanted to address.

THE ASC WHO WENT FOR HELP

I described Rob's sexual experience with his then two-year-old daughter in Chapter 9. After several such experiences, he stopped, and continued his other addictive sexual activities. His guilt over being sexual with his daughter outweighed her convenience as a sex object.

Several years later, Rob became frightened about his sexuality, and decided that he wanted to get help. He didn't know if his behaviors were normal or abnormal. He also didn't have anyone to ask about it because sex addiction isn't a subject that one casually brings up with coworkers or friends.

Rob went to see a psychiatrist at his company's HMO. The psychiatrist knew little about "deviant" sexual behaviors. He listened attentively, and made notes as Rob filled him in on his sexual concerns, including exposing himself to women, going to peep shows, masturbating in his car, and trying to have sex with his wife while she slept. He told about the crisis that occurred because his wife had become pregnant as the result of one of his night time approaches. The abortion that resulted, and his feelings about his own actions, lead him to seek help. As he talked, he felt better, relieved that he could share his secret life for the first time.

The next day Rob received a call at work from the psychiatrist. He was told that a report had been made to child protective services about the abuse of his daughter. A social worker would be calling to make a report. The police department had been alerted and, along with CPS, would decide if Rob should remain in his home.

Rob's daughter was interviewed by the social worker, who found no evidence that Rob was continuing his activities with her. But the fact that he had in the past meant that CPS could play a role in making sure the daughter was safe. The social worker gave Rob the name of a therapist (a man I will call Dr. Y) who worked with sex offenders, and told him to call for an appointment.

Rob went to his first session with fear and hope. At last he was going to see an expert on the subject that disturbed him. He was also frightened of looking at his sexuality and finding out that perhaps he was mentally ill.

Dr. Y uses behavioral methods. He set out to evaluate Rob, and spent several weekly sessions giving him tests and asking him questions. Rob was sent for a polygraph test and a plethysmograph.

THE PLETHYSMOGRAPH

A penile plethysmograph is like a lie detector test for sexual arousal. Rob was put into a tiny room with a small window which allowed an experimenter to see him from the back. Given only brief explanation of the reason for the test by Dr. Y, he was told to put a loop with a strain gage over his penis so that when his penis became erect the changes in diameter would be recorded on a graph in the next room. He was then exposed to visual and auditory pornographic scenes, including child porn. A record was made of the degree of response to each stimulus. From this record, Dr. Y prepared his treatment program to reduce arousal to each of the stimuli that elicited an erection.

Taking this test is harmful. The shaming of all kinds of sexuality in our culture, even the healthy kinds, makes this procedure massively shameful. Instead of reducing shame around sex so that the person can begin healing, it reinforces shameful feelings for having sexual responses to pornography in the presence of a person who thinks this is wrong.

Rob was shocked by the test and the results. He responded to a graphic story of sexual activity with an adolescent girl, and to an erotically-told rape scene. He protested, saying he thought that most men would respond to the scene with the thirteen-year-old girl. I agree. I believe that the majority of people (men and women) would also respond sexually to rape scenes. Producers of the movie *Thelma and Louise* used that information when they decided to include close-ups of the rape scene at the center of the plot. By talking openly about it, I have found that men and women alike will say they were aroused by this scene if someone else says they were first.

Rob asked Dr. Y if his responses would be compared to those of a normal sample of men, a standard procedure when evaluating a person's test results. Dr. Y told him that his responses were used as a baseline to compare with changes to be made. There are no studies that describe how an average group of men would respond to these scenes. I found myself shocked by this, so I examined recent data published on the plethysmograph to find out if this was indeed the case. It is.

In a review of the literature on the use of this test, the authors (James Barker and Robert Howell, "The Plethysmograph: A Review of Recent Literature," *Bull. Am. Psychiatriy Law*, 1992) tell us that this test is used in courts to support the guilt of a person on trial for child molesting, and is used to predict recovery. Yet there is no research indicating that the test is predictive of anything. *No studies have been done to establish a relationship between arousal in response to particular pornographic stimuli and the possibility of acting in ways demonstrated in the porn scenes.* It's the same as assuming that if any person responds sexually to pornography that details certain sex acts, that person is likely to commit those same acts. This is quite absurd since we know that even people who limit themselves to sex with a mate in the missionary position will be aroused by a variety of sexual stimuli, because we live in a culture that prevents us from discovering our healthy sexuality. We are all reactive to stimuli of many sorts. The kinds of stimuli that each of us is reactive to is vital information about our childhood experiences. But it doesn't indicate that we are doing the acts that arouse us in the form of pictures or sounds or words.

For instance, many women are encouraged by sex therapists to use rape fantasies to become and remain aroused sexually. While women don't want to be raped, most will find themselves aroused by a fantasy of being raped. Living in a culture where children are owned by parents, are made to do what the parents want, and are humiliated and shamed if they don't cooperate, sets us up for cross-wiring of sexuality to violence, humiliation, and control.

Force is frightening, but the fantasy of being forced can be translated into sexual arousal. Examples can be seen in old movies where the man couldn't resist the woman, kissed her forcefully, while saying things like "shut up" in a lustful, "loving" way. The woman melted into the kiss. Women used to be aroused by these movie scenes, yet being kissed like that may not be at all pleasant. The movie is the equivalent to pornography shown to men with a strain gage attached to their penis.

If the assumption is made that a person's response to sexual stimuli indicates the kind of sex they are likely to engage in, then many women would be seeking hard, controlling kisses, and rape. In this case we can see that the assumption of a connection between arousal to porn and choice of sexual activity doesn't make sense.

Research also shows that the plethysmograph doesn't predict acting out. Barker and Howell cite studies indicating that the test lacks reliability and validity, the two major measures of a test's effectiveness. Researchers have found that men are capable of inhibiting their sexual response to the test. Rob wasn't able to do this, but some men are. Men have had to learn since their first unbidden, public erections how to distract themselves from sexual stimuli to prevent evidence of arousal. In addition, men who respond sexually to illegal stimuli have even more motivation to learn how to prevent erections. These studies demonstrate the fallacy of believing that erection always accompanies arousal.

When men are shown "appropriate" sexual stimuli to see if they respond—or to see if they don't respond—a man can fantasize about something that will arouse him, thus invalidating the test.

THERE ARE NO PLETHYSMOGRAPH STUDIES ON WOMEN

As I read studies on the use of the plethysmograph for men, I began to think about how this test could be used to learn more about the numbers of people who have sexual attraction to children, even if they don't act on it. Studies that would establish norms for a general population—in other words, establish what percent of people around us become erect when exposed to child pornography—would involve administering the plethysmograph to a large number of men. As I discussed this with my friend and researcher, Matthew, he pointed out that the same study needs to be done with women too. I found myself reacting with distaste at the idea of putting a strain gage in my vagina, and asking other women to do the same. At the same time, I knew he was right. To do otherwise is to support the cultural belief that men are perverts deserving of having their genitals violated, and women aren't. It is also consistent with the belief that girls are violated by sexual contact and boys aren't. We think nothing of putting a strain gage on a penis, but are shocked at the thought of putting one in a vagina.

Apparently researchers have the same qualms, because there are no studies about women's sexual feelings toward children that use the plethysmograph. The female plethysmograph is used only in studies that are conducted to help women learn how to have more arousal—not less!

ROB IS FORCED TO MASTURBATE TO FANTASIES OF HIS DAUGHTER

Rob didn't succeed in convincing Dr. Y that while he reacted to fantasies of these activities, he wasn't drawn to acting them out as part of his addictive choices. They didn't fit with the function of his addiction. He was "treated" for all the sexual stimuli that brought erections.

The treatment consisted of masturbating in a private place, such as his home, to fantasies of the scenes that arouse him, to fantasies of sex with his sister with whom he had been sexual in childhood, and to fantasies of being sexual with his daughter. He was told to continue masturbating even after orgasm. He did so until his penis hurt. As Rob told me about this, he shook his head, and tears came to his eyes. He said he knew it was wrong, but he had wanted to believe that working with this professional held real hope. He had been cursed by his sexual acting out, and hoped that someone knew how to help. He didn't know yet that there was more than one approach to his problems.

The principle of the masturbation exercises is that by doing something over and over in ways that are no longer pleasurable, even painful, the behavior will lose the positive, rewarding value. This was supposed to happen by repeatedly masturbating, even after orgasm, to the fantasy. As one or more orgasms make it impossible to enjoy stimulation, the fantasy is supposed to lose its ability to arouse because it is no longer pleasurable, and is in fact now actually accompanied by pain.

While the behavior does decrease as a result of this treatment, I don't agree that it's for these reasons. Instead, I believe what happens is that by consciously deciding to have the fantasy and masturbate, and to satiate the sexual urges instead of fighting against them, shame drops. The behavior is no longer secret, and so the feeding of shameful addictive behaviors through secrecy stops.

Secrecy is further impaired by the requirement to make audio tapes of the fantasies while the ASC masturbates. They say outloud what they are thinking and what they experience as they do the exercise. Random segments of the tapes are then played in the therapist's office to make sure the man is really doing what he has been told. This set up interrupts the addictive environment, preventing the addictive trance state that is the addict's reward. The person must become more conscious of his behavior when he wants to use another person as a sexual stimulus.

While this form of treatment can in some respects be viewed as successful, the price is too high for the benefits. The unhealthy behavior of masturbating to fantasy of illegal and/or unethical acts forces the man to do the behaviors he already knows are harmful. How can a therapist in good conscience force a person to do the very thing he is trying to cure him of? Perhaps when helping a person stop checking to see if the stove is still on, or stop frequent hand washing, it may not be harmful to increase the symptom to break up the pattern. But when the behavior is illegal, harmful to the client, and the object of masturbation, this approach must be questioned.

I was particularly distressed by the requirement to masturbate to fantasy of sex with Rob's daughter. Rob found this distressing too, and rightly believed that this was not a good thing for him to do. Rob had had no sexual interest in his daughter for over five years, and now was required to think of her sexually, while masturbating to orgasm. I could image what it was like for him to find privacy to do this exercise perhaps while she was in the house, and then what it might feel like to see her again knowing he was having sex with her in his mind.

Dr. Y's exercise created incest. The behaviors he required of his patient constitute pedophilia. He must have been subject to the same thinking errors of his patients when he thought that Rob's daughter wouldn't be affected by her father's sexual fantasy of her. He didn't take into account the fact that sexual energy can be transmitted without physical contact.

Dr. Y Did Not Like Sex Offenders

Dr. Y's negative attitude toward sex offenders came through in his work with Rob. When Rob asked him about it directly, he indicated that he thought a certain amount of guilt was a good thing in this kind of therapy. His approach to working with Rob indicates that not only did he hold Rob responsible for his actions and for changing his behaviors (a valid expectation), but he also felt a personal disgust for Rob and his sexual behaviors. He saw himself as a disciplinarian, which left Rob feeling dehumanized and uncomfortable in his presence. Rob cried with deep grief as he told me how he felt abused by Dr. Y, that he felt like a freak in the man's eyes. Rob had thought he should be a tough guy, able to take the treatment and survive it, even while he perceived Dr. Y as wanting to get the goods on him, searching for evidence that he was really a pervert. The conflict was very painful.

As Rob told me these details, I thought about what it would be like for a therapist to feel compelled to make sure he hasn't overlooked his client's denial. It was easy for me to see how the therapist can make the person go through a series of emotionally and physically painful exercises in the service of preventing further violation of children. Dr. Y's obvious inability to see the differences in his clients—not all were trying to con him— might come from years of dealing with addicts who don't want to admit what they are doing so they can avoid their own shame, and perhaps to continue some of their behaviors. With no methods to address the addiction, there is no effective way for Dr. Y to know the client has been "cured." When I was in training as a psychologist, this kind of work was considered among the least desirable career choices. The kind of methods that were offered then were not appealing to me or many other therapists. It is only in the past few years that working with sex offenders has become potentially enriching.

In 1990, I attended a continuing education workshop required for yearly re-licensure as a psychologist. I spent seven hours listening to an "expert," who had already told us he was burning out, explain how to evaluate and treat sex offenders. He showed us his pornography collection of pictures that he used to establish a person's arousal patterns. Near the end of the presentation, he recommended that we tell our clients to masturbate to *Hustler* magazine in order to change their sexual response from children to women. He didn't know that he was merely offering a change in the focus of the addiction, and doing nothing to help people heal their sexuality. How could he not burn out? All he could help people do was create more socially-acceptable lies.

I haven't met a person yet who told me they had a basically positive, or even neutral, relationship with a behavioral offender therapist. The opinion of SA group members is to avoid that kind of approach in favor of working with therapists who understand the nature of addiction recovery.

ROB WANTED TO CHANGE

To put each person who has been sexual with children through this routine is damaging to the self-esteem of the person, and this damage will actually prevent the person from healing their sexuality in ways that allow them to replace old, harmful behaviors with new, healthy ones.

Rob should not have been treated as a conscienceless criminal who needed to be subjected to an impersonal, degrading, controlling set of tests and assignments. He was ready to do anything he could to change, which he has since proven. If Dr. Y had been able to look at Rob as a person, he would have seen this. Rob had been writing about his sexual issues in his diary for some time before going for help. His need to tell was strong, but the fear of telling limited him to writing privately for a time. He brought me many pages of journal entries from the weeks before he sought help. They are filled with descriptions of exactly what he had been doing, and his despair at not being able to tell the whole story. He had told his wife most of it, but couldn't bring himself to tell her about how he had been sexual with their daughter until he was forced to by CPS.

Dr. Y asked to see this writing, and when Rob reluctantly parted with it for a week, he didn't read it. Dr. Y missed an opportunity to see the inside workings of a man who hated what he was doing, who felt isolated by his behaviors, and who was ready to face anything in order to change. But I gather from Rob's reports that Dr. Y might not have been able to see the person reflected in those pages even if he had read them.

Rob describes Dr. Y as aloof, unfriendly, impersonal, and matter-of-fact. His description matches that of a therapist who has burned out on treating people who don't change—the common experience of those working with sex offenders.

When Rob asked for information from the results of the tests, and from Dr. Y's personal response, he received none. I read about Rob's feelings, recorded in week after week of diary entries, of fear and frustration. His distress grew over a period of three months. He finally decided to contact a lawyer in the yellow pages who specialized in sex offenses to see if it was possible to abandon this treatment.

He quickly found out that he had the choice to see whoever he wanted, and immediately set out to find a new therapist. At this time he learned that there are two different ways that offenders are approached by therapists. He chose one that employed the more humanistic model. His diary entry reflected great relief after only 20 minutes with the new therapist. Rob described his therapist as open and nonpunitive. He had a structured workbook that Rob found supportive of the work he wanted to do. When he asked questions he got answers. He felt no shaming, and instead, was highly supported. He was surprised and pleased that there was no talk about lie detector tests or the plethysmograph. This therapist and his co-therapist trusted what Rob said, but at the same time held each client accountable for their actions and their recovery work. People in groups hear inconsistencies in voice tones, and eventually deceit will come out. Rob said that some men can be good liars for a time, but once people get to know a person in this honest setting, it will catch up with them.

Since beginning this therapy he has seen a total of three therapists for individual therapy and group therapy, and recently began seeing me with his wife for couple issues, working on healthy sexuality, and is working toward telling his daughter about what happened when she was a baby.

Rob has changed greatly during the past three-and-a-half years. His therapists see him as taking full advantage of his therapy, and with a good prognosis for fully reclaiming healthy sexuality.

BEHAVIORAL THERAPY WAS THE ONLY OPTION

Behavioral therapy was the only therapy available for sex offenders until the past decade, when treatment for sexual addicts was designed by Patrick Carnes (see his books in Suggested Readings). This humanitarian approach allows the therapist to be involved in a way that does not create burn out, and offers hope for change in the culture. But the old style was all there was for decades. It will take time for the courts and other institutions who are involved in the prevention of further child abuse to change over to a new style. I have compassion for Dr. Y because what he learned about treating sex offenders was all that was available when he began his practice. He will have to abandon his entire approach to working with these men if he is to move to a more humanitarian way of dealing with this culturally-created epidemic. It is easier for those of us who didn't have behavioral training in the first place than it is for those who have to give up an approach that helped to reduce symptoms and immediate danger to the community.

MEDIA ATTENTION

As I talked with friends and colleagues about the plethysmograph, and lack of norms, and required masturbation that harm both the person fantasizing and the person being fantasized about, the universally horrified response helped me see that something needs to be done to change this approach. While it will change in time, as the public becomes aware, and influences therapists using these methods, it may be possible to speed up this change. If a group of ASC's who have gone through this kind of treatment were to gather together to write magazine articles and letters to editors of newspapers, the publicity that could result would serve to educate the general public about its existence.

I would like to function as a clearing house for such an endeavor. I know that the humiliation of admitting publicly that one has been required to go through treatment as a sex offender prevents each person from taking action on his own. Perhaps if no individual has to name themselves to the media, each can add their number to the list to establish that this is a common experience. Media attention can provide information to people about what is going on in the name of treatment. Some compassion may be elicited, and perhaps a beginning shift in the opinions of the public.

If you are interested in being involved, either as an ASC or as a writer who has access to magazines or newspapers, please write to me at the address in the front of the book. Include your name, address and phone number and the story of what happened in that treatment that felt wrong to you. If enough people write, I will select a writer with compassion about these issues, and turn the letters over to her or him.

Chapter 16

Drunk and Homeless:
The Man Who Had Sex with His Stepson

I want to close with a wonderful story of a man who was as far down the sickness continuum as a person can be, and who is now leading a powerful, satisfying life and having healthy sex with his wife. Stories like this are proof to me that change really is possible for adults who are sexual with children.

Randel, forty-six years old, lives in an Oregon town where he works in a mill preparing lumber to make homes. He is married to a woman who understands his ASC history, and joins him in recovery. They recently bought their first place, an old one-bedroom house they are working on together to make into a home. Ellie drives a school bus, a job she sought for some time while working as a clerk in a department store.

Randel doesn't hide his past. To the contrary, he speaks out in AA meetings and even in his church. The twelfth step of the Twelve Step programs, begun with AA, is to bring the truth about addiction to others in a way that might help them address their own addiction. He also talks because bringing his story into the open helps prevent him from acting out his illegal behaviors. He learned this repeatedly by telling his wife or another program person every time he felt the urge to think sexually about a child. He no longer does.

I became acquainted with Randel two years ago when he met with me to tell his story for this book after responding to my article in a recovery magazine. He is an earnest man, joyful that he has been able to recover from a curse that lead him to deep feelings of shame and a long period of severe alcoholism. By the time we met he was able to talk without shame as he described his early years of sexually abusing his adopted son, and of the consequent life on the street, drinking to numb the unbelievable emotional pain that emerged when he became sober. Sitting across from me for several hours, he laid out the story. His second wife sat next to him. She had already heard the stories, both when alone with him and in AA meetings where they met.

Randel was one of the first people I interviewed, and one who has done very abusive things to a young child. I didn't want to shame him, but I was aware that this man was guilty of the very acts done to me that had troubled me throughout my life. Could I have empathy and compassion for such a person?

While I sat with him I saw the man who had controlled a child from age five to seven, who used the child's sexuality in ways that were harmful to his life, and were sure to affect him in vital ways. At the same time I saw a man who had suffered deep shame from his actions, and who had faced that shame and terror in order to free himself from his illness. I witnessed his courage in admitting he had done these acts and in his willingness to live with the shame instead of ending his life— a choice made by others in his position. I could see that Randel was a model of the point this book makes—his life was as devastated as that of his victims, and he deserved to have treatment so that he could recover and become a member of society. His recovery has gone far beyond that. Randel, through telling his story, has touched the lives of many ASC's—other alcoholics who had been unable to come forward because their stories were unacceptable even to most AA members with their own shame-filled histories.

Randel discovered a gift that became available to him after he had been facing himself for some years. He realized he could intuit the stories of some people who had been sexually abused, or who were being sexual with children. When such a person attended AA meetings or his church, Randel paid special attention, letting it be known he was available to talk if the person had an interest. Most have not responded, but many have. From his disclosures, a core gathering of sex addicts gradually developed into a Sex Addicts Anonymous Twelve Step self-help program. Randel told me that more than 15 men have come to one or two meetings, but didn't stay. These figures are significant for a town with a population of under 15,000.

RANDEL'S STORY

Randel began his story by describing his period of alcoholism that included living on the street, homeless. At that time he was in an Eastern Washington town with cold winters, yet when I asked him how he slept and stayed warm he had difficulty answering. The effect of the alcohol prevented him from remembering or from knowing how miserable his existence was. Randel described sleeping next to a broken window of a bar from which some heat escaped. He worked at the bar checking I.D.'s. For wages, he was given all the wine he could drink. When it closed he slept wherever he happened to lie down. For seven years he remained within a three-block area, his life a blur of drunkenness.

Alcohol had been a common part of his life by age twelve, numbing feelings that stemmed from the abuses he experienced in his childhood. Clearly an alcoholic from early in his life, the evolution of the disease into the final state of dysfunction didn't begin until he introduced sexual contact with the stepson he adopted after marrying the boy's mother.

Randel grew up in an abusive family. He observed his father frequently beating and raping his mother, brutally humiliating her. She killed herself when she was fifty-two. He was sexually abused by an uncle who threatened him with harm if he told. The uncle burned his hand, making the point that it would be worse if Randel revealed the sexual activity going on between them. This left Randel with the belief that sex was bizarre and repulsive. He couldn't understand during his teen years why his friends found kissing desirable when they were beginning to date. Only recently has he discovered that kissing can be a loving and sexual way to relate with his wife.

Randel's neighborhood was fraught with adults and teens being sexual with younger children—the unspoken intuiting of shared sexual damage brings like people together. In addition, during grade school and junior high years he had frequent sexual encounters with other boys, many of them forced on him. Some seemed voluntary, such as giving sexual favors in order to belong to a special club. Randel wanted to tell about the distress he was experiencing, but belonging was more important than being taken care of.

While sex seemed to be a strange way to relate with people, Randel was able to invent fantasies about sex that allowed him to become aroused and have orgasms. While he did this on a regular, addictive basis, he felt deep shame after he ejaculated.

Orgasm ended the intense drug of sexual arousal, allowing his sexual shame to re-emerge.

Randel's fantasies had a number of subjects, one of which was innocent boys between the age of three and seven. Once the child was older he was no longer stimulating. Randel also said that most children even in that age range did not arouse him. A very specific facial expression was necessary to get his attention. The child had to be a boy with a sweetly innocent face, vulnerable, and trusting adults to take good care of him. Randel realized even before therapy that this was the child he was when he was abused by his uncle during those years. Now he was taking on the role of the one in power instead of the one who was powerless.

Even though sex with a person seemed strange and disgusting, Randel married for the first time in his mid-twenties. His wife had a son who was four at the time they began dating, and five when they married. At first Randel didn't let himself know that he was sexually attracted to the boy, but after they lived together he could no longer avoid the awareness.

Don was the youngest of Ruth's four children, and at age five, the only one young enough to appeal to Randel's "addict." Randel put up walls between himself and the boy in hopes that he could avoid being a sexual abuser. But Donny didn't let that continue. Probably the object of sexual abuse before he met Randel, Donny knew how to elicit the new father's "caring." When children are deprived of real caring, they take what they can find, and if they have received sexual approaches or response to their natural sexuality, they will perceive the power to attract that is within their control. Many people who are recovering from damaged sexuality feel they brought it on. In some cases the adult will tell them this, but even if the adult doesn't, the child will still believe it because they actively sought out sexual contact. In truth, the rules for children are

different than for adults because children are literally dependent. They have to get their needs met any way they possibly
can. ***Children are never responsible for sexual exchange with
an adult.***

RANDEL ABUSES HIS STEPSON

Donny approached Randel with an innocent, sweet look, asking
for affection. The combination of innocence and the right age
pushed Randel to act on his cross-wiring. Once begun, the
behaviors escalated from sexualized relating to actual sexual
contact. His shame was so deeply triggered that he was unable
to perceive the difference between activities suitable for children
and those that are not.

Now ready to have this child as a sexual partner, he focused
his "love" on Donny. He gave him baths, took him shopping for
special things, and set out to win his trust. When sexual with
Donny, he paid the boy to do things for his pleasure. In his
warped way, he was trying to pay for the guilt by giving
something to the child in return. Deep inside he knew it wasn't
possible to make things fair.

As the two years proceeded, Randel wanted desperately to
stop, but wasn't able to. He knew that if he were caught he
would have to stop, and so he turned himself in. But as the legal
process was begun, he was too terrified of the consequences,
and ran. This was the beginning of seven years of heavy
drinking and complete loss of himself.

Each time Randel tried to give up alcohol during this
devastating time, his emotional pain was so intense that he
returned to drink. Finally he couldn't take any more, and, one-
month sober, he went to a therapist. The therapist told him that
he had to face the pain of long-repressed memory in order to
heal himself so that he could tolerate being sober. This lead to
a dream in which Randel saw his mother lying passed out on the

floor, and his uncle holding him, his fingers digging into Randel's ribs. The uncle fondled him sexually, and if Randel resisted, the fingers dug deeper. When he was finished, he held Randel's fingers over fire while admonishing him to keep the secret. The dream allowed the memory of similar events to return and stay.

When Randel told the therapist about his feelings for his stepson, and innocent young boys, the therapist called Child Protective Services, as he is required to do by state law. Randel then went through a lengthy and trying court process resulting in a two-year sentence which was suspended as long as he was in treatment. The therapist assigned by the court spent the next two years trying to change Randel's cross-wiring from children to women. He did this by telling Randel to fantasize naked women in sexual activities while masturbating, to use pornographic magazines, and go to adult bookstores to see videos in order to be aroused by those things that are acceptable to our culture. It failed. He had no cross-wiring to women, and so the pictures just looked like pictures. No amount of masturbation changed that. Randel is very glad this "treatment" failed because he is happy that he isn't now addicted to sex with women instead of with children. His current sex life with his wife doesn't include fantasy or pornography—instead, he has learned how to really be with her as the unique person he loves. This therapist didn't understand sexual addiction and the recovery process that is necessary for a person to find healthy sexuality. He was attempting to use a behavioral approach to change cross-wiring, a common technique among therapists who work with offenders.

After two years, the therapist dismissed Randel, telling him he was well. Within a week Randel acted out with another child, and returned to the therapist. In a few weeks Randel moved to another town in Washington and arranged to see a new therapist—Steve Zimberoff, whose work is described in Chapter 13—one who held the keys to his recovery. Steve understood sexual addiction, encouraged Twelve Step recovery, and knew the need for uncovering the past and freeing Randel from the feelings still bottled up. Over a period of years, Randel's addictive feelings diminished, replaced with growing comfort loving a woman. This change lead to his second marriage to Ellie, a person who understands the process of recovery.

SEXUAL RECOVERY

Randel told me about his two-year marriage, and the joy he experiences in their sexual relationship. On his wedding night he prayed to his "higher power." He asked for help in learning how to love his wife. Through this affirmation of his wish for healthy sexuality, accompanied by his years of recovery, which included learning to be completely honest, he has been able to contain his entire sexual energy in his relationship. He glowed as he told me that he has even had orgasm after orgasm. Randel said that if I had told him years ago this was possible he would have thought I was crazy.

I asked about the process he went through to reach this place. What he said is now familiar to me as I have heard many stories of sex addicts in recovery. At first he had no sexual interest in women because of the dominance of his cross-wiring to children. But once he began discovering his childhood contact with adults, things started to change.

His first experience of shame-free sex occurred when he was eager to find out what mature sex was like, having known only what his first therapist called immature sexual behavior. Not knowing how to do this, he followed his intuition, and called on his developing understanding of prayer. He imagined talking to God, asking what was healthy sex. Immediately he saw that he was hiding himself under the covers, and pulled them off. Hiding his body was part of his shame. Staying in touch with his view of God as shame-free and accepting, he masturbated with no shame for the first time in his life. Through this experience, he found out how to begin the process of removing shame from sex. With repeated shame-free self-stimulation, the shame could no longer remain attached to sexual activity. This automatically led gradually to a healthier expression, and to removal of the cross-wiring to children. A therapist helped get the process started, but it took Randel's intuitive understanding of spiritual healing to open himself to discovery of how to remove the obstacles to the unfolding of healthy sexuality.

Now in his marriage with Ellie, he is going though his second adolescence, only this time the way it should be for all of us. As he is able to bring his sexual energy to his love for his wife, he is finding himself attracted to her body, loving her breasts, events he thought were not possible for him. Kissing, once repulsive, is so pleasurable he has had orgasms with that stimulation alone. The intimacy that comes with kissing and staying present no longer scares him.

As the cross-wiring fades, he gets to have the natural experience of loving the body of the person he is in love with. No longer is he pulled away from that by fantasies of children. He is also delighted that his first therapist didn't succeed in getting him hooked on women's bodies. It is one woman's body he loves and finds sexual.

I asked Randel how he and Ellie decide when to have sex, and his answer didn't surprise me. The decision is often made when he finds himself in a light mood, giggling like a kid. In moments Ellie's little girl comes out playfully. Neither one "initiates" sex, instead, their playfulness leads into sexual contact, making it possible to go further if it feels right to do so.

I asked Randel if he no longer had fantasies about children. He said that occasionally he will see a child who is a trigger, but now only the thought is there. He doesn't become aroused and is able to prohibit fantasies. He also knows that the guilt that comes with the thoughts will leave as soon as he tells Ellie about it. He is still afraid she will be upset because he feels like he is committing adultery, but she, a recovering addict too, understands and supports him. He has the foundation in place to prevent himself from relapsing, and is enjoying life in a way that will also inhibit relapse.

Since he is able to have intimate, bonding sex with Ellie, no fantasies even try to emerge when he is with her. He has a commitment to himself and to her that if thoughts of children come up he will stop having sex and talk it through. So far it hasn't been necessary.

RECOVERING ASC'S CAN TEACH US ABOUT HEALTHY SEX

Randel's story is an example of how the recovery of sex addicts is preparing an understanding for all of us about the nature of unhealthy sex. Randel's cross-wiring isn't the only sexual desire that isn't healthy. Most sanctioned sexual interest is just as far from the healthy variety as the unsanctioned kind. But only people who have an intense need to change are forced to scrap the old kind and make way for the new. Randel gets to have more wonderful sex than any of those people in movies or television who moan and thrash in apparent ecstasy.

Randel's discoveries show how it is possible to begin with the most painful, socially unacceptable cross-wired sexual preferences, suffer from complete moral corruption, and then enter a recovery process that not only eliminates the attraction to children, but also permits a discovering of healthy sexuality. Complete recovery will automatically yield healthy sex.

I believe that as we allow ASC's to face their shame and heal, they will be the leaders in the discovery of healthy sex. ASC's and other sex addicts have such distorted, miserable, life-interrupting use of sex that they have no choice but to stop and do the painful work of healing. As I listen to stories of people who have been able to face the severe shame of directing their sexual energy toward children, I believe they hold the seeds to cultural change that will make sexual activity with children impossible.

People like Randel hold the only real hope for child abuse prevention. As it stands now, our culture is so intensely negative and shaming of people like him that it is incredibly difficult for a person to turn himself in and begin the process. Most people like Randel don't manage to do the kind of recovery work he has accomplished. A major reason for this is that our culture won't allow it. Anyone who reveals their story—an act that is necessary to recovery—will be shamed by our culture as a whole. This threat is enough to prevent most from getting in touch with their feelings. Why would they? The predominant feeling of shame will override all else, and push the person back to acting out in addictive ways to prevent that very feeling of shame.

The ASC is not solely responsible for damaging children's sexuality. Our culture is—the culture that won't allow them to heal. It is our task, as members of a damaging culture, to change our perceptions and actions so that we can allow the process that will eliminate the use of children for sexual gratification of adults.

Chapter 17

Our Culture Perpetuates Sexual Violation at All Ages

As I listen to people's stories and write their experiences, I feel as if I were pushing against a tremendous wall of water. It reminds me of dreams where I must run but my feet flail and I can't move. I want to show the stories of the ASC's and their partners so you will see that they were the victims too. I want to scream out to you that you have to know they didn't choose to do these things. Their childhoods of sexual boundarylessness, and this culture that you and I perpetuate from generation to generation, set them up for it. Yes, they have to take responsibility for it now, and stop, but they also need our full support and compassion in order to have the opportunity to heal.

CULTURAL SUPPORT FOR INCEST AND OTHER SEX WITH CHILDREN

Because we are members of our culture we have difficulty seeing it—seeing the rules and myths that dominate so much of our thinking and beliefs. It is much easier to see another culture, such as those studied by anthropologists who have been able to identify damaging choices.

For example, it is easy to see that adolescents in Africa are physically and emotionally harmed when they are circumcised with no anesthetic as a ritual of reaching adulthood. But in our own culture we believe that circumcising an infant right after birth does not hurt and is good for him. Only recently has this belief been questioned. I benignly agreed to this procedure twenty-three years ago when my son was born, and never gave it any thought. Only now can I know that they cut his skin, brought him great pain, and communicated to him that this was for his own good. In my work with clients who retrieve memory of their early days, through guided imagery, I get to see that we know on a deeply primitive level what is going on even the day we are born and before. But in 1970 I had never heard anyone suggest that circumcision wasn't good for a child, or that it might cause physical pain.

In the 1960s, when I was in college, I read a chapter in an anthropology book about a culture called "Nacirema." When we finished reading about these people who painted their faces and had many garments made out of woven cloth and animal skins and furs, each assigned for specific occasions, we were told that Nacirema was American spelled backward. The author had found a way to give us some objectivity. But face makeup and clothing are easier to see through the anthropologist's filter. Describing our culture as outwardly condemning incest while covertly creating and supporting it is more difficult to manage.

I struggled along with my discomfort for many more years, knowing that my perceptions didn't match the definitions of our culture, until I read a book by Anne Wilson Schaef in 1986 called *Codependence: Misunderstood, Mistreated* (Harper and Row). A chapter on our culture opened my eyes. Every word rang true. She followed this chapter with an entire book on the subject, a bestseller called *When Society Becomes an Addict*, in 1989 (Harper and Row). While these books aren't about adult/child sexual interaction, they provide an understanding of how culture sets us up to act out its edicts, and prevents us from knowing what is true for each of us. My very reading of Schaef's books demonstrated this principle—I was more able to see after she put words to my intuitive knowing. I wasn't able to do that without a mirror.

I want to recommend that you read these books if you want to grasp the role of our culture in perpetuating damaging beliefs and actions. They will be particularly interesting if you are recovering from addiction because Schaef couches her observations in the language of addiction. She differentiates addictive process from living process. Addictive process prevents us from living richly and fully, expressing our creativity and creating community in optimal ways. Living process is living in this moment, a way of life that will automatically yield healthy sexuality and a creatively-evolving culture. Schaef's perceptions make clear that we have a solution in hand. ***We know how to recover from addiction. Millions are doing it. As we take this recovery further, we will also heal our culture.***

Psychoanalyst Alice Miller has written an entire book— *Thou Shalt Not Be Aware: Society's Betrayal of the Child* —in an effort to bring to consciousness how we set up parents and others to be sexual with their children, and then shame them mercilessly when they are caught. I recommend it if you want to see how our culture is capable of holding two opposite views at the same time. I also recommend *For Your Own Good: Hidden Cruelty in Child-rearing and The Roots of Violence*. This book, and several others, are listed in Suggested Reading. All her books focus on cultural blindness—or, rather, our individual blindness that is supported by our families and culture, and that we pass on from generation to generation.

I will not try to duplicate Alice Miller's writing here, but I do want to express some of my own realizations about how we can submerge information in the service of membership in a family and then in a culture. I feel deep passion about how we have scapegoated those who are discovered and arrested for abusing children sexually. ***These people are not the few perverted ones who are outside the norm. They are the symptom of a culture that represses sexuality and at the same time stimulates it.***

INCEST ISN'T THE WORST THING IN THE WORLD

When an adult is sexual with a child, it is very harmful. This is well established. But it isn't as harmful as growing up starving, as millions of children do. It isn't as harmful as growing up in Vietnam during the war, watching people be killed and living in constant fear of disruption or death, with parents who are always afraid. Unless it includes violence, it isn't necessarily as harmful as being beaten and hurt as a child. It can be no more harmful than emotional abuse that constantly belittles a child, removing all self-esteem—abuse that goes on in front of others with no shame or apology. Yet we react to sexual abuse of children as if it were far more horrendous than any other abuse. And we react to those who have sexual feelings toward children as if they were the worst people on earth. This overreaction is part of what prevents us from seeing that having sexual feelings for children is just a fact, and that it is something that can be healed.

When I was writing the story of Sheila, who masturbated when her son was nursing, I had two strong and contradictory feelings. One was the urge to paint a striking picture so you would believe the child's sexuality was affected by it, and the second was the desire to underplay the story because I was afraid this scene was so distressing that you wouldn't want to believe it was true. My opposite feelings are responses to two reactions common in our culture. One is denial that adult sexual interaction actually goes on more frequently than we imagine, and the other is overreaction to these common behaviors.

Why do we react so strongly to one form of abuse? Why does the intensity of the reaction far outweigh the relative significance in a child's life? Why do we condemn the perpetrator of sexual abuse to a far greater extent than the perpetrators of other abuses? Why do we have such strong reactions?

I believe one answer lies in an attempt to create false sexual boundaries so that each one of us doesn't act on cross-wiring to be sexual with children. If we have the programming, we can make sure we don't respond to it by creating intense reactions to those who do. ***By hating people who are sexual with children, many adults make sure they don't accidentally act on their programming to do the same.*** Until each one of us can acknowledge that we have some programming to use sexual energy with children because we live in a culture that covertly condones doing so, we will have to react with great disgust to signs of someone else's sexual activity with children. But when we can look and know and feel, and reduce our shame, then we can place this behavior in its correct position. And we can allow those who acted on the cross-wiring to speak out, get help, and heal their sexuality.

CONVICTED SEX OFFENDERS ARE PEOPLE TOO

I sat in a room with nine convicted sex offenders, men, each of whom recited their sexual activities with children, as well as other "deviant" behaviors, as I describe in Chapter 13. My presence brought up incredible shame for them. They had already told their stories over and over, week after week, adding new information as they discovered it, and were working to reduce shame. But the presence of a new person, particularly a woman, put them in touch with the way society views their acts. My work with sex addicts made little difference to them. I was a new face, and every new listener will bring up shame that has not yet been discharged. This was not a roomful of men who had a good time being sexual with children. They weren't people who might sit around a bar swapping stories of how they lured another child into their car. They lived lives of isolation, keeping secrets and creating lies to themselves so they could figure out how not to kill themselves. Suicide is often the only option to people who are unable to have self-compassion, and to know they have the right to an environment in which they can heal from their curse.

CULTURAL BLINDNESS

How can a person not know their partner is being sexual with their child? Common sense tells us that of course we would be able to perceive such a vital activity going on in our home with those we know best. But it is more common not to know than to know. We live in a culture that requires blindness to simple truths, and distorts communication so that one kind of statement really means another. We as children had to learn the rules. We had to accept that the truth wasn't true, and that lies were.

We are told that when people marry they will have sex only with each other, yet most people have sex outside the marriage. Then they lie about it so that it looks like our society matches the spoken norm. Children learn not to listen to their intuition because they have to choose between the truth they perceive and the lies they are told. Children cannot afford to stay with their own truth.

When I was about twelve, a friend of my parents told me he really liked a singer that was popular, and I felt a bond with him because of it—a cross-generational bond, something that a child and adult could share which was rare in my life. The next time we saw him I asked him about the singer, and he told me he had just been teasing, he really hated him. I was crushed. I felt betrayed, and naive. I had not been able to differentiate his teasing from the truth because I hadn't been exposed to the sound in the voice that indicated the truth was the opposite of what was being said. He belonged to a culture that allowed people to communicate by expressing the opposite of the truth. I, as a young teen, had not yet learned about this.

During the week that I first interviewed Joyce (whose husband had been sexual with her daughter from the time she was born until she was eight) and attended the sex offender therapy group, I read a book that made the same point I was learning—when our culture uniformly tells us that something terrible is really healthy, we believe it.

Alice Walker (Pulitzer-Prize-winning author of *The Color Purple*, 1982) wrote a book called *Possessing the Secret of Joy*. She presents us with young people living in an African tribe she calls the Olinkas, who circumcise their adolescent girls. (While she fictionalized the story, the events she described actually happen to millions of girls.) Not only do they cut off the clitoris, they scrape away the labia and sew the vagina shut. Menstrual blood is reabsorbed in the vagina, or leaks out if their is any room left to do so. The vagina is painfully re-opened by intercourse after marriage. Walker introduces a black brother and sister about the same age as missionaries from the United States, which provides us with the contrast between the cultures.

After frequently enjoying sex with the American boy, the main character, Tashi, who had somehow not gone through the anesthetic-free operation, decides to have it done so that she won't be laughed at by her peers. She was seen as different, and told that as she grew older her vulva would grow too, and soon a man wouldn't be able to enter. This cultural "wisdom" had been passed down for centuries, supported by the beloved, idealized spiritual leader.

We can say that this method was designed so that men had control over women, but this kind of thinking is truly naive. *The women were the ones who perpetuated this abuse.* Women did the surgery, women led the mocking of the ones who didn't want to have it, and women passed down to the next generation the need for this purification of "undesirable" parts of the female body. *We pass on to the next generation the institutionalized abuses done to us.*

As I read this book, I was horrified that they didn't know better. Why didn't someone just stand up and say, no, we aren't going to do this any more. We can love our vulvas and the role they play in bringing sexual pleasure and inviting new lives into the world.

These thoughts were going through my mind in the early morning before I got out of bed to bathe and start the day. As I rolled over, raising the down comforter, I could faintly smell my own vulva. I frowned with distaste, wanting to get up and remove it with soap and water. As I looked at my body getting out of the bed, I saw that I was responding to our culture's form of the same thing Tashi was faced with. I didn't smell bad. It wasn't so strong that another person would be offended. Yet my reaction to vaginal smells was distaste for my vulva and for my whole body.

I had been telling women for years that they had a right to love their bodies just as they are. I offer a workshop called "Love Our Bodies." Obesity and dieting are evidence of the harm of body hatred. But we can't decide, just by intellectual understanding, to stop hating our bodies. The Olinkas couldn't decide to go against centuries of history in order to reclaim a healthier use of sexuality, and defend their bodies. People who are sexual with children can't just decide they are good people, worthy of not being victims or victimizers, and give up their acting out. The necessary healing process is a long one. It requires leaders who can see the whole picture, individuals being held accountable for the harm that is being done, and a culture that is willing to examine itself to see what must be changed to make room for health.

We can't dismiss the African culture's practices as primitive and weird, assuming that if we were born there we wouldn't accept them. We would. In our own country we cannot see that what is taught to us, and that which we teach to children, is harmful. Reading Alice Miller's examples of what she calls "poisonous pedagogy" are easier for Americans to see because her examples come from European culture. But they are harder to see than the African example because our culture is more similar to European than Black African tribes.

We Can't See What We're Trained Not to See

My own blindness showed up when I dated a man in the early 1980s who was attracted to children. The two jobs he worked while we were seeing each other were both with children, which in itself means nothing. But other information was available that I misinterpreted.

I lived in an apartment in a family neighborhood. When Franklin visited me, he went for walks with his dog, and made friends with a girl about seven. He talked about her in glowing terms, with a big smile on his face. I was jealous. Because I had no idea that a normal looking man might really be attracted sexually to a seven-year-old, I assumed that anything I felt must be patterns of mine from some unknown source.

The day I moved from that apartment, I returned after the place was entirely empty to spend a little time saying good-bye. While I was sitting on the raised hearth reflecting over the time I had lived here, Franklin and his friend walked in. He focused intensely on her as he showed her around my apartment. He didn't introduce her or act as if I were even present. I was enraged. I thought he was being passive aggressive, or perhaps just lacking in social skills. I was jealous of this girl, this person who got all his attention while I got none.

I didn't know that I was reacting appropriately to being confronted with the "other woman." I wonder what it was like for her to be the center of his interest while the woman in his life was feeling hateful toward her and him. I abandoned her through my ignorance. I was unable to say to her that his interest was more than just friendly, that the energy he gave to her belonged with me. I couldn't ask her if more than just sexual energy was being delivered. I cannot guess from what I know if he had touched her in sexual ways.

Another time I was driving behind Franklin on the way to meeting him at a restaurant for dinner. I saw him look into a car next to him at the light. A woman was driving with a child in a car seat beside her. He looked lustfully, trance-like, into the car. Again I went into a rage. Having no understanding of how addictive trances can take a person entirely out of the present, I assumed that he knew I was behind him and could see him sending sexual energy toward another woman. I took it personally, questioning if he was trying to express anger at me or hurt me.

When we met minutes later at the restaurant, I asked him about it, describing what I had seen. He said he wasn't looking at the woman, he was looking at the child. *I stopped feeling jealous because I thought I had made a mistake.* I stopped believing my perception that he was sending sexual energy. I couldn't consider that he was telling the truth about looking at the child, and at the same time, know that he was sending sexual energy from an addictive trance.

I didn't realize until years after we broke up that he was sexually interested in children. It didn't make sense that someone I would be in a relationship with, who was having sex with me on a regular basis, would be interested in children. I now know that this is a common means for partners of pedophiles to dismiss concern. I didn't understand about cross-wiring.

I had considered having a baby with this man. I took his interest in children at face value, and thought he would make a good father. While I could see that he spent time with children to entertain himself with their interest in him, rather than to meet the child's needs, I couldn't translate this into understanding that it is not at all good for the child. I could have been the dominant breadwinner, leaving him home with the child, believing the child was in very good hands. I could have been in Joyce's position.

I also know that Franklin was trying to heal himself. One time he told me that he had been sexual with a nine-year-old girl when he was a young teenager. If I knew what I know now, I could have helped him remove the shame from that experience, and listened to his stories and his feelings which would have automatically reduced his further sexual interest in children. He was ready to experience his feelings about this, and was looking for a shame-free audience. Instead I cried, feeling hurt and violated by his cross-wiring. He didn't bring it up again. We separated soon after that.

SEXUAL BONDING ENERGY IS DIFFERENT FROM SEXUAL AROUSAL

One of the ways our culture fools us is by defining sex as sexual arousal. In this way, flirting, suggestive remarks, and monogamously bonding energy can't be seen as being sexual with children.

Rex and I had a sexual experience that demonstrated to me the power of the non-arousal component of sexual bonding. We began by having sex, but it wasn't pleasurable because Rex was working on issues of his childhood. We stopped, and instead lay together looking into each other's eyes, intimate, and really seeing how bonded we were. Married six years, we fully knew we were together no matter what, and each of us was relinquishing our fear that we will be abandoned. We had no arousal, and no interest in being sexual, but at the same time we both felt sexual bonding energy. We coupled again, using it as the glue.

Sexual bonding energy isn't appreciated as sexual energy because it isn't accompanied by arousal and so it is easy to deny. Sexual arousal is only an addition to this feeling. As we choose the person we want to bond with, we look into each other's eyes and bond. Then we follow that with sexual arousal and intercourse. The purpose of arousal is to intensify the bond, and to take the family another step—possibly inviting children. But the violation of a child's sexuality can occur purely with the violation of the bonding energy—using it for monogamous, one-on-one bonding instead of family/community bonding.

CHURCHES SHAME SEXUALITY

Strict religious institutions create intense shame about sexuality, in an attempt to stop unhealthy sexual activity. The Catholic Church, in particular, has produced large numbers of people who feel so shamed around sexuality that they become sex addicts, or have secret sex with children where they can be in the power position, or lose their ability to have sex altogether. Those in my practice with the most intense disturbance around sexuality came from families who believed that sex was wrong, and who subjected their children to the influence of priests and nuns whose sexuality had also been seriously damaged while they were growing up.

Few people can tell me exactly how the communications were made to them, except for a few stories about how nuns acted when the subject came up. But everyone knew they weren't to masturbate, they weren't to lust, and of course, weren't to have sex until married. These were known subjects to take to confession even though they weren't described beyond phrases such as "impure thoughts." Men who tell about going to confession either did confess, do their assignment, and then promptly commit the same "sins" again, or they didn't tell. Either way, the association of sexuality and badness was strengthened weekly from the time puberty arrived.

Some people, including men, became unable to have sex. A client I will call Roger was single in his late thirties because he couldn't get erections or arousal even when he tried to masturbate. He remained capable of sexual bonding energy, however, and so became attached to women he knew he could never couple with. Women, through time, have been able to marry and bond without accessing sexual arousal. This has been prescribed by many cultures, at different periods. Most notably for us is the recent Victorian era.

The sexual trance state allows a person to continue to be sexual in spite of church prohibitions. In this way, *sex addiction is created by and supported by strict religious institutions.* (This is perhaps the cause of the fact that religious communities have among the highest percentage of reported sexual activity with children.) If a person isn't allowed to have healthy sex, and is being sexual only in a trance state, it becomes difficult or impossible to see the child's needs. Sex itself is so bad that doing it with a child doesn't seem much worse. Sexual addiction has allowed our species to continue. If everyone responded as Roger had, no pregnancies would occur. Instead, many millions of people have discovered how to incorporate shame into sex so they don't feel it as shame, and are able to express this undeniable facet of being human.

Religious Shaming

The Catholic Church, and other religious organizations, attempt to use shame to stop unhealthy sexual activity. The fact that severe shaming will stop evidence of behavior has been interpreted to mean that real change has taken place. This is tragic. *The more sexuality has been shamed in order to control it, the more unhealthy it has become for each of us.* Then as more and more unhealthy signs of it appear, the churches set out to further shame the evidence. The result is that everyone is taught to hide their sexuality to prevent further shaming. This very hiding lays down another layer of shame. *The secrecy that must go with the shame prevents open discussion of sex in a way that can truly allow healing.*

This entire process has made it easy for adults to be sexual with children and to not know they are doing anything worse than touching their own genitals to bring arousal. If masturbation is a terrible sin, and so is incest, what's the difference? Secrecy prevents each person from knowing they are harming children. Once the secrecy is broken, it becomes possible for individuals to see what they have been doing, and, as with the men in the offenders group, be amazed that they had been able to think they weren't hurting children.

We Can Learn to See by Talking

I sat for the second time with Joyce, listening to how she has progressed from the state typical of women in our culture— unable to believe her intuition when it told her something was wrong in her daughter's life—to a woman who is filled with a beast who refuses to let an addict control her and harm her child. She spoke out angrily about how she told Greg's "addict" that he won't win ever again. Sitting over coffee, she looked at Greg, the man who is in recovery, whom she loves. And she knew that underneath his recovering, loving self his addict lives, listening. She told the addict that she is more powerful than he is. She will rip him to shreds if he touches their daughter or a woman ever again. It is over, he is out.

I grew as I listened to her. I thought about the times I haven't said anything when I watched parents do abusive things to their children. The shield is gone that instructs me not to know. I recognize abuse, yet I don't have the courage to walk up to a parent and tell them.

I know this inhibition, the fear of offending, the belief that I will be abandoned by everyone if I tell the truth all the time, is what keeps mothers like Joyce from believing their intuition about what is happening to their children. And even when they know, they are unable to take the next step to protect and defend the child. Instead, they turn into shallow, safe people, non-threatening to their partners or to anyone else of importance. We as a culture have trained women and men to not see when abuse is taking place. Until we see how this feeds the partner's silence, and creates the inability to protect, child abuse will not stop. We cannot change anything by training children to refuse to be touched in ways that feel bad. We cannot change anything by merely putting the convicted offender in jail or treatment. We must see that we as a whole people teach parents to "live and let live," and otherwise dismiss or diminish the seriousness of what is happening. We must know that Joyce isn't alone with the experience of having a partner who had a sexual relationship with her daughter.

As I hear about Joyce's fear of letting the "beast" out to protect herself and her daughter, I know that she still struggles with our culture's perception of people, especially women. We aren't allowed to speak out, to yell, to look unfeminine, to assert the truth, to swear. It is against the rules. Yet at the same time we are supposed to be angry mother bears and protect our children—even when our partner is telling us we are crazy.

Intuition is the element that is necessary to know what is happening, yet "female intuition" is said in a degrading tone. It is "just intuition," not scientific fact. By our culture's ideals, we have to see our partners having sex with our children before we have a case. And their "addicts" are very good at making sure we don't see. We have two needs at the same time, and we can meet only one. *Either we fit in and sacrifice our children and ourselves, or we speak out and are shunned by family members and by society.* Which will it be? The forerunners of cultural change are people like Joyce who don't have our culture's support yet, much as the first feminists didn't. In a decade or two things will be different. There will be groups of people supporting each other, and the truth will be obvious. But until then, Joyce and I and others will have to push the truth out, free our beasts to speak, and take the consequences.

PROGRESSING THROUGH THE CULTURAL SHIFT

Our culture is in the midst of a revolution. Millions of us are recovering from childhood sexual activity with adults, and sex addicts are identifying themselves in order to heal their sexuality. The onslaught of sex in the media is a symptom of the death struggle of unhealthy sexuality. Now we can make room for another facet of our culturally distorted views—sexual feelings for children. As our culture is allowed to heal this facet, we can move to a place of self-love that will prepare us to heal all human-caused disturbances.

Suggested Reading

I. Books About Sexual Recovery

Allen, Charlotte Vale, *Daddy's Girl*. Berkley Publications, 1984.

Bass, Ellen, and Laura Davis, *The Courage to Heal*. Harper and Row, 1988.

Carnes, Patrick, *Contrary to Love: Helping the Sexual Addict*. CompCare, 1989.

Carnes, Patrick, *Don't Call It Love*. Bantam, 1991.

Carnes, Patrick, *Out of the Shadows: Understanding Sexual Addiction*. CompCare, 1983.

Davis, Laura, *Allies in Healing*. Harper Perennial, 1991.

Earle, Ralph and Gregory Crow, *Lonely all the Time*. Pocket Books, 1989.

Engel, Beverly, *The Right to Innocence*. Jeremy Tarcher, 1989.

Fraser, Sylvia, *My Father's House*. Harper and Row, 1987.

Gil, Eliana, and Toni Kavanaugh, *Sexualized Children*. Launch Press, 1993.

Hastings, Anne Stirling, *Reclaiming Healthy Sexual Energy*. Health Communications, 1991.

Hastings, Anne Stirling, *Discovering Sexuality That Will Satisfy You Both: When Couples Want Differing Amounts and Different Kinds of Sex*. The Printed Voice, 1993.

Hastings, Anne Stirling, *Healthy Sex* (audio cassette). The Printed Voice, 1994.

Hunter, Mic, *Abused Boys: The Neglected Victims of Sexual Abuse*. Lexington, 1990.

Kasl, Charlotte *Women, Sex and Addiction*. Ticknor and Fields, 1989.

Love, Patricia, *The Emotional Incest Syndrome*. Bantam, 1990.

Mellody, Pia, *Facing Love Addiction*. Harper San Francisco, 1992.

Miller, Alice, *Thou Shalt Not Be Aware: Society's Betrayal of the Child*. Meridian, 1986.

Schaef, Anne Wilson, *Escape From Intimacy*. Harper and Row, 1989.

Schnarch, David M., *Constructing the Sexual Crucible: An Integration of Sexual and Marital Therapy*. Norton, 1991.

Schneider, Jennifer P., *Back From Betrayal*. Hazelden, 1988.

II. Books About General Recovery

Beatty, Melody, *Codependent No More: How to Stop Controlling Others and Love Yourself More*. Harper/Hazelden, 1987.

Bradshaw, John, *Healing the Shame that Binds You*. Health Communications, 1988.

Farmer, Steven, *Adult Children of Abusive Parents*. Contemporary Books, 1989.

Forward, Susan, *Toxic Parents: Overcoming Their Hurtful Legacy and Reclaiming Your Life*. Bantam, 1989.

Goldberg, Herb, *The Hazards of Being Male: Surviving the Myths of Masculine Privilege*. Signet, 1977.

Goldberg, Herb, *The Inner Male: Overcoming Roadblocks to Intimacy*. Signet, 1988.

Goldberg, Herb, *The New Male Female Relationship*. Signet, 1983.

Goldberg, Herb, *The New Male: From Self Destruction to Self Care*. Signet, 1980.

Hendrix, Harville, *Getting the Love You Want*. Henry Holt, 1988.

Hendrix, Harville, *Keeping the Love You Find*. Pocket Books, 1992.

Kellogg, Terry, *Finding Balance*. HCI, 1991.

Lee, John, *I Don't Want to Be Alone*. Health Communications, 1990.

Mellody, Pia, *et al, Facing Codependence*. Harper and Row, 1989.

Miller, Alice, *For Your Own Good: Hidden Cruelty in Child-Rearing and the Roots of Violence*. Farrar, Strauss & Giroux, 1984.

Miller, Alice, *The Untouched Key: Tracing Childhood Trauma in Creativity and Destructiveness*. Doubleday, 1990.

Miller, Alice, *Banished Knowledge: Facing Childhood Injuries*. Doubleday, 1990.

Schaef, Anne Wilson, *Codependence: Misunderstood, Mistreated*. Harper and Row, 1986.

Schaef, Anne Wilson, *When Society Becomes an Addict*. Harper and Row, 1989.

Schainess, Natalie, *Sweet Suffering: Woman as Victim*. Pocket Books, 1986.

III. Fiction Useful to Recovery

Bryant, Dorothy, *The Kin of Ata Are Waiting For You.*
   Random House, 1976.

Piercy, Marge, *Woman on the Edge of Time,* Fawcett, 1985.

Redfield, James, *The Celestine Prophecy.* Warner Books, 1993.

Walker, Alice, *Possessing the Secret of Joy.* Pocket Books/Div. of Simon &
   Schuster, 1992.

SUPPORT GROUPS FOR
SEX ADDICTION RECOVERY

Sex Addicts Annonymous (SAA)
PO Box 3038
Minneapolis, MN 55403

Sexaholics Anonymous (SA)
PO Box 300
Simi Valley, CA 93062

Sex & Love Addicts Anonymous (SLAA)
PO Box 88, New Town Branch
Boston, MA 02258

S–Anon (for families of sex addicts)
PO Box 5117
Sherman Oaks, CA 91413

Adult Children of Sex Addicts & Sexually Dysfunctional Families (ACSA)
PO Box 8084, Lake Street Station
110 East 31st
Minneapolis, MN 55408

About the Author

Anne Stirling Hastings, Ph.D., a licensed psychologist in private practice in Bellevue, Washington, is the author of *Reclaiming Healthy Sexual Energy, Discovering Sexuality That Will Satisfy You Both: When Couples Want Differing Amounts & Different Kinds of Sex,* and *Healthy Sex: Real Life Stories of Bonding, Monogamous, Joyful, Shame-free, Rule-free Sex* (audio cassette). She specializes in sex addiction and sexual abuse, and teaches classes and workshops on reclaiming healthy sexual energy. She is married to Rex Holt, sculptor, painter and certified Rolfer.

If you would like information about classes, workshops, speeches or training for therapists, please drop me a note.

My address is:

>Integrity Resources
>P.O. Box 40083
>Bellevue, WA 98005

If you would like to share your experiences after reading this book, I would appreciate receiving them. Thanks.

Anne Stirling Hastings

DISCARD

The Printed Voice is a new company formed on cooperative principles between authors and publisher. The Printed Voice is committed to serving authors' creative process, changing the world one voice at a time. For a complete list of titles, please write to:

The Printed Voice
98 Main Street No. 538
Tiburon, CA 94920